Research and Counseling: Building Strong School Counseling Programs

Edited by
Garry R. Walz

**American Association for
Counseling and Development**

Serving the counseling,
guidance and human
development professions
since 1952

American Association for Counseling and Development
5999 Stevenson Avenue
Alexandria, Virginia 22304

Library of Congress Cataloging-in-Publication Data

Research and counseling.

 Revision of papers originally presented at a conference held in 1987 and sponsored by the Counseling and Personnel Services Clearinghouse and the American Association for Counseling and Development.

 Bibliography: p.
 1. Personnel service in education—Congresses.
 2. Counseling—Congresses. Walz, Garry Richard.
II. ERIC Clearinghouse on Counseling and Personnel Services.
III. American Association for Counseling and Development.
LB1027.5.R445   1988   371.4   88-19447
ISBN 1-55620-051-X

Printed in the United States of America

CONTENTS

Preface

"Building Strong School Counseling Programs" was the topic of 1987's collaborative midyear conference with ERIC/CAPS. But, going beyond what the title implies, it tried to capture the essence of the past 20 years of ERIC/CAPS' involvement with guidance and counseling information and research, the APGA/AACD stimulation of such information and research, and what the next 20 years might foretell—hence 20/20!

The future was envisioned by David Pearce Snyder, and the past and present were chronicled by John Krumboltz, Norman Gysbers, Dave Capuzzi, and Claire Cole. Discussion sessions, reactor panels, and Q and A sessions with participants were the mode and format for learning, growing, and knowing. What are the outcomes of such sessions? That remains to be seen.

Research has been denigrated in some circles because some individuals view research as dry and boring, not exciting or stimulating. This conference refuted that "old saw." Research and the search for new ideas and techniques are alive and well in AACD and within the counseling and human development profession. My hope is that the readership of this book will gain as much as I did by participating in the 20/20 conference.

—Patrick J. McDonough
Executive Director, AACD

Introduction

The Educational Resources Information Center (ERIC) was established in 1966 to provide a wide range of users such as students, educators, researchers, teachers, and the public with ready access to educational resources. The Counseling and Personnel Services (CAPS) Clearinghouse in the School of Education at The University of Michigan was one of the 14 original clearinghouses. Since its establishment it has worked to offer current and viable resources to counselors, student personnel workers, and human resource specialists at all age levels and in all settings—educational, agency, business, and government. Since its inception over 2 decades ago, CAPS has emphasized the need not only to disseminate information (ensuring that persons who need a particular type of information receive it) but especially to facilitate it use—to assist persons to apply relevant information and resources to their urgent needs. One way that we have done this has been through the publication of monographs that synthesize large bodies of information on critical topics and identify desirable practices and programs. Another way is through the development and sponsorship of local, regional, and national workshops and conferences. A particularly well received model adopted by CAPS has been to offer workshops and conferences where savvy researchers and developers join with practitioners to review and discuss strategies for the adoption and adaptation of the available resources.

It seemed to us at ERIC/CAPS, however, that something special was needed to celebrate 20 years of ERIC/CAPS service to counseling. In initial discussions with Dr. Patrick J. McDonough and Dr. Charles Lewis, the idea of a conference that analyzed the past 20 years of counseling research and looked 20 years into the future (hence, "20/20') was born.

AACD volunteered to cosponsor such a conference, and AACD staff, coordinated by Dr. Sharon Alexander, expertly managed the conference logistics. The initial drafts of the material in this publication were presented at the conference. ERIC/CAPS staff provided the presenters with computer searches of the ERIC database and edited the final manuscripts.

We believe that the papers in this monograph, authored by distinguished members of the counseling profession, provide a window into the best practices of the past and the most compelling resources for the future. As ERIC/CAPS enters its third decade, we hope that the ideas and visions in the pages of this monograph will assist school counselors to demonstrate a 20/20 acuity in retrieving and using the most powerful resources and choosing the most promising directions to target their future goals and efforts.

The Key to Achievement: Learning to Love Learning

John D. Krumboltz

Professor, Educational Psychology
Stanford University, Palo Alto, California

Introduction

Schools could be happy places where young people learn new ideas and skills enthusiastically under the tutelage of creative teachers and supportive administrators. Indeed, for some youngsters schools are just such places. However, for all too many others, schools are places where fear and failure pervade the atmosphere.

Counselors are in a key position to help make learning a positive experience. Counselors are sensitive to individual differences. They realize that a given classroom environment can help one child but not another. Counselors can facilitate essential kinds of communication with teachers and administrators as well as with students.

Counselors can and should play a central role in helping young people learn and achieve. Some people have the notion that counselors work only with emotional problems, or career development, or college planning, and that counselors leave academic achievement in the hands of teachers. Such an attitude would put counselors on the fringe of the educational endeavor, whereas in fact they belong at the hub. Counselors serve in a capacity that enables them to integrate the contributions of teachers, administrators, parents, educational specialists, and the students themselves to create a school environment where children can learn and achieve successfully.

The purpose of this paper is to derive from the pertinent research literature some ideas on which counselors and the educational team can build positive learning programs so that children can achieve happily. With the aid of Garry Walz, Jeanne Bleuer, and Kathy Bidelman, I relied heavily on the ERIC database. I also read extensively in cognitive psychology (Anderson, 1983; Norman &

1

Rummelhart, 1975; Rummelhart, McClelland, & the PDP Research Group, 1986), but let me assure you that the theories of cognitive psychologists have little applicability so far. They are still wondering how the word "lamp becomes associated with lamps" (Miller & Johnson-Laird, 1976, p. 2), or "What happens when we understand a sentence?" (Johnson-Laird, 1983, p. ix). These are complex questions, and the answers may someday enlighten educational practice. One attempt to relate cognitive psychology to education is the book *Cognition and Instruction* by Dillon and Sternberg (1986). Chapters by various authors explore the relationship of the research in cognition to writing, second language learning, mathematics, science, social studies, art, music, and reasoning. But Sternberg in his final chapter cautions us not to expect too much.

I will share here what I have learned, but, not to worry, there is much left to discover. The nightmare of the ancient wise man that someday all truths would be known has not yet become reality.

The Enjoyment of Learning

Now you may be saying: Why all this emphasis on learning "happily"? Can't people learn while they're unhappy? Can't they learn while they're scared? Can't they learn because they are being threatened with dire consequences? Yes, of course they can. People can learn under all kinds of circumstances. However, the emotional concomitants of learning have long-term implications. Young people can learn to love the process of learning or they can learn to hate it. Their emotional reactions to the process of learning will influence the extent to which they will continue the process or quit. People who learn to love reading will continue to read throughout their lives. People who learn to hate reading may never voluntarily pick up a book again. The goal of education is not to forcefeed a set of facts into the malleable heads of young children, but rather it should be to inspire a love of learning that will motivate a lifelong eagerness to acquire new knowledge and skills.

Definition of Enjoyment

It is important to note that when I speak of students being happy in school, enjoying school, and loving learning, I do not mean that they are not working hard, are not serious, or are not concentrating. On the contrary, I am talking about the enjoyment of disciplined study, in the sense developed by Csikszentmihalyi (1975), where the experience is one of complete but easy concentration without distraction from personal problems, where time seems to fly, and where there is a feeling of being competent and in control. Enjoyment in the sense in which I am using the term does not involve frivolity, laziness, or lack of serious purpose. Enjoyment involves intense concentration on important tasks that challenge individuals to do their best.

Case Study in Learning to Enjoy Reading

Can counselors be effective in helping young people to learn and achieve? Shortly I am going to review some of the research evidence that indicates clearly how counselors can be effective in promoting learning and achievement, but I don't really need to look at the evidence to be convinced myself. I'd like to tell you a story about how a counselor helped me when my daughter Ann was having some difficulties in learning how to read. Like any proud father I wanted Ann to do well in school. When she was in the second grade she seemed to be having some difficulty in reading. The teacher thought it would be valuable for her to practice reading at home. I cooperated eagerly in the effort.

Ann and I would pick out a book that we thought appropriate for her reading level. She would sit on my lap and I would ask her to read to me. When she came to a word that she did not know, she would ask me to tell her the word. I would say, "Let's sound it out." I wanted her to learn how to figure out the words by herself. Painstakingly Ann would try to make sense of the black squiggles on the white page. Patiently and lovingly I would lead her through the process of phonetically sounding out the pronunciation of each difficult word. Ann quickly became impatient and frustrated by this process. Sometimes she would even break into tears when she could not figure out what a word meant. I began to find it increasingly difficult to persuade her to spend time reading with me.

Fortunately the school district in which we resided had a school counselor in the elementary school, Mr. Ken Sanner. I took my problem to him and explained what I had been doing to help Ann with her reading. I told him about Ann's frustration. He listened to me patiently and understandingly.

"So you are wondering whether to tell her words when she asks or have her continue sounding them out?" he paraphrased empathetically.

"Exactly!" I replied. "What do you think I should do?" (No nondirective nonsense for me—I wanted answers!)

Ken then said something that I have never forgotten, and it changed the course of my parental intervention in reading.

"What is your goal?" he asked.

"My goal is that I want Ann to enjoy reading," I answered without hesitation.
"So. . . ."

Instantly the light bulb above my head clicked on. If I wanted Ann to enjoy reading, I was going to have to make reading an enjoyable activity. What I had been doing was making reading a feared and hated activity. I had been doing the exact opposite of what my goal had been. I saw it all in an instant.

The next evening when I invited Ann to read with me I said, "We're going to do reading differently now, Ann. I'm going to tell you any word that you want. We're just going to read the story together and enjoy it." The new approach worked much better. Ann was able to focus on understanding the story rather than on whether she could please her father by sounding out difficult words. Although there was still a long road ahead to develop Ann's reading ability, that key intervention by the counselor enabled me to see that the connection between my goal and my actions made all the difference in the world. Now 25 years later Ann is a lobbyist working in Washington, DC. I called her on the phone one Sunday night not too many weeks ago and asked her about her weekend.

"I spent the whole weekend reading."

"Don't you want to get out and have some fun?" I inquired.

"I was having fun reading," she said.

Learning to Hate School

In recent years education bashing has become a popular sport and has been used as a justification for withholding the money schools need to do a better job. As an educator myself I don't want to knock my hard-working colleagues who are making splendid efforts in the most difficult circumstances. We do need to look at our own profession critically and compassionately, however, to see how we can improve it.

What troubles me is that in all too many schools teachers and administrators, just as I did with Ann, affirm that they want youngsters to love learning but then engage in activities that defeat the goal. For some educators the process of learning is like taking bitter medicine—you hate it but it's good for you.

Other teachers feel that it's not their responsibility to ensure learning, let alone the love of learning. Their responsibility is to "cover the subject." If they cover the subject, talking about it and assigning readings in it, then students should learn it. If students don't learn, the teacher's job is to assign low grades equitably. Students are penalized for failure to learn—a classic case of blaming the victim.

Just for a minute let's imagine how we would go about designing an educational program if our purpose were to make students hate to learn. How would we teach them so that when the teaching was finished they would hate the subject matter, hate the teacher, and hate the building in which the experience took place? First, we would hide from them the exact purpose of what it was we were trying to accomplish. We wouldn't tell them the goal. Second, we would give them some impossible tasks. No matter how hard they might try, they couldn't succeed. Third, when we discovered that the students were failing to master the impossible tasks, we would ridicule them and report their failures and shortcomings to their friends and relatives. Fourth, just to pour some salt in the wounds, we would identify one individual in the class who was doing the tasks better than any of the others and say, "If Frank can do it, why can't you?" This would isolate Frank and make all the other children hate him. Finally, if we should happen to catch any student helping another in trying to master these impossible tasks, we would punish such cooperative behavior unmercifully, insisting that each youngster work in silent solitude separated from the support and encouragement of fellow students. Under circumstances like these I can assure you that it would not take long for students to hate the entire learning process.

But isn't this, in effect, exactly what we do for all too many youngsters in our schools? We don't make clear to them exactly what it is they are supposed to be learning. We give them assignments that are too difficult for them to master, and thus they face the prospect of certain failure. (Failure does not necessarily mean getting an F grade. For some, failure is simply not being "Number One," not getting an A, or not being in the top half of the class.) When students fail, everyone else in class knows it, and we send reports home to parents pointing out their child's failures. When too many youngsters in a class do not succeed, we repeat the tasks again. Those who have mastered them the first time become bored. The incentive system and the social structure isolate youngsters from each other, discourage cooperation, and, in effect, cast aspersions on those who help each other with their homework.

Under circumstances like these isn't it understandable that large numbers of youngsters become alienated from school, hate teachers and learning, vandalize school property, and drop out as soon as they can? Other societal forces contribute to these unhappy outcomes—parental abuse, drugs, poverty—but clearly the results are not what we want. The schools need a Ken Sanner to come along periodically and ask, "What is your goal?"

Love of Learning as an Educational Goal

Suppose we were to answer, "Our goal is for children to love learning." Just consider that possibility for a moment. Suppose our goal was not that children learn—but that children love learning.

How then would we evaluate the success of the schools? Instead of just giving achievement tests to youngsters and reporting the relative rank order of schools on reading achievement and mathematics achievement, we would also ask, for example, "How much do you enjoy reading?" We would tally the percentage of youngsters in each school who reported pleasure in learning. We would honor and reward those teachers and administrators who were able to create the greatest love of learning. Perhaps you are thinking now, "This is an impossible pipe dream, let's get real." Maybe it's not as impossible as it sounds.

Politicians and journalists watch carefully public opinion surveys of the popularity of the President of the United States. Politicians use polls like these as an indication of whether or not they should run for office. What people like and don't like has profound implications for our political process.

In education, inquiries about student attitudes toward learning are certainly not a new idea. At Stanford University student ratings of teacher performance are required and are used as one indication of faculty merit. The California

Achievement Tests at the elementary school level include questions inquiring about the extent to which students enjoy each subject. (A discouraging fact is the progressive decline in the joy of learning with increasing grade levels.) The Michigan school assessment program similarly collects evidence of student enjoyment of reading.

The problem is not that we don't collect evidence about how much students love learning. The problem is that we just don't consider such evidence to be important. Love of learning has not been clearly articulated as an educational goal.

Are positive attitudes toward learning important to people? Definitely yes, according to a recent survey of parents, teachers, and students in five California high schools (Krumboltz, Ford, Nichols, & Wentzel, 1987). Asked how large a role the school should play in achieving 40 broadly stated and important educational goals, parents, teachers and students alike agreed that two attitude goals belonged in the top half of the list: "Appreciate the importance of education," and "Engage in and enjoy learning for its own sake." There is no doubt that the vast majority of the population endorses the goal that students should enjoy learning. Putting the goal into practice is the next step.

Counselors would certainly join administrators and teachers working with parents and students in taking steps toward a common goal—children should learn while enjoying the process. Do we ever succeed in reaching this goal? Yes, occasionally we succeed brilliantly. But our successes seem to be all too few. I came across an essay by a high school senior entitled "How I'm Different from the Rest of the Kids." Juana Arcelia Sainez wrote as follows:

"How I'm Different from the Rest of the Kids"

If I were to become a world famous heart surgeon, or if I were to drop out of school to marry Mr. Wonderful, either way my parents would still consider me their perfect baby girl. My parents never judge me by my literacy nor my success in school. Because my parents, raised on a farm in Mexico, never attended school, they haven't found reading and writing an essential part of their lives. While growing up, my dad planted corn seeds in the field with other men in the family; my mom cooked tortillas, like all Mexican peasant women.

Now, in California, my dad, a laborer, stirs cement for a living; my mom shows me, the youngest girl, how to cook refried beans using her secret spicy recipe. They've managed by scribbling their signatures on documents, but they depend on me to write out their checks, read important mail, translate for them when they confront an English-speaking individual, and make phone calls.

Although my parents can neither read nor write, they live happy, traditional lives. My parents enjoy monthly get-togethers for a family member's birthday. The 20 or more relatives devour my mom's homemade tamales; the stereo plays

Mexican rancheras; the women in the family gather in the kitchen, gossiping about a relative in Mexico; the men, discussing living costs in Mexico, sit around the dining room table playing poker; the grandchildren play house in the family room. The action begins when everyone dances to salsa music while the very young clap their hands to the beat. The party ends the next morning after the guests eat breakfast and head homeward. During all this time no one has talked about a book.

Because my sister and brother like my parents' traditional lives, they consider my parents their ideal role models. My sister, who never learned to read beyond the fourth-grade level, graduated from a San Francisco public high school and decided to work as a file clerk, a job that demands little reading. At 19, she was married and gave birth to her first child. Presently she still works, but she sees herself as a mother, not a cosmopolitan business woman. Often she calls me up to help her spell words such as "necessary." Recently, I had to correct her grammar in a letter she had written to her daughter's principal. When the principal wrote back I had to translate the letter into spoken English because my sister couldn't understand the formal content of the letter. She depends on me for all of these reading and writing tasks.

My brother, who reached high school not knowing how to read, dropped out because he wanted to earn money working as a laborer. At 25, he hated not knowing how to fill out a job application when necessary. I tried to teach him to read and write by sounding out the letters of the alphabet. I have no teaching skills and had the feeling I was leading him into a black hole—a feeling that was confirmed. Writing a Christmas card, he asked me if he spelled "from" correctly, when in fact he had spelled it "furm." He still doesn't have a hold on reading and writing. My other brothers and sisters more or less fit the same pattern I've described. Why am I different? I think it's because I've had different school experiences that have encouraged me to find out my interests through reading and writing.

In elementary school, my teachers convinced me that reading was fun. When the teacher announced, "We are walking down to the library to get a free book from the Reading is Fundamental program—R.I.F.," my classmates and I ran to form a single line, folded our hands in front of us, and shushed the noisy kids so we could be the first class down there. On the way, we whispered about our favorite "Curious George" book we hoped to find in the gold mine of books stacked on the tables, or about the new "Sammy the Seal" books we saw in an R.I.F. pamphlet. After reading my free book, I swapped with my friends so I could read another of Snoopy's adventures. The books were like healthy, sugary lollipops, and no one took them away.

In middle school, my reading became related to my future goals. I remember the day I decided to become a doctor. In science class, my classmates and I were dissecting a frog. I didn't close my eyes and say "gross"; instead, I was fascinated. Recognizing the frog's heart, I thought, "Wow, here's a real heart that looks nothing like a Valentine heart!" Since that day, I've been reading everything about science and medicine I can get my hands on.

In high school, my teachers indirectly help me reveal my individuality through reading and writing. In English class, my teacher inspires my classmates and me to use writing to discover who we are. That's why, when I wrote my college essay, I was easily able to discuss my own experience in terms of that quote from "The Breakfast Club": "What we learned today is that each one of us is a brain, an athlete, a basket case, a criminal, and a princess." Writing has helped me become my own person.

Unfortunately, my sister and brother never encountered the pleasures of writing, nor any of the other positive school experiences I've had with reading and writing. But, examining these experiences, we can get some clues toward a solution to the problem of illiteracy. We can see what would have helped my sister and brother. If schools make reading and writing fun, if they use reading and writing to help students find future goals, and if they encourage students to read and write as a way of finding out about themselves, more students will grow up with ambitions to be world-famous surgeons, and fewer will be dropouts and illiterates.

● ● ●

Note that Juana sees herself as unusual, as different from the rest of the kids. Unlike them, she finds learning to be fun. She had positive school experiences with reading and writing. Clearly Juana is one of our successful outcomes. But why are there so few like her? Why is she in the minority?

Two Necessary Conditions for the Enjoyment of Learning

What is it that schools might do to help students enjoy learning? It seems to me that there are two fundamental needs that are being ignored for too many youngsters in our schools:

1. Youngsters need to feel important, but certain types of school experiences make some of them feel degraded and unimportant.
2. Youngsters need to cooperate in friendly ways with their peers, but the traditional school structure often forces them into isolated competition against each other.

It should be possible to design school experiences that address both needs. School environments could be designed to make every child feel important and to enable youngsters to cooperate with each other in the achievement of school goals. I would like to explore in the remainder of this paper some counselor activities that might move us in these directions.

The Need of Every Child to Feel Important in School

When parents of students at five California high schools were asked to rate the importance of 40 broadly stated educational goals, the one they rated as the most important, number one in the list, was "Have feelings of personal worth and self-confidence" (Krumboltz, Ford, Nichols, & Wentzel, 1987). How successful are schools in promoting this important outcome?

Certainly some young people have experiences in school that make them feel valued and important. They receive recognition from teachers and peers. They participate in group activities. Their academic efforts are rewarded with good grades and praise. But many others share few of these rewards. What could we do to increase the percentage of youngsters who have positive school experiences? What are the obstacles within the school environment?

Structural Impediments to Student Self-Esteem. Part of the problem is rooted in the structure of the school system itself. Perhaps some dormant assumptions need to be reexamined.

Grading Systems. For some reason it has been determined that we must rank order students on their accomplishment of each type of task. It is not clear to me why it should be so important to rank order student accomplishments, but for the moment that is the system under which we operate in most school districts. Rank ordering students has no serious emotional consequences for those students who come out ranking number one. Indeed, it is a satisfying experience to be number one in a class or in the school. It's not even horrible to be in the top half of the class. The trouble is that a full 50% of the population ranks below average!

A few people seem not to mind that they are considered below average in some subjects, but the system produces some youngsters, far too many, who are below average in every academic subject. In a recent study (Duckworth et al., 1986) students in 69 high school classes were asked to respond to the statement: "No matter how hard I work in this class I can't do as well as I would like." An average of 37% of the high school students agreed with that statement, and the percentages were almost identical whether they came from students in biology, geometry, English, or history classes.

Test Score Reports. Some achievement test scores are reported in "grade equivalents." Grade equivalent scores carry more meaning than is warranted. For example, suppose you hear that Joey is a sixth-grade student who is reading at the fifth-grade level. You immediately assume that poor Joey is one year behind schedule and that a serious problem exists. The unstated presupposition in the minds of most lay people and many professional educators is that all sixth-grade students should be reading at the sixth-grade level. (Remember that Juana Arcelia Sainez was distressed that her sister read at the fourth-grade level.)

What is a grade equivalent score? It is an average, not a standard. Scores on a reading test are averaged for all sixth graders; that mean is designated as the sixth-grade equivalent. Fifty percent of the sixth graders score above average and 50% score below average by definition. Furthermore, many fifth graders score higher than the average of the sixth graders, and many sixth graders score lower than the average of the fifth graders. There is a wide range of achievement in every class—always has been, always will be. Different levels of accomplishment are as normal as different heights and weights.

Reporting scores in grade equivalent terms, however, produces an undue and inappropriate emotional impact. Fear and misunderstanding are created when children are reported scoring at some grade equivalent level less than their actual grade. Because, by definition, 50% of the population is below grade level, grade equivalent scores cause youngsters to feel less important, less valued, and less competent than they need to feel. (Some students of course score "at grade level," but only because of rounding errors. If grade equivalents were reported precisely, e.g., 6th grade, 5th month, 22nd day, 3rd hour, almost no one would score exactly "at grade level.")

Labeling Systems. Another educational practice is to apply labels to youngsters who are experienceing particular difficulties. Labels such as "learning disabled" or "emotionally disturbed" are not intended to stigmatize students. They are intended to be helpful so that such students can receive special services for their special needs. Unfortunately the labels often are applied to the youngsters themselves, not to the programs designed to help them. As a consequence, teachers may have different expectations for youngsters when they learn about the label that accompanies each youngster.

Algozzine et al. (1977) reported that the behaviors of emotionally disturbed youngsters seemed more disturbing and less accepted when subjects thought they were exhibited by a "learning disabled" child than when they were thought to be the behavior of an "emotionally disturbed" child. Disruptive aggressive behavior was seen as less tolerable if it came from a "learning disabled" rather than an "emotionally disturbed" child. Algozzine (1979) has warned that biases are generated by categorical labels and that these biases affect the perceptions of individuals who will be working with these children.

In another study (Ysseldyke & Foster, 1978) a 12-minute videotape of a normal youngster was shown to elementary school teachers. Some of the teachers were told that the child was normal, a second group that he was learning disabled, and a third group that he was emotionally disturbed. The teachers rated the boy more negatively when he was labeled as either learning disabled or emotionally disturbed than when he was labeled as normal.

Perhaps progress has been made since these studies were done, but even when such clear-cut labels are not used, teachers can develop expectations about student performance on the basis of test scores, prior grades, or other stereotypical attributes such as sex or race. The possibility that some teachers are more "alterable" than others in changing their expectations was provided in one small scale study (Cooper, 1977).

Counselor Actions That Can Affect Self-Esteem and Academic Achievement. Because the system has so many built-in mechanisms to stigmatize and diminish the self-esteem of a large number of its constituent members, one might become pessimistic about the possibility of counselors ever being able to do anything constructive. We counselors, however, are resilient and are not easily discouraged by difficult circumstances.

Can counselors do anything to improve academic achievement? In a review of the literature covering a 10-year period Gerler (1985) cited three studies (Gerler, Kinney, & Anderson, 1985; Gerler & Locke, 1980; Downing, 1977) documenting that elementary school counselors have had a positive effect on academic achievement. So there is evidence that counselor actions can have a positive impact.

Let's focus now on some of the research findings that support specific kinds of counseling services and activities that have some likelihood of making a difference. Counselors can exert their influence in three ways: (1) by consulting with teachers about individual or classroom concerns, (2) by counseling with students themselves (or with parents), and (3) by influencing school policy within the system.

Consulting with Instructional Staff. Teachers bear the responsibility for helping the children in their classroom to learn. It's a tough job. It's a complicated job and it is amazing that it is done as well as it is given the tremendous obstacles that teachers face every day. Teachers need all the help they can get. Counselors are often in a position to lend support and encouragement when teachers feel frustrated, unappreciated, overwhelmed, angry, or discouraged.

Teachers are always going to be crucial to the learning process because they perform some functions that the written word can never provide and that computers probably will never be able to provide (though computers are making steps in that direction).

Schallert and Kleiman (1979) wrote an interesting paper pointing out the essential activities that teachers perform that textbooks cannot. Teachers can adapt to what children already know. They can interact with the children, ask them questions, listen to questions, note puzzled looks, and pick up on body language. When a lesson needs more clarification, they can explain more fully. Teachers can bring to bear knowledge that the children already have and help them see how new information relates to it. Teachers can focus attention on important learning segments by asking direct questions, eliciting guesses, and encouraging comments. Teachers can check to see whether learning has been successful. Schallert and Kleiman quote Socrates in the dialogue *Phaedrus*: "Written words seem to talk to you as though they were intelligent, but if you ask them anything about what they say . . . they go on telling you the same thing forever" (p. 9).

If teachers do their job well the results are stimulating and pleasant for members of the class. But what portion of the class is really experiencing pleasant events in school? A study by West et al. (1981) summarized several other studies that examined the reactions of some 1,500 adolescents. The adolescents were to recall important actions occurring to them in school within the past 5 school days. They reported who elicited them and how pleasant they were. In one rural high school Eggleston (1973) found that 37% of teacher actions were perceived as pleasant and 63% unpleasant. In a larger city high school, 41% of teacher behaviors were deemed pleasant versus 59% unpleasant. Students were no more pleasant to each other in school than the teachers were. The picture emerging from these studies is that the majority of student-perceived actions in school are unpleasant. What possible actions can counselors take to deal with this problem?

1. Encourage teachers to experiment with giving alternative choices about learning activities to students. How much should teachers structure the learning and how much power should students themselves have in picking their learning activities? It is possible that some students in a classroom can be given more power to choose than others. An investigation by Greene (1979) gave some students a choice of when to do their work, the sequence in which to do the work, and the standards that would be used for judging their performance. Other students had no such choice. The most important finding that emerged from this study was that in high-ability classrooms students can be given more choices, but in lower-ability classrooms the students benefit more from teacher-structured activities. This study confirms some of Cronbach and Snow's (1977) findings about aptitude treatment interactions. The results are suggestive but not conclusive.

When I was a student teacher in an inner-city New York junior high school, I remember struggling with discipline and lack of interest in an eighth-grade social studies class. I tried to apply the principles I was learning at Teachers College—arousing students' motivation, leading them in stimulating discussions, and presenting them with alternatives from which they could choose. My efforts seemed unavailing.

Then one day I tried something completely different. Before the students entered the classroom, I put on each desk a pencil, a blank piece of paper, and a textbook. On the blackboard I wrote a list of questions and the page numbers in the textbook where the answers to these questions could be found. When the students entered the classroom I directed them to sit down, read the questions on the blackboard, find the answers in the textbook, and write the answers on their piece of paper. The students followed the instructions, and for the first time in my experience the classroom was quiet. The students loved the experience. They didn't like the choices I had given them earlier. When given those choices, they would too often choose to do the wrong thing, and they knew it.

In some classrooms certain individuals can be given more choice, but Greene's finding suggests that the level of talent in the classroom as a whole is the determining factor in deciding how much choice to give students. When the entire class is made up largely of high-ability students, more choices are possible. In other classrooms teachers might well be encouraged to devise more highly structured activities.

Generalizations on issues as serious as this ought not to be based on a few research studies, however well conducted. Classrooms do not fall neatly into two categories, high ability and low ability. Teachers differ in their skill in defining limits for student choices. In some circumstances, "Linda, would you like to make your presentation today or tomorrow?" would constitute an upper limit on freedom of choice. "Shall we study 17th-century English history or astronomy?" might exceed the limit in most classrooms.

The same kinds of choices are probably not appropriate in classrooms of markedly different ability levels, but that is not to say that lower-ability students should not be taught how to make choices. These students will grow up with the right to one vote just like everyone else. The schools have a responsibility to teach wise decision making to everyone, and a good place to start teaching the relationship between choices and consequences is with permissible alternatives within the classroom.

2. Encourage teachers to set appropriate standards of performance for each individual. The research I have examined indicates clearly that standards of performance for students need to be set at a moderate level for each student. If the standards are set too high, discouragement and diminished performance result. If standards are set too low, boredom and diminished performance result. A rigorous experimental test of this hypothesis has been contributed by Burkman and Brezin (1981), who studied 32 classes taught by 12 teachers for 588 students. The percentage of correct answers required to get a passing grade was experimentally manipulated. For most of the content in this physical science course a medium performance standard produced the most achievement. When the content was easy, however, a higher performance standard produced better results. When the content was difficult to learn, a lower standard produced the best results.

Similar findings were discovered in quite a different way by Mayers et al. (1978). In this creative study, 85 adolescents were given "beepers" that served as a stimulus for filling out a report about what they were doing at the instant the beep occurred and how much they were enjoying it. The adolescents were monitored for an entire week, in school and out, from 7:30 in the morning until 10:30 at night. Among the fascinating findings in this study was that students did not dread taking tests. On the contrary, during tests their concentration was extremely high and they felt challenged.

Self-reports from students based on their perceptions of the skills and challenges in individual classes were examined. Classes in which student skills were high but the challenges were low were labeled "boredom" classes. When the skills and challenges were both high, the label given was "flow" classes. Where the challenges were high but the skills were low, the investigators gave the label "worry" classes. Students felt the most "energy"—strong, active, alert, involved, and excited—in the "flow" classes where there was a match between challenge and skills. They tended to have positive feelings (happy, cheerful, friendly, and sociable) even in the "boredom" classes, as well as the "flow" classes, but the "worry" classes reduced those positive feelings.

Clearly, a good match for one student was not necessarily a good match for another. The problem that teachers have is adjusting to individual differences. I taught ninth-grade algebra for 2 years, and one of my most difficult problems was providing appropriate challenges for the wide range of talent. Counselors can help teachers to realize that some students may be bored in class because they are not sufficiently challenged, whereas others in that identical class are fearful, worried, and anxious because the same activities to them are overwhelmingly difficult. Teachers need encouragement, support, and appreciation for taking the extra effort to tailor learning activities to individual needs. Griggs (1985) made a number of constructive suggestions for adapting learning activities to different learning styles.

3. Structure ways for teachers to learn how better to manage time. "Time-on-task" is widely known to be an important component of achievement (Bloom, 1976). It seems almost self-evident to say that children learn those things on which they spend time in learning. The old proverb "practice makes perfect" states the idea even more succinctly. But if you prefer scientific evidence, the notion that time spent on a task improves performance on that task was supported in a study of the Follow Through Program (Stallings, 1974) and in a re-analysis of data from 22 nations on children 10 to 14 years of age and high school seniors (Tedesco et al., 1979). As Duckworth (1983) pointed out, time-on-task by itself is an empty concept without considering the nature and appropriateness of the task and the students' readiness for it.

It takes great organizational skill to keep 30 youngsters busily occupied at learning tasks suitable to their level of attainment 6 hours a day—especially so when extraneous duties (collecting lunch money, listening to loudspeaker announcements) are added to a teacher's normal responsibilities. Student time spent on task is time not spent creating discipline problems, so double benefits accrue to teachers who can keep everyone busy at challenging tasks. Workshops or building-level inservices might be ways of bringing together teachers to share their methods of structuring tasks and activities efficiently.

4. Encourage teachers to accept credit for student accomplishments. Is student accomplishment in the classroom the result of the teacher's behavior? Some teachers believe strongly that their own actions have a powerful influence on student behavior and student academic achievement. As conceptualized by Rotter (1966), such teachers would be said to have a high internal locus of control.

Other teachers see student behavior and accomplishment as resulting from external sources not under teacher control; such teachers would be said to have a high external locus of control.

Do the beliefs of teachers about the extent to which they have control over student accomplishments relate to actual student accomplishments? The answer seems to be a strong "yes." Students who have "internal" teachers tend to achieve more than do students assigned to "external" teachers (Murray & Staebler, 1974; Vasquez, 1973). Subsequent work has attempted to confirm these earlier findings while trying to isolate the exact behaviors that enable the "internal" teachers to perform better. Sadowski and Woodward (1981) showed that the "internal" teachers tended to generate more of an "origin" atmosphere among the students. That is, the students saw the teacher as encouraging student goal setting, responsibility, and self-confidence. Rose and Medway (1981) again confirmed that the "internal" teachers tended to have classes with higher achieving students than did "external" teachers, but they were unsuccessful in identifying specific teacher behaviors that distinguished the two groups. The study was well done in that achievement gains in the fourth grade were based objectively on the Comprehensive Test of Basic Skills administered at the end of the third grade.

Here is an intuitively appealing and only slightly overstated conclusion: Teachers who believe they have the power to affect student achievement do in fact affect student achievement; those who think they can't, don't. Yet we are not exactly sure what it is the teachers do that makes a difference.

The fact that people who believe they have the power to influence student behavior do in fact influence student behavior does not indicate the direction of causality. Beliefs may influence performance, or performance may influence beliefs. Successful teachers might well want to believe that success is due to their efforts, whereas less successful teachers would prefer to cast the blame elsewhere, and perhaps justifiably so. There is some evidence that children can be trained to change their internal beliefs (Dweck, 1975), but whether teachers' beliefs can be changed so as to affect student achievement remains untested.

Should counselors then encourage teachers to adopt a more internal locus of control? We don't know if the effort could succeed, but it might be worth a try. Even if teachers' locus of control can be modified, we don't know whether such changes would have an effect upon student achievement. However, until we get some research answers, what should counselors be doing? We have only correlational evidence, but I can see little harm in encouraging teachers to take credit for student accomplishments and to believe that renewed efforts on their part can help students who are having trouble. Simple appreciation of the teacher's talent and energy will help the teacher feel better and build a better counselor-teacher relationship.

Individual Counseling with Students. Counselors see their major role as working directly with students. What kinds of interventions are most effective in helping students who are having difficulty learning in school? Goodstein (1979) has written a perceptive paper on the diagnosis and treatment of underachievement. He makes it clear that underachievement is not simply a matter of lacking skills—it is often a profound psychological coping mechanism.

When I was in the seventh grade I was required to enroll in a music course. As part of the introductory exercises the music teacher asked each student in the class to sing a few notes solo. She went around the room, each student singing a few notes as requested. When she came to me I refused to sing. She tried to flatter me. I refused. She coaxed and cajoled me. I refused. She threatened me with possible failure in the course. I refused. She asked me why I refused. I told her that I did not want to sing. She could have had me drawn and quartered, but I was not going to sing. Furthermore, I was not going to tell her or anyone else why I was not going to sing. I am now prepared to tell the real reason why I refused so adamantly to sing in seventh grade: My voice was changing at that time and I was afraid that I would squeak or squawk and make a fool of myself to the laughter and ridicule of my peers. Fortunately the teacher did not make a federal case about my refusal. I wonder now how many other youngsters in school fail to try because they are afraid of ridicule.

Goodstein cites an article by Iscoe (1964) that describes the "double bind" situation of a bright underachieving child who is told over and over by parents and teachers that he can succeed if only he would try. The child is given credit for being able to succeed but is excused for his failure because he doesn't try. The child is in a terrible dilemma. What if he did really try and still failed? His only excuse for failure would then disappear. He is already receiving credit for being able to achieve, so there is nothing to be gained by trying. He has everything to lose if he does try and still fails. Under the circumstances his only alternative is to continue refusing to try.

Counselors need to be sensitive to the complex issues that underlie low academic achievement. Some youngsters fail from lack of skill; others fail because failure is the only way they see to preserve their self-respect. Counselors who can see behind facades generated by fear and can gently confront self-defeating thinking are in a powerful position to help youngsters reshape their lives.

1. Counsel students to accept responsibility for their own outcomes. In the last 10 to 15 years, a large number of studies, based on attributional theory (Weiner et al., 1971), have been conducted on the concept of students' locus of control. As we have seen in the case of teachers, locus of control refers to the degree to which people believe they have control over their own destiny. The "internals" believe that whatever they accomplish is due to factors inside themselves—their own ability and effort, for example. "Externals," on the

contrary, believe that factors outside themselves determine their destiny—luck, task difficulty, life circumstances, and the behavior of other people.

Does it make any difference whether students adopt internal or external beliefs? An overwhelming amount of evidence shows that internals achieve better than externals. Several reviews of the literature (Greene, 1976; Lefcourt, 1976; Stipek & Weisz, 1981) have confirmed a consistently low but positive association between an internal locus of control and achievement.

At the elementary school level internals achieved more than externals (Bar-Tal et al., 1978; Bar-Tal et al., 1982; Cauley & Murray, 1981; Cunningham, Gerard, & Miller, 1978; Kennelly & Mount, 1985). However, the outcomes have not always been identical for both boys and girls (Crandall et al., 1962; Stipek & Hoffman, 1980).

Mitchell (1979) asked 143 students from the 10th, 11th, and 12th grade to explain the reasons for the grade point average they received and found that the low-achieving students often cited luck or being disliked by the teacher. Mitchell decries this self-defeating attribution to luck. Those who believe in luck are less likely to exert effort and take actions that could improve the situation. He endorsed Weiner's (1976, p. 199) contention that attributional training programs possibly could be used to improve achievement-related behavior.

Saunders-Harris (1981) found that internal subjects achieved significantly better than externals in seventh-grade science classes. Similar findings were reported in Britain for 1,000 9- to 11-year old children (Reid & Croucher, 1980). The study used the Crandall Intellectual Achievement Responsibility (IAR) questionnaire (Crandall et al., 1965), which showed substantial correlations between the British children's acceptance of responsibility for their own achievement and the quality of that achievement. Furthermore the IAR was relatively independent of measures of intelligence. Again the suggestion was made that children could learn to accept more responsibility for their successes and failures in the classroom.

Do children accept responsibility for their failures as well as they accept responsibility for their successes? Definitely not. In a review of 38 studies on this topic, Zuckerman (1979) found 71% of the studies showed that subjects take more responsibility for success than for failure whereas only 5% of the studies reported results in the opposite direction. Marsh (1986) labels this tendency to accept responsibility for success but not for failure the "self-serving effect" (SSE). (The labels of "attributional egotism" (Snyder, Stephan, & Rosenfield, 1978) and "self-serving bias" (Bradley, 1978; Miller & Ross, 1975) also have been used to identify this tendency.) In studying fifth and ninth graders in Australia, Marsh found that academically able students were more likely to attribute their successes internally and their failures externally than were students who were less academically able. Furthermore these self-serving effects seemed to be content-specific. "Students who were more able in reading had larger SSEs for attributions of ability in reading, and students who were more able in mathematics had larger SSEs for attributions of ability in mathematics" (p. 198).

Other work (Greene, 1985; Johnson, 1981; Marsh, 1984; and Marsh et al., 1984) has shown that students with the best self-concepts were most likely to exhibit these self-serving effects. In other words, children with high self-concepts accepted responsibility for their successes but blamed their failures on outside factors much more than low self-concept children did. A meta-analysis conducted by Whitley and Frieze (1985) confirmed that adults also are motivated by a need to enhance their self-esteem by means of attributing success to internal factors and failure to external factors. It would seem that if you want to feel good about yourself, you should blame others for your failures and accept total responsibility for your successes!

A review of the literature by Fahey (1984) reported that learning disabled children are more external in their locus of control than are normal children in regard to attributions toward success. Citing Pearl et al. (1980), Fahey reported that "learning disabled children attribute their successes to external factors (task difficulty), while they attribute their failures to internal factors (ability) and not to the difficulty of the task" (p. 436). Other related studies on the learning disabled have been conducted by Blau and Loveless (1978), Dean (1985), Dembinski and Mauser (1977), Dickson (1976), Dudley-Marling (1985), Gallagher (1972), Johnson et al. (1981), Murray (1980), Omizo et al. (1985), Rubin et al. (1986), Swanson (1980), and Tolliver (1979).

As one might expect, students who have discipline problems in high school tend to have a more external orientation whereas those judged by their teachers to be helpful facilitators in the classroom tend to have a more internal orientation (Gnagey, 1981). The same basic results were obtained in Nigeria (Maqsud, 1980) where 12- and 13-year old academic achievers were more internal in their attributions whereas the delinquents were more external.

The concept of locus of control has some important implications for the work of counselors and school psychologists (Chan, 1978). Although it is clear from this mass of evidence that a belief in one's own powers to influence outcomes is associated with successful outcomes, we have not shown which is chicken and which is egg. Does the belief affect the performance or does the performance influence the belief? If a child's belief that her fate was governed only by luck could be changed to a belief that she had some measure of control over her own destiny, then perhaps she could be motivated to exert more effort to improve her performance. To make that case we would have to see evidence that (1) the belief could be changed, and (2) higher academic achievement occurred as a result. What does the evidence show?

A study by Smith and Troth (1975) showed that a program of direct cognitive teaching of achievement motivation thinking and acting strategies was successful among 12th graders in a vocational training center in reducing external control feelings and increasing achievement motivation. However, the training program had no effect on academic grades or on ratings given by instructors.

A path analysis based on 22,660 high school seniors seemed to indicate that, in addition to intellectual ability, locus of control had a strong relationship to achievement. The suggestion was made that improving general self-concept may not be an effective means of improving achievement but that helping students achieve a more internal locus of control might offer more hope (Keith et al., 1985). The evidence was only correlational, not experimental.

Fadiman (1979) suggested one possible treatment. The problem is caused because people use inaccurate language to state their generalizations; therefore, reframing needs to be taught. If a child says, "I am not good at math," the counselor should help the child reframe the statement to "You mean, you *used* to not do well at math." The child cannot be accurate in stating "I am not good at math" because the child is not doing math at the time she is speaking to the counselor. The child may have a history of failing at math, but it is incorrect to let past events justify a present generalization. Using the present tense to describe the past has serious consequences, according to Fadiman. It perpetuates the presupposition that one's history must continue to be repeated. It prevents change in growth and therfore limits future possibilities. Fadiman cited one case study of a 11-year old Little Leaguer who thought "I can't hit." After the parents and the coach corrected his grammar, the boy finished in the top tenth of the League in batting. The idea is appealing, but the evidence is weak.

Sparta (1979) gave a sketchy description of a study that experimentally compared three treatments for altering achievement and self-concepts with a sample of 54 elementary school youngsters from a heterogeneous (Anglo and mixed minority) population. The experimenter stratified according to sex and degree of learned helplessness, and randomly assigned to either an attribution treatment, a self-management treatment, or a positive reinforcement treatment. The treatment that produced the best results was the attribution treatment in which the trainer "used specific interpretations and exhortations to foster personal responsibility within achievement situations, through guiding attributions increasingly toward greater effort and less toward low ability" (p. 5). The report, however, did not make clear on which outcome measures the best results were obtained.

Attempting to persuade children that their hard work and effort will pay off seems to have some effect. Schunk (1984) wondered whether children should be given feedback on their arithmetic problem solving by comments on their ability or about their effort. Some of the children received comments from the proctor who, upon finding what page number they were working on, remarked, "You're good at this." Children who received the effort feedback were told, "You've been working hard." The main conclusion was that "children who initially received ability feedback demonstrated significantly higher levels of self-efficacy and subtraction skillful performance compared with subjects initially given effort feedback'' (p. 14).

Schunk explains the finding as follows: "As children solve problems during training they begin to develop a sense of efficacy. Telling them early in a course of skill development that ability is responsible for their task successes supports their self-perceptions of progress and substantiates this sense of efficacy'' (p. 17). Giving effort feedback early in a task was not as effective as giving ability feedback, even if ability feedback was given later. There seems to be a primacy effect operating.

Another effort to change locus of control was reported by Bradley and Gaa (1977), who studied 36 students in two 10th-grade English classes. The most successful treatment was a goal-setting (GS) conference procedure that promoted a more internal control orientation in students toward academic activities but did not affect social or physical types of activity. The technique was described as follows:

> For five weeks members of the GS group participated in weekly individual goal-setting conferences during which they received feedback on their progress in attaining previously set goals. The material to be studied during the coming week was briefly discussed, as well as any activities, evaluations, or assignments which were to occur. The student then set goals related to discussed areas as outlined by a goal-setting checklist. This list was constructed weekly in conjunction with the classroom teacher and provided a format for the selection of relevant goals as well as structure for the following week's feedback.
>
> During the goal-setting conferences, the student not only set goals but also discussed appropriate actions in accomplishing the goals. The student had some measure of control over reinforcements in the academic situation for two reasons: (1) the goal-setting conferences allowed students a reasonable measure of control over certain outcomes directly related to achievement in the classroom, and (2) they were designed in such a way that the student should become aware that a significant amount of control over those outcomes was possible. (p. 20)

The fact that this treatment was better than the two control treatments in developing more internal attitudes toward academic affairs while not affecting attitudes in other domains constitutes further evidence of the domain specificity of locus of control beliefs. Apparently it is quite easy to believe that one has power to accomplishment in one area but not in others. Although locus of control beliefs were affected by the treatment, no evidence was presented that academic achievement itself changed.

So what have we learned? We know that internals achieve more and have fewer discipline problems than externals. We know that people with good self-concepts tend to exhibit a strange inconsistency: They are responsible for successes but not failures. We know that external beliefs can be changed to internal beliefs by persuasion, exhortation, goal-setting exercises, cognitive restructuring, and telling children, "You're good at this." We cannot yet be sure that changing beliefs changes academic achievement.

We need to avoid overgeneralizing the results of these studies. Many variables such as task difficulty, length of time on the task, source of feedback, and wording of the attribution can affect the outcomes. Clearly, researchers need to isolate the effects of these and other variables before we will know exactly what actions have which effects. In the meantime, counselors can encourage children and teachers to accept responsibility for their successes without fear of doing harm.

2. Counselors can teach children how to take tests. Some children cannot show what they know because they have not learned how to take academic tests. Test-wiseness is a skill that has long been known and investigated (Ebel, Millman, & Bishop, 1965). The problem has been perceived as particularly acute in the testing of minorities (Samuda, 1975; Mercer & Brown, 1973).

A study that showed quite conclusively that test-taking skills can be taught to Black second-grade children was conducted by Kalechstein and Docter (1981). Youngsters were randomly assigned to a test-taking techniques group or to a control group. The test-wiseness training included instructions on "(a) following orally administered directions, (b) marking responses, (c) time-using strategy, and (d) guessing strategy" (p. 199). Those taught the test-wiseness techniques then scored remarkably higher on the Stanford Reading Achievement Test. Test-wiseness seems to be a skill that teachers and counselors can teach.

3. Adapt counseling to the individual learning styles of each student. Griggs (1985) has written an intriguing monograph on ways of adapting counseling to the learning styles of the counselees. Learning style variables include preference for sound, light, and temperature during counseling; amount of motivation, persistence, and responsibility during counseling; preference for high or low structure, learning alone or with others, and amount of variety; use of auditory, tactual, kinesthetic, or visual approaches; and preferred time of day for high energy. A Learning Style Inventory was constructed to measure preferences for these 22 elements. Detailed descriptions of how counselors can adapt their counseling to these individual learning styles are described. One chapter summarizes a large number of research studies that demonstrate the effectiveness of adapting counseling to different learning styles for different age groups. The advantage of the learning style approach is that it helps counselees appreciate how they are unique. Failure experiences can be attributed to a mismatch of style with program rather than to a lack of ability. The approach encourages young people to find environments that are compatible with their style.

Attempts to identify different attributes or learning styles and adapt instruction or counseling to them are not new, nor have they always been successful. The whole aptitude-treatment-interaction (ATI) line of research (Cronbach & Snow, 1977; Greene, 1979) was founded on the hope that learner attributes would be differentially related to instructional methods. Part of the problem has been the different conceptions of what constitutes a learning style.

Bolocofsky (1980) asked whether classroom competition or lack of competition would have differential effects on the achievement of field-dependent and field-independent 10th-grade students. Field-dependent individuals' perceptions tend to be influenced more by the context in which they occur than do those of field-independent individuals (Witkin et al., 1977). The "competitive" students were told that their grades would be based on how well they performed relative to others in the class. The "noncompetitive" students were told that their grades would be based on their total number of correct responses regardless of how well others in the group performed. The "competitive" environment produced generally higher reading comprehension, with the effect being more pronounced for field-dependent subjects than for field-independent subjects.

The same concepts with different names were used by Glenn and Ellis (1982), who classified children as either stimulus-free or stimulus-bound to see which group of elementary school children would learn problem-solving techniques more effectively. The method of instruction itself was the most powerful factor. They concluded that the direct method of instruction "works effectively with both stimulus-bound thinkers and stimulus-free thinkers" (p. 136).

Crawley and Trout (1985) tried to match students to instruction on the basis of Maslow's need model in ninth grade physical science. They found themselves unable to identify a set of variables useful for matching purposes. Their study gave little support for matching personality with instruction. Morris and Melvin (1981) also developed a measuring instrument to Maslow's levels. Although they advocated adapting instruction to individual needs, their study did not provide any evidence of its effectiveness. Attempts to adapt instruction to growth spurts have even been advocated (Pulvino & Jurovic, 1986).

Studies that fail to show the differential effectiveness of learning styles are not evidence that the learning style approach might be necessarily ineffective. Griggs (1985) indicated that further research is needed and suggested several useful approaches.

There is no shortage of possible categories into which people can be subdivided. The problem is identifying classifications that really make an important difference in whether counseling or instruction is effective. Any attempt to respond sensitively to individual differences is bound to be appreciated. Griggs recommends that counselors use case study techniques to see whether certain counseling interventions work better with different individual learning style preferences. Rigorous control-group designs will be necessary too.

Influencing Changes in the System via Technology. Counselors, as members of the school team, can be consistent advocates for adapting the school system to individual needs. Indeed, if there is any one thing that makes people feel appreciated and important, it is that others are sensitive to their needs, preferences, and values.

Computers and related technologies have tremendous possibilities for adapting education and counseling to meet individual differences. Walz (1984) described some of the future uses of computers in tutoring, diagnosing, gaming, and networking. Computers are being used for career guidance and development, dissemination of career information, administration of guidance programs, personal counseling, and testing. I have gone on record as being somewhat skeptical of present computer development (Krumboltz, 1985), but I am enthusiastic about future possibilities and have currently begun a research project to simulate occupations on videodisc to provide vocationally undecided students with realistic work samples in various occupations.

The critical need is not the development of better computers but the development of better software. Papert (1987) suggested the development of a discipline of computer criticism similar to literary criticism. Pea (1987) responded that "software criticism is more at issue than the computer itself" (p. 4). The development of effective educational and counseling software is an art form that has just begun. It will need articulate critics as well as creative and sensitive developers.

Counselors might well want to be at the forefront of attempts to introduce and adapt computers to educational and counseling purposes. Computers are useful tools—not magic wands. If used wisely, the new tools should better enable us to help individuals feel important, cared for, and productive.

Mocros and Russell (1986) conducted a survey of computer use in special education. Among their findings was that teachers who were using educational software did not generally learn through inservice programs but more often through a colleague or friend who shared knowledge and enthusiasm and then continued to provide support. Counselors who learned to use computer software would be one source of inspiration for teachers who are just developing skills. Organizing small groups of teachers who want to learn and support each other in developing computer application could be another useful step at the building level.

The Need of Every Child to Cooperate with Others

Human beings are social animals. We love to attend conferences, talk and commiserate with each other, share ideas, and plan and work together. Schools are institutions that, to all outward appearances, put people together. In reality, the social structure of the school contributes to keeping people apart. Teaching is a lonely occupation. Teachers spend the vast portion of every working day solely responsible for the learning activities of a heterogeneous group of youngsters. There is no opportunity to share the work, discuss individual student problems, or make plans together. The presence of 30 youngsters in a classroom does not satisfy the social needs of a teacher. A teacher needs colleagues who share the same responsibilities and values.

Counseling is a lonely occupation also. A counselor working all day long with students or teachers, individually or in groups, does not have the opportunity to compare notes with other counselors, share concerns, and brainstorm solutions.

Students, at least, have other students sitting next to them, playing with them, and walking and talking with them in the halls. But appearances are deceptive. Students can talk with each other, but do they talk about subjects the school wants them to be learning? How often do students walk out of a classroom and say, for example, "Wow, I can hardly wait to find out how *Hamlet* ends," or "The periodic table of the elements—what a fantastic way to show how atoms are related!"? People in business talk shop with each other. What is there about the school environment that discourages "shop talk" among students?

Structural Impediments to Student Cooperation. School tasks themselves require cooperative activity on the part of students, but the structure of the school inhibits natural tendencies to cooperate.

Assessment. Students are evaluated on the basis of what they do alone, not what they do as part of a group. Writing a term paper is usually done alone, not as a group effort. Taking an examination is done alone. In fact, cooperation of certain types is severely punished.

Program Planning. In high school each student pursues an independent schedule for the day. In large high schools few students have the same sequence of courses and teachers during a typical week. Individual adaptation of the curriculum is to be applauded, but the consequence is that each youngster approaches the school day alone.

Availability of Special Interest Groups. Only part of what young people need to learn is taught in the regular school curriculum. In addition to the major subjects, some schools offer a rich variety of extracurricular activities. Other schools offer very little. Students have, or could develop, many other interests. Student interests could be surveyed. Interest groups could be organized around common interests. How about a Future Lawyers of America Club? A major activity for counselors could be planning and organizing group activities to broaden learning opportunities and make school attractive to more students.

School Policy toward Group Membership. Schools usually have no stated policy about the desirability of students becoming group members. However, group skills are highly valued by high school students, parents, and teachers. In responses to the goal, "Get along comfortably and cooperatively with members of different racial, cultural, and ethnic groups," the mean importance rating for all three groups was shown to range between "critical" and "very important" (Krumboltz, Ford, Nichols, & Wentzel, 1987).

The groups that do exist usually enroll a minority of the total student body. Membership in each group is voluntary and usually must be sought out by the student. Group organizing skills are not systematically taught—how to recruit, how to get new members involved. As a consequence many students lose interest in the school and feel alienated from it.

Counselor Actions to Promote Student Cooperation and Academic Achievement. Peer pressure is intense among adolescents. They are strongly influenced by the values of whatever group they join. Adolescent gangs exert tremendous power over their members and seldom for educationally approved activities. Educators seldom capitalize on the power of the peer group in achieving educational aims. They could. Let's see what ideas counselors might derive from the research literature.

Consulting with Teachers about Group Methods. The competitive individualistic structure of American education has been criticized before but specific alternatives have not achieved much popularity. What could counselors do?

1. Encourage teachers to experiment with forming student teams. An excellent meta-analysis comparing cooperative, competitive, and individualistic goal structures on achievement was reported by Johnson et al. (1981). They reviewed 122 studies and classified and identified four types of goal structures: (a) cooperation— an individual can attain his or her own goal if and only if the other participants can attain their goals (orchestra members playing a symphony); (b) cooperation with intergroup competition—all members of the same group achieve the same outcome but some groups can achieve their goals only if other groups do not (members of a football team); (c) interpersonal competition—an individual can attain his or her own goal if and only if the other participants cannot attain their goals (tennis players in a tournament); and (d) individualistic efforts—whether an individual accomplishes his or her goal has no influence on whether other individuals achieve their goals (library patrons reading books).

Findings from the 122 studies were analyzed in three different ways with comparable results. The results of this meta-analysis are so impressive that I would like to quote directly some of the most significant findings: "Cooperation promotes higher achievement than does interpersonal competition. The results hold for all subject areas (language arts, reading, math, science, social studies, psychology, and physical education), for all age groups (although the results are stronger for pre-college than for college students), and for tasks involving concept attainment, verbal problem solving, categorizing, spatial problem solving, retention and memory, motor performance, and guessing-judging-predicting" (p. 56–57).

In comparing cooperation with individualistic efforts they report, "All three meta-analyses indicate that cooperation promotes higher achievement and productivity than do individualistic efforts. These results hold for all subject areas and age groups. The results are so strong that identifying mediating or moderating variables is difficult" (p. 57).

There is some indication that cooperation without intergroup competition promotes higher achievement and productivity than cooperation with intergroup competition, but the number of studies is too small and the findings may be true only for shorter durations of time when a group product is required. The researchers tended to find no significant difference between interpersonal competitive and individualistic goal structures on achievement and productivity. In their conclusion the authors state, "Given the general dissatisfaction with the level of competence achieved by students in the public school system, educators may wish to considerably increase the use of cooperative learning procedures to promote higher student achievement" (p. 58).

Specifically, how are classes organized in these cooperative approaches? A number of variations are possible. One approach investigated by Slavin (1977) involved 205 seventh-grade students in eight intact English classes. Some of the students were formed into "student-teams-achievement" divisions (STAD). Team members were assigned adjacent seats and given the task of preparing each other for quizzes. They were encouraged to work together to help each other to learn the academic material. The students took quizzes individually, and individual scores were added to form a team score. However, the individual scores were based on how well each team member performed in relation to other students (on other teams) who previously had achieved at the same level. In this way even members of the team who had not performed very well in the past had an equal chance of being able to contribute points to their team's standing because they were competing, not with other members of their own team, not with the entire class, but with other people in the class who had achieved at their own level in the past. This team approach produced positive effects on variables such as time-on-task, liking for others in the class, number of classmates named as friends, and amount of peer support for academic performance. Unlike most studies on cooperative learning, this particular study produced no evidence of academic improvement.

Slavin (1980) reviewed 17 studies that measured student achievement under a team-learning approach in comparison to an individualistic control group and found greater achievement in 14 of them. The remaining 3 studies showed no significant differences.

One of the questions in the use of cooperative team approaches is whether the positive effects found are due to their novelty or whether they would have a more long-lasting effect. Slavin and Karweit (1981) investigated this question in schools where team methods were used most of the instructional day for one entire semester. The subjects were 456 fourth- and fifth-grade students and 17 teachers. Although random assignment to treatments was not possible, efforts were made to match experimental schools with control schools on relevant test scores. Compared to the control group the cooperative team members liked school more, named more friends in school, and increased their self-esteem. The team approach also produced significantly higher academic achievement on three tests (reading vocabulary, language mechanics, and language expression) but no significant differences on four other tests.

Is cooperation more effective with "internals" than with "externals"? A study by Nowicki (1982) showed that in a digit symbol substitution task, cooperative teams of two achieved the highest score increase whether teams consisted of students who attributed their outcomes to internal or external causes. In contrast, when individuals were competing against themselves or competing against other individuals, the internals tended to improve more than the externals, though neither improved as much as they did under the cooperative condition.

Kohn (1986a) presented a persuasive case for the use of cooperation in schools. Portions of the book were abstracted in *Psychology Today* (Kohn, 1986b). One technique, attributed to Elliot Aronson and his colleagues, was called the "jigsaw" method of learning. Students form teams to study the life of a well-known person. Each student receives partial information about the subject, so students must share and integrate their information to make their final report.

Mathematics inspires fear in many students—perhaps because precise answers in a competitive environment reveal failure so clearly. A UC Berkeley-based group called EQUALS has developed a cooperative way of learning math (Booth, 1987). The Director of EQUALS, Nancy Kreinberg, stated, "A cooperative learning environment helps all kids—bright kids, slow kids, competent kids and scared kids—because it sets up a situation in which they are free to explore, to make guesses, to fail and have it be OK" (p. 9). Students in the program are organized in teams of four and work together to solve such problems as how to build the highest tower using two sheets of paper, 10 paper clips, and a pair of scissors.

If we were to take these findings seriously, we would alter drastically the way in which American education is conducted. Each student would be assigned to a team in every class, members of the team would be expected to help each other, and the performance of the whole team would determine the grade of each individual member.

Under team-learning conditions, peer pressure works toward the accomplishment of the educational goals, not in opposition to them. There is, of course, much research left to be done on the exact way to structure classes for optimum output. May I suggest, however, that the evidence is so overwhelmingly favorable that little harm and much good can be derived from starting sooner rather than later to encourage teacher use of cooperative groups.

Some may argue that there is something vaguely un-American in encouraging cooperation instead of competition. Americans, however, are pragmatic if nothing else. Americans like to do what works. In recent years American leaders have wondered why the Japanese have been outproducing us. Many have studied management techniques in Japan. One of the imported ideas is the use of "quality circles," groups of workers who are assigned responsibility for improving production or performance. Group procedures like this have now been started in many U.S. industries.

Athletic teams are prime examples of cooperative efforts where all members of the group benefit if the team is successful. What is more American than football, baseball, and basketball?!

Military people have often testified to the power of the group in holding a platoon together in combat. Individualistic motivations alone could inspire only flight. There is no shortage of examples of ways in which Americans cooperate with each other to accomplish important goals. If learning and academic achievement are important goals, then Americans should be the first to jump on the cooperation bandwagon. The techniques improve academic achievement and students enjoy learning.

2. Organize peer tutoring programs. If school districts had more money, they could hire more teachers, arrange smaller classes, and provide students with more individual attention. Because schools don't have more money, we need to look for less expensive ways to accomplish some of the same purposes. One logical approach to the problem is to arrange for children to teach other children.

A large number of peer tutoring programs have been devised over the years. The quality of the research has not always been the best, but despite that, a consistent picture has emerged that peer tutoring produces both academic and social gains for the tutors as well as the tutees (Devin-Sheehan, Feldman, & Allen, 1976; Feldman et al., 1976; Gartner, Kohler, & Riessman, 1971; McGee, Kauffman, & Nussen, 1977; Mize, Ladd, & Price, 1985; Paolitto, 1976).

James and Sanderson (1979), after reviewing the results of a number of other studies on peer tutoring, devised a tutoring and academic counseling program that consisted of one 3-hour tutoring and counseling session with a minority student each week for 16 weeks. The tutors also met with a coordinator for 1 hour a week. Tutors were assigned to students on a one-to-one basis, and the tutoring sessions included both academic teaching and counseling. The tutors would help tutees with mathematics problems, writing assignments, or vocabulary development. The third hour of each counseling session was devoted to issues such as study habits, time management, attention to the homework assignment, peer influences in a classroom, relationships with teachers and parents, classroom behavior, test anxiety, and test-taking skills. A matched, but apparently not randomly assigned, control group provided some comparison. The grade point average of the tutees improved significantly more than that of the control group (.5 versus .1).

Because previous research had shown as much benefit for the tutor as for the tutee, Chandler (1980) experimented with reverse peer tutoring. Instead of using high achievers as tutors, he used seventh- and eighth-grade low achievers and matched them with second- and third-grade children who were similar in temperament, type of problem, and academic achievement. Chandler reported that the tutors were skeptical until they were convinced that they, and only they, could really understand how the tutees would think and feel because they had "been there." Each tutor spent 45 minutes a day, 4 days a week for 6 weeks at the tutee's school. The tutor was responsible for making up quizzes and reporting progress to the program supervisor.

A major weakness of the study was that no control group was used because the elementary school principal thought it would not be ethical to prevent some children who needed help from obtaining the benefits of a useful program. (Everyone understands that a "lottery" is a fair way to decide who gets some benefit first—random assignment is just one variation of a lottery.) Unfortunately we can't be sure whether the program was useful or not because of the principal's decision, but the pre-post comparisons were nevertheless favorable. Ratings by the teachers of both tutors and tutees indicated substantial improvement in academic subject matter mastery and in a more positive attitude toward school. One of the major findings of the study was that the tutors, who initially had tended to attribute causes to external factors, moved significantly toward a more internal belief system after the tutoring experience.

Two experiments reported by Medway and Lowe (1980) looked further at the attributions of tutors and tutees. In their studies all groups of students saw tutee effort as the primary cause of the beneficial outcomes and tutor effort as the secondary cause. There was also a sportsmanlike tendency for the children to view their partner as responsible for their own benefits and to accept any blame for failures. This finding might seem to be somewhat inconsistent with findings of the self-serving-bias studies in which subjects tended to accept credit for success and blame external factors for failure. However, in these peer tutoring experiences the "external factor" was the partner. Blaming another individual human being is not the same as blaming abstract external factors.

If you were to set up a peer tutoring system and you wanted the tutees to model themselves after the tutors, what kind of children would you choose to be tutors? An excellent review of the literature by Schunk (1987) shows that children tend to emulate competent models. The actual age of the model seems not to matter as long as the model is competent at the task under consideration. However, if the tutees have doubts about their ability to complete the task successfully, a same-age peer may be more effective than an older peer or adult.

Should the peer tutors be of the same sex? Not necessarily, according to the evidence uncovered by Schunk. "Children learn from models of either sex, but may perform behaviors displayed by models who they believe are good examples of their sex role" (p. 167).

Conducting Group Counseling Sessions with Students.   A long established method for helping people solve problems is group counseling. Group counseling enables students to help each other and to perceive first hand that their own problems are not unique. They also learn to give and receive help. A well conducted group conseling session gives people a sense of belonging and the satisfaction of working together to solve common problems.

Dyer (1979) claims that as a result of group counseling, "students learn to believe in themselves, to understand why they think and behave in the ways they do, to develop alternatives to the thinking and behavior that they identify as self-depriving, to actively set goals to change, test out, evaluate, and either incorporate or reject their new behaviors, and to set priorities for themselves that will optimize their own personal living in every area of their existence'' (p. 148).

Whether group counseling actually achieve all of these outcomes is subject to test. None of Dyer's claimed outcomes included academic improvement.

One large scale study of the effects of group guidance procedures in elementary schools was reported by Gerler and Anderson (1986) who recruited 18 counselors throughout North Carolina to conduct group guidance sessions. Previous studies on the effectiveness of group guidance activity in schools showed that group guidance activities had beneficial effective outcomes (increased enjoyment of school, better attitude toward school) but not necessarily improved academic outcomes. The Gerler and Anderson study took on the challenge of academic achievement as well as the more effective outcomes.

The counselors were asked to assign at random one classroom as the experimental group and another as the control group. Data were presented showing the matching to be reasonably effective.

The treatment was composed of 10 sessions of 30 to 40 minutes each. School-related topics included succeeding, being comfortable, being responsible, listening, asking for help, improving, cooperating with peers, and cooperating with teachers. The final sessions dealt with positive and negative aspects of school and allowed students to discuss their personal strengths.

The unit of analysis in this study should have been the classroom, but the individual was apparently used inappropriately as the unit of analysis, thereby making smaller differences statistically significant. The students who received this experimental group counseling were rated as having better classroom behavior by their teachers, received higher ''conduct'' grades, and had more positive attitudes toward school than did children in the control classes. However, no statistically significant differences in academic grades in either language arts or mathematics appeared.

Any one of a variety of problems can serve as a focus for group counseling. Freeman and Couchman (1985) identified problems originating from divorced or divorcing families. They strongly recommended that schools play an important role in assisting children to cope with separation and divorce. They recommended that counselors provide opportunities for these children to discuss their feelings and provided a bibliography of age-appropriate resource materials for both parents and children. Reiss (1981) provided a model of how a family's assumptions affect each member's behavior.

Learning disabled first and second graders were provided group counseling by Amerikaner and Summerlin (1982). The children were randomly assigned to one of three groups: a social skills training group, a relaxation training group, and a control group. The social skills training group consisted of 12 sessions that involved getting the children to talk about characteristics they admired, their favorite activities, their feelings, their strengths, and their differences. Self-ratings by the children showed that their "social self" improved most under the social skills training, but not personal or academic self-esteem scores. The relaxation treatment was most successful in helping children reduce their acting-out behavior (temper tantrums, physical aggressiveness toward others, and lying).

In conventional group counseling, youngsters sit around in a circle and talk to each other and to the counselor. Some radically different approaches to group guidance have been suggested. Hillman and Runion (1978) experimented with activity group guidance with 120 fifth-grade students. Concrete activities, not just talk, constituted the focus for these sessions. Planning and constructing a mural, making a toothpick sculpture, teaching a physical education skill to others, creating a play, writing poetry, and tasting unusual foods were some of the activities described. Thirty pupils from each of four schools were randomly assigned to three groups of 10 students each: activity group guidance, placebo discussion, and control. Outcomes were assessed by sociograms administered to all members of the fifth-grade classes from which the participants were selected. The activity group guidance method was shown to be more effective than the control groups for "increasing social power" (presumably, being chosen more often by peers).

At the high-school level, a similar idea was suggested by Casella and Schrader (1975), who described activity counseling in which potential dropouts are taken to various parts of the city to learn about their community (the courts, the harbor, the county hospital, people employed in various occupations). Youngsters had a chance to interview significant people in the community and to talk with each other about what they had learned. Evaluation of the experiment was sketchy but the authors were enthusiastic.

Group counseling tends to produce the outcomes intended for it—not more, not less. Social skills training increases the social self-concept, relaxation training reduces acting out behavior, activity groups generate more peer friendships, and cooperation training improves attitudes toward school. These are valuable outcomes by themselves and tend to make the school environment a more enjoyable place to work whether academic achievement is affected or not.

Summary

If we want our schools to produce more skillful achievers, reduce dropouts, and inspire lifelong learning, we will have to construct school environments where more children learn to love learning. Schools need to be places where children enjoy working on important tasks. But children cannot enjoy the process of learning if they feel threatened with humiliation and failure or if they are required to work in academic solitude and isolation.

School counselors are in an influential position to help arrange school environments where every child is made to feel important and part of a working team. Working with students, parents, teachers, administrators, school board members, psychologists, and educational researchers, counselors can make some important contributions.

To help children feel valued and important counselors can:

- consult with teachers and encourage them to experiment with giving choices to students, set appropriate performance standards, structure better ways to manage time, and accept credit for student accomplishments; and
- counsel individually with students and teach them to accept responsibility for their outcomes, take tests wisely, and adapt to their individual learning styles; and use technology to provide for individual differences.

To help children learn teamwork and cooperation counselors can:

- consult with teachers and encourage them to experiment with teams within classrooms, sponsor peer tutoring programs, and conduct group counseling programs.

If we are successful in our efforts, children like Juana Arcelia Sainez will no longer feel that they are different from the rest of the kids. Each will feel a valued and important part of the team that is learning important skills. Each will be enjoying the process. Loving to learn need no longer be restricted to the minority.

References

Algozzine, B. (1979). *An analysis of the disturbingness and acceptability of behaviors as a function of diagnostic label.* (ERIC Document Reproduction Service No. ED 185 748)

Algozzine, B., et al. (1977). The effects of labels and behavior on teacher expectations. *Exceptional Children, 44,* 131–132.

Amerikaner, M., & Summerlin, M.L. (1982). Group counseling with learning disabled children: Effects of social skills and relaxation training on self-concept and classroom behavior. *Journal of Learning Disabilities, 15,* 340–343.

Anderson, J.R. (1983). *The architecture of cognition.* Cambridge, MA: Harvard University Press.

Bar-Tal, D., et al. (1978). Effect of an innovative science program on perceptions of locus of control and satisfaction. *Science Education, 62,* 349–357.

Bar-Tal, D., et al. (1982). Consistency of pupils' attributions regarding success and failure. *Journal of Educational Psychology, 74,* 104–110.

Blau, H., & Loveless, E. (1978). *Medication, predelinquency, and delinquency: An eight-year study.* Paper presented at the International Conference of the Association for Children with Learning Disabilities, Kansas City, MO.

Bloom, B.S. (1976). *Human characteristics and school learning.* New York: McGraw-Hill.

Bolocofsky, D.N. (1980). Motivational effects of classroom competition as a function of field dependence. *Journal of Educational Research, 73,* 213–217.

Booth, G. (1987, July 26). Beating the numbers. *Image,* pp. 9–10.

Bradley, G. (1978). Self-serving biases in the attribution process: A re-examination of the fact or fiction question. *Journal of Personality and Social Psychology, 36,* 56–71.

Bradley, R.H., & Gaa, J.P. (1977). Domain specific aspects of locus of control: Implications for modifying locus of control orientation. *Journal of School Psychology, 15,* 18–23.

Burkman, E., & Brezin, M. (1981). Effects of expectation level on achievement in high school physical science courses (ISIS) employing a quasi mastery teaching method. *Journal of Educational Research, 75,* 121–126.

Casella, D.A., & Schrader, D.R. (1975). "Tripping" with borderline dropouts. *School Counselor, 23,* 48–50.

Cauley, K., & Murray, F.B. (1981). *Structure of children's attributes of school success and failure.* Paper presented at the annual meeting of the American Educational Research Association, Los Angeles, CA.

Chan, K.S. (1978). Locus of control and achievement motivation—critical factors in educational psychology. *Psychology in the Schools, 15,* 104–109.

Chandler, T.A. (1980). Reversal peer tutoring effects on powerlessness in adolescents. *Adolescence, 15,* 15–22.

Cooper, H.M. (1977). *Intervening in expectation communication: The "alterability" of teacher expectations.* (ERIC Document Reproduction Service No. ED 165 079)

Crandall, V.C., Katkovsky, W., & Crandall, V.J. (1965). Children's beliefs in their own control of reinforcements in intellectual-academic achievement situations. *Child Development, 36,* 91–109.

Crandall, V.J., Katkovsky, W., & Preston, A. (1962). Motivational and ability determinants of young children's intellectual achievement behavior. *Child Development, 33,* 643–661.

Crawley, F.E., & Trout, J.S. (1985). *Attitude and achievement in ninth grade physical science of low need level students: A reexamination of the matching hypothesis.* Paper presented at the annual meeting of the National Association for Research in Science Teaching, French Lick Springs, IN.

Cronbach, L.J., & Snow, R.E. (1977). *Aptitudes and instructional methods: A handbook for research on interactions.* New York: Irvington.

Csikszentmihalyi, M. (1975). *Beyond boredom and anxiety.* San Francisco, CA: Jossey-Bass.

Cunningham, J.D., et al. (1978). Effects of success and failure on children's perceptions of internal-external locus of control. *Social Behavior and Personality, 6,* 1–8.

Dean, R.S. (1985). *The interaction of neuropsychological and emotional variables in LD children.* Paper presented at the Annual Conference of the Association for Children and Adults with Learning Disabilities, San Francisco, CA.

Dembinski, R.J., & Mauser, A.J. (1977). What parents of the learning disabled really want from professionals. *Journal of Learning Disabilities, 10,* 578–584.

Devin-Sheehan, L., Feldman, R.S., & Allen, V.L. (1976). Research on children tutoring children: A critical review. *Review of Educational Research, 46*, 355–385.

Dickson, R.L. (1976). The relationship between attitudes and reinforcers: An investigation with emotionally disturbed children. *Journal of Special Education, 10*, 365–370.

Dillon, R.F., & Sternberg, R.J. (Eds.) (1986). *Cognition and instruction.* Orlando, FL: Academic Press.

Downing, C.J. (1977). Teaching children behavior change techniques. *Elementary School Guidance & Counseling, 11*, 277–283.

Duckworth, K. (1983). *Intelligence, motivation, and academic work: An operations perspective.* (ERIC Document Reproduction Service No. ED 227 109)

Duckworth, K., et al. (1986). *The relationship of high school teachers' class testing practices to students' feelings of efficacy and efforts to study.* (ERIC Document Reproduction Service No. ED 274 676)

Dudley-Marling, C. (1985). Perceptions of the usefulness of the IEP by teachers of learning disabled and emotionally disturbed children. *Psychology in the Schools, 22*, 65–67.

Dweck, C.S. (1975). The role of expectations and attributions in the alleviation of learned helplessness. *Journal of Personality and Social Psychology, 31*, 674–685.

Dyer, W.W. (1979). The case for group counseling as the means for eliminating erroneous zones. *Elementary School Guidance and Counseling, 14*, 145–148.

Ebel, R.L., Millman, J., & Bishop, C.H. (1965). An analysis of test-wiseness. *Educational and Psychological Measurement, 25*, 707–713.

Eggleston, L.P. (1973). *A study of the role and importance of interaction in a high school setting.* Unpublished paper.

Fadiman, J. (1979). Reframing reality: A transpersonal approach. *Elementary School Guidance and Counseling, 14*, 113–117.

Fahey, D.A. (1984). School counselors and psychological aspects of learning disabilities. *School Counselor, 31*, 433–440.

Feldman, R.S., Devin-Sheehan, L., & Allen, V.L. (1976). Children tutoring children: A critical review of research. In V.L. Allen (Ed.), *Children as teachers: Theory and research on tutoring* (pp. 235–252). New York: Academic Press.

Freeman, R., & Couchman, B. (1985). Coping with family change: A model for therapeutic group counseling with children and adolescents. *School Guidance Worker, 40*, 44–50.

Gallagher, P.A. (1972). Structuring academic tasks for emotionally disturbed boys. *Exceptional Children, 38*, 711–720.

Gerler, E.R., Jr. (1985). Elementary school counseling research and the classroom learning environment. *Elementary School Guidance and Counseling, 20*, 39–48.

Gerler, E.R., & Anderson, R.F. (1986). The effects of classroom guidance on children's success in school. *Journal of Counseling and Development, 65*, 78–81.

Gerler, E.R., Kinney, J., & Anderson, R.F. (1985). The effects of counseling on classroom performance. *Journal of Humanistic Education and Development, 23*, 155–165.

Gerler, E.R., & Locke, D.C. (1980). Multimodal education: A model with promise. *Phi Delta Kappan, 62*, 214–215.

Glenn, A.D., & Ellis, A.K. (1982). Direct and indirect methods of teaching problem solving to elementary school children. *Social Education, 46,* 134–136.

Gnagey, W.J. (1981). High school facilitators and inhibitors. *Clearing House, 54,* 370–375.

Goodstein, M. (1979). *The diagnosis and treatment of underachievement.* Paper presented at the B'nai B'rith Career and Counseling Services Professional Staff Conference, Washington, DC.

Greene, J.C. (1976). *Choice behavior and its consequences for learning: An ATI study.* Unpublished doctoral dissertation, Stanford University.

Greene, J.C. (1979). *Class effects in ATI's.* Paper presented at the annual meeting of the American Educational Research Association, San Francisco, CA.

Greene, J.C. (1985). Relationships among learning and attribution theory motivational variables. *American Educational Research Journal, 22,* 65–78.

Griggs, S.A. (1985). *Counseling students through their individual learning styles.* Ann Arbor, MI: ERIC/CAPS.

Hillman, B.W., & Runion, K.B. (1978). Activity group guidance: Process and results. *Elementary School Guidance and Counseling, 13,* 104–111.

Iscoe, I. (1964). I told you so: The logical dilemma of the bright underachieving child. *Psychology in the Schools, 1,* 282–284.

James, W.H., & Sanderson, L.A. (1979). *A multi-dimensional tutoring and academic counseling model: Applications and effects upon minority high school students.* (ERIC Document Reproduction Service No. ED 194 677)

Johnson, D.S. (1981). Naturally acquired learned helplessness: The relationship of school failure to achievement behavior, attributions, and self-concept. *Journal of Educational Psychology, 73,* 174–180.

Johnson, L.S., et al. (1981). The uses of hypnotherapy with learning disabled children. *Journal of Clinical Psychology, 37,* 291–299.

Johnson-Laird, P.N. (1983). *Mental models.* Cambridge, MA: Harvard University Press.

Kalechstein, P., et al. (1981). The effects of instruction on test-taking skills in second-grade Black children. *Measurement and Evaluation in Guidance, 13,* 198–202.

Keith, T.A., et al. (1985). *Effects of self-concept and locus of control on achievement.* Paper presented at the annual meeting of the National Association of School Psychologists, Las Vegas, NV.

Kennelly, K.J., & Mount, S.A. (1985). Perceived contingency of reinforcements, helplessness, locus of control, and academic performance. *Psychology in the Schools, 22,* 465–469.

Kohn, A. (1986a). *No contest: The case against competition.* Boston, MA: Houghton Mifflin.

Kohn, A. (1986b). How to succeed without even vying. *Psychology Today, 20*(9), 22–28.

Krumboltz, J.D. (1985). Presuppositions underlying computer use in career counseling. *Journal of Career Development, 12,* 165–170.

Krumboltz, J.D., Ford, M.E., Nichols, C.W., & Wentzel, K.R. (1987). The goals of education. In R.C. Calfee (Ed.), *The study of Stanford and the schools: Views from*

36

the inside: Part II. The research. Stanford, CA: School of Education, Stanford University.

Lefcourt, H.M. (1976). *Locus of control: Current trends in theory and research.* Hillsdale, NJ: Lawrence Erlbaum.

Maqsud, M. (1980). The relationship of sense of powerlessness to antisocial behavior and school achievement. *The Journal of Psychology, 105,* 147–150.

Marsh, H.W. (1984). Relationships among dimensions of self-attribution and dimensions of self-concept. *Journal of Educational Psychology, 76,* 1291–1308.

Marsh, H.W. (1986). Self-serving effect (bias?) in academic attributions: Its relation to academic achievement and self-concept. *Journal of Educational Psychology, 78,* 190–200.

Marsh, H.W., Cairns, L., Relich, J., Barnes, J., & Debus, R. (1984). The relationship between dimensions of self-attribution and dimensions of self-concept. *Journal of Educational Psychology, 76,* 3–32.

Mayers, P.L., et al. (1978). *The daily experience of high school students.* (ERIC Document Reproduction Service No. ED 159 583)

McGee, C.S., Kauffman, J.M., & Nussen, J.L. (1977). Children as therapeutic change agents: Reinforcement intervention paradigms. *Review of Educational Research, 47,* 451–477.

Medway, F.J., & Lowe, C.A. (1980). Causal attribution for performance by cross-age tutors and tutees. *American Educational Research Journal, 17,* 377–387.

Mercer, J., & Brown, W. (1973). Racial differences in I.Q.: Fact or artifact? In C. Senna (Ed.), *The fallacy of I.Q.* New York: Third Press, Joseph Okapaku Publishing.

Miller, D.T., & Ross, M. (1975). Self-serving biases in the attribution of causality: Fact or fiction? *Psychological Bulletin, 82,* 213–225.

Miller, G.A., & Johnson-Laird, P.N. (1976). *Language and perception.* Cambridge, MA: Harvard University Press.

Mitchell, J.V., Jr. (1979). Causal attribution and self-assessment variables related to grade point average in high school. *Measurement and Evaluation in Guidance, 12,* 134–139.

Mize, J., Ladd, G.W., & Price, J.M. (1985). Promoting positive peer relations with young children: Rationales and strategies. *Child Care Quarterly, 14,* 221–237.

Mokros, J.R., & Russell, S.J. (1986). Learner-centered software: A survey of micro-computer use with special needs students. *Journal of Learning Disabilities, 19,* 185–190.

Morris, R.C., & Melvin, E.A. (1981). *An assessment of student perceptions of needs deficiencies.* (ERIC Document Reproduction Service No. ED 256 836)

Murray, H., & Staebler, B.K. (1974). Teacher's locus of control and student achievement gains. *Journal of School Psychology, 12,* 305–309.

Murray, J.N. (1980). Understanding and use of chemotherapy by learning disabilities and behavior disorders teachers. *Journal of Learning Disabilities, 13,* 356–360.

Norman, D.A., & Rummelhart, D.E. (1975). *Explorations in cognition.* San Francisco: W.H. Freemen.

Nowicki, S., Jr. (1982). Competition-cooperation as a mediator of locus of control and achievement. *Journal of Research in Personality, 16,* 157–164.

Omizo, M.M., et al. (1985). The effects of rational-emotive education groups on self-concept and locus of control among learning disabled children. *Exceptional Child*, *32*, 13–19.

Paolitto, D.P. (1976). The effect of cross-age tutoring in adolescence: An inquiry into theoretical assumptions. *Review of Educational Research*, *46*, 215–237.

Papert, S. (1987). Computer criticism vs. technocentric thinking. *Educational Researcher*, *16*(1), 22–30.

Pea, R.D. (1987). The aims of software criticism: Reply to Professor Papert. *Educational Researcher*, *16*(5), 4–8.

Pearl, R., Bryan, T., & Donahue, M. (1980). Learning disabled children's attributions for success and failure. *Learning Disability Quarterly*, *3*(1), 3–9.

Pulvino, C.J., & Jurovic, M.C. (1986). Being aware of student growth spurts: Implications for counseling and research. *Elementary School Guidance and Counseling*, *21*, 52–58.

Reid, I., & Croucher, A. (1980). The Crandall Intellectual Achievement Responsibility questionnaire. A British validation study. *Educational and Psychological Measurement*, *40*, 255–258.

Reiss, D. (1981). *The family's construction of reality*. Cambridge, MA: Harvard University Press.

Rose, J.S., & Medway, F.J. (1981). Teacher locus of control, teacher behavior, and student behavior as determinants of student achievement. *Journal of Educational Research*, *74*, 375–381.

Rotter, J.B. (1966). Generalized expectancies for internal versus external control of reinforcement. *Psychological Monographs*, *80*(1, Whole NO. 609).

Rubin, S.S., et al. (1986). *Independent diagnosis of learning disability and emotional disorder: Rationale, method, and results*. Paper presented at the Annual Conference on the American Psychological Association, Washington, DC.

Rummelhart, D.E., McClelland, J.L., & the PDP Research Group (1986). *Parallel distributed processing: Explorations in the microstature of cognition* (Vol. 1). Cambridge, MA: MIT Press.

Sadowski, C.J., & Woodward, H.R. (1981). *Teacher locus of control and students' perceptions and performance*. Paper presented at the Annual Convention of the American Psychological Association, Los Angeles, CA.

Samuda, R.J. (1975). *Psychological testing of American minorities*. New York: Dodd, Mead.

Saunders-Harris, R., & Yeany, R.H. (1981). Diagnosis, remediation, and locus of control: Effects on immediate and retained achievement and attitudes. *Journal of Experimental Education*, *49*, 220–224.

Schallert, D.L., & Kleiman, G.M. (1979). *Some reasons why teachers are easier to understand than textbooks*. (ERIC Document Reproduction Service No. ED 172 189).

Schunk, D.H. (1984). *Sequential attributional feedback: Differential effects on achievement behaviors*. Paper presented at the Annual Meeting of the American Educational Research Association, New Orleans, LA.

Schunk, D.H. (1987). Peer models and children's behavioral change. *Review of Educational Research, 57,* 149–174.

Slavin, R.E. (1977). *Student teams and achievement divisions: Effects on academic performance, mutual attraction, and attitudes.* (ERIC Document Reproduction Service No. ED 154 020)

Slavin, R.E. (1980). Cooperative learning. *Review of Educational Research, 50,* 315–342.

Slavin, R.E., & Karweit, N.L. (1981). Cognitive and affective outcomes of an intensive student team learning experience. *Journal of Experimental Education, 50,* 29–35.

Smith, R.L., & Troth, W.A. (1975). Achievement motivation: A rational approach to psychological education. *Journal of Counseling Psychology, 22,* 500–503.

Snyder, M.L., Stephan, W.G., & Rosenfield, D. (1978). Attributional egotism. In J.H. Harvey, W.J. Ickes, & R.F. Kidd (Eds.), *New directions in attribution research* (Vol. 2, pp. 91–120). Hillsdale, NJ: Erlbaum.

Sparta, S.N. (1979). *Treatment of helpless children: Examination of some potentially therapeutic influences.* Paper presented at the Annual Convention of the American Psychological Association, New York, NY.

Stallings, J.A. (1974). *Follow through classroom observation evaluation, 1972–73— Executive summary.* (SRI Project URU-7370). Stanford Research Institute, Menlo Park, CA.

Stipek, D., & Hoffman, S. (1980). A causal analysis of the relationship between locus of control and academic achievement in first grade. *Contemporary Educational Psychology, 5,* 90–99.

Stipek, D.J., & Weisz, J.R. (1981). Perceived personal control and academic achievement. *Review of Educational Research, 51,* 101–137.

Swanson, L. (1980). Cognitive style, locus of control, and school achievement in learning disabled females. *Journal of Clinical Psychology, 36,* 964–967.

Tedesco, L.A., et al. (1979). *School and classroom processes: A secondary analysis.* Paper presented at the Annual Meeting of the American Educational Research Association, San Francisco, CA.

Tolliver, J.H. (1979). *Impact of an educational crisis center on some elementary school children in a residential treatment program.* (ERIC Document Reproduction Service No. ED 176 517)

Vasquez, J. (1973). *The relation of teacher locus of control to teacher characteristics and student learning gains.* Doctoral dissertation, University of California at Los Angeles.

Walz, G.R. (1984). Role of the counselor with computers. *Journal of Counseling and Development, 63,* 135–138.

Weiner, B. (1976). An attributional approach for educational psychology. In L. Shulman (Ed.), *Review of research in education* (Vol. 4). Itasca, IL: F.E. Peacock.

Weiner, B., Frieze, I.H., Kukla, A., Reed, L., Rest, S., & Rosenbaum, R.M. (1971). *Perceiving the causes of success and failure.* Morristown, NJ: General Learning Press.

West, C.K., et al. (1981). Who does what to the adolescent in the high school: Relationship among resulting affect and self-concept and achievement. *Adolescence, 16,* 657–661.

Whitley, B.E., Jr., & Frieze, I.H. (1985). Children's causal attributions for success and failure in achievement settings: A meta-analysis. *Journal of Educational Psychology*, *77*, 608–616.

Witkin, H.A., Moore, C.A., Goodenough, D.R., & Cox, P.W. (1977). Field-dependent and field-independent cognitive styles and their educational implications. *Review of Educational Research*, *47*, 1–64.

Ysseldyke, J.E., & Foster, G.G. (1978). Bias in teachers' observations of emotionally disturbed and learning disabled children. *Exceptional Children*, *44*, 613–615.

Zuckerman, M. (1979). Attribution of success and failure revisited, or: The motivational bias is alive and well in attribution theory. *Journal of Personality*, *47*, 245–287.

The Counselor as Facilitator of Learning

Shirley A. Griggs

Professor, Counselor Education
St. John's University, Jamaica, New York

The area of "learning and achievement" is extremely broad, and John Krumboltz has performed a yeomanly task in putting these concepts in operation, identifying and synthesizing the significant research, and generating practical applications and recommendations for school counselors. As practitioners on the firing line, school counselors are more concerned with "what works" rather than exclusively with theory and research. However, the thoughtful counselor is not content with "the bag of tricks" approach to effecting change and growth in counselees, and needs to feel confident that the strategies and techniques advocated are supported by a solid research base. Krumboltz has achieved an optimal balance here by abstracting and critically reviewing the research related to learning and achievement and generating creative approaches to enhance student growth and development in these areas. Indeed, his paper entitled, "The Key to Achievement: Learning to Love Learning," is in keeping with his reputation for excellence and practicality and should be used as a road map for school counselors who aspire to make a positive difference in the lives of youth.

The central theme, learning to love learning, needs to be articulated as an educational objective. Krumboltz (1986) is skilled in advancing the alternative hypothesis and asks: "How would we go about designing an educational program if our purpose was to make students hate to learn?" His ensuing description is uncomfortably close to the reality in many of our schools.

The reader should be aware that when developing this reaction paper, I chose to react selectively because the topic is very broad. In addition, Dr. Krumboltz's major ideas, findings, insights, or recommendations have been highlighted with quotation marks.

Consulting with Teachers about Individual Classroom Concerns

"Teachers bear the responsibility for helping the children in their classrooms to learn." During my research leave last semester, a colleague and I visited 15

41

secondary schools across the nation to identify exemplary schools that were using a learning styles-based instructional approach (Dunn & Griggs, in press). In most schools, a dichotomy existed between faculty members who embraced the learning styles approach and those who practiced traditional total-group instruction with the teacher maintaining the pivotal role as described by Goodlad's (1984) observations of thousands of classrooms. In our talks with conventional teachers we uncovered two concerns that seemed to underlie resistance to change: academic standards and issues of control. These teachers exuded pride when adhering rigidly to standards that ensured a high rate of student failure. Over the years, it became clear to supervisors and administrators that these teachers were not successful with challenging students who were learning disabled, lacking in basic skills, or below average in ability or achievement. Hence, they were frequently assigned to teach honors, advanced placement, or academically gifted classes. Conversely, it was not unusual to find that the teachers who embraced learning styles instruction were assigned to the resource room or general track classes. Thus, in many schools, a system seems to exist wherein incompetence is rewarded. I am not the first to suggest that teachers who succeed with challenging students need to receive the rewards, and that teachers who consistently fail with difficult-to-teach youngsters need to alter their instructional methods. "If students don't learn the way we teach, we need to teach them in the way that they learn," a position advocated by Dunn and Dunn (1977), clearly defines the educators' responsibility.

"Encourage teachers to experiment with giving alternative choices about learning activities to students." From kindergarten through graduate school we tend to delimit and focus student learning activities too rigidly. Frequently, students are given identical homework assignments, term projects, or experiential activities—all of which are carefully defined and highly structured by the teacher. The student becomes a master at identifying teacher expectations, which is not synonymous with learning. Witness the doctoral candidate, who has completed all coursework and blocks at the dissertation stage, which requires a high degree of independent learning, autonomy, innovation, and motivation—characteristics that frequently are underdeveloped throughout the educational process. Drawing from my own school experience, I recall both stifling and expanding learning activities. A seventh-grade French teacher assigned a home project that required submission of a soap carving of the Eiffel Tower, the purpose of which escaped me. After chipping away at some 20 odd bars of Ivory soap and failing to come up with a reasonable facsimile, I had to abandon the assignment. In sharp contrast, I recall an 11th-grade social studies project that involved developing a paper entitled, "A Career in ____(blank)" and, for me, the "blank" became nursing. (At that time, college-bound women tended to select between two visible careers: teaching or nursing.) After becoming familiar with a variety of resources, we set about data collecting, which for me involved observing nurses in the local hospital, interviewing neighbors who were a nurse-doctor team, sending for information from the American Nurses' Association, and reading about the profession. For me this project was a peak learning experience, as characterized by Maslow. Obviously, it was compatible with my learning style!

"Encourage teachers to set appropriate standards of performance <u>for each individual</u>." (Underlined for emphasis). Counselors tend to be concerned with the *individual*. We are trained to identify each individual's uniqueness, strengths, assets, and personality characteristics in order to facilitate learning, growth, and development. Most teachers tend to be concerned with *groups*, as reflected in their attention to discipline, management, control, structure, norms, and competitive versus cooperative environments. However, groups don't learn and achieve: individuals learn and achieve, sometimes independently and frequently in groups. Herein lies a possible source of conflict. In my experience, no student, no matter how angry, hostile, or troublesome, exists who cannot be accepted, understood, and emphathized with in a one-to-one counseling relationship, if we understand his or her phenomenological world. However, accepting and supporting this same student within a group, in which the student may be defiant, rebellious, disruptive, and hostile becomes problematic. To bridge this dichotomy, counselors need to encourage teachers to respond more directly to the individual learning styles, needs, cognitive styles, and personality requisites of each child. Special education teachers are mandated by law to make such provisions by developing individual education plans (IEPs) for each child—a provision that should be authorized for the student population at large.

Krumboltz addresses the relationship between achievement and self-concept and cites the work of Shunk (1984), which suggests that when students are given feedback on their performance, with an emphasis on their ability rather than their effort, the result is an increased sense of self-efficacy and empowerment. Educators have wrestled with the relationship between academic achievement and self-concept for some time. Does the child's failure to achieve result in feeling poorly about self, or does the child initially have low esteem that translates into a lack of confidence and low achievement? Pottebaum, Keith, and Ehly (1986) examined longitudinal data from a large representative sample of high school students to determine if there is a causal relation between self-concept and academic achievement. The results suggested that there may *not* be a causal relationship but that a third variable, possibly social class or ability, may be causally predominant over both self-concept and achievement in relation to learning. Bloom (1964) has recognized for some time the critical importance of cultural differences in relation to learning. He observes that the differences are most dramatic in the contrasts between culturally deprived children and those who come from more culturally advantaged backgrounds. Noting that longitudinal studies reveal that much of the child's development with regard to basic learning prerequisites to later learning has been completed by the end of the third grade, which accounts for approximately 50% of the variance at grade 12, he advocates early childhood education, small classes in grades one to three, and individualization of learning and instruction. Dunn and Dunn (1978) in their text entitled, *Teaching Students Through Their Individual Learning Styles*, offer concrete suggestions for putting these concepts into operation.

Individual Counseling with Students

"Counsel students to accept responsibility for their own outcomes." Krumboltz cites a number of research studies that identify locus of control as an important construct in the learning process. Students with an internal orientation are higher achieving than those who are external, and evidence suggests that counselors can help students to move toward an internal orientation.

Additional research, showing promise of affecting student learning, is in the area of achievement motivation (Aronson, 1982; McClelland, 1961; McClelland & Winter, 1969). In 1961, McClelland began to design and implement motivational training programs, despite his earlier conviction that the level of achievement motivation is a relatively stable personality disposition. To facilitate his investigation, McClelland (1965) developed a total of 12 propostions for a training program. These propositions encompass the areas of self-study, goal setting, and interpersonal supports. Following a decade of research, Johnson and McClelland (1984) designed a structured program approach to raising the level of achievement motivation, entitled *Learning to Achieve*. This research established the importance of well-defined, achievable task objectives as well as the strong linkage between achievement motivation and self-esteem (Blaney, 1977; McClelland, 1971; Purkey, 1970). Counselors can apply these approaches in group counseling settings with underachieving, unmotivated students.

"Counselors can teach children how to take tests." Test taking is a component of study skills, and counselors can facilitate skill development in reading, vocabulary, test taking, writing, thinking, problem solving, listening, note taking, and time management by ensuring that the curriculum addresses these areas in content courses or through developmental group counseling. The National Association of Secondary School Principals (NASSP, 1982), in collaboration with the American Council on Education, has developed valuable study skills program materials for use in grades 5 through 12.

"Adapt counseling to the individual learning styles of each student." Krumboltz observes astutely that there are different conceptions of what constitutes a learning style. Additionally, many learning style models lack a research base that would demonstrate that accommodating individual learning style preferences makes a difference in terms of improving student achievement and attitudes toward learning. During the annual convention of the Association for Supervision and Curriculum Development (1987), five nationally prominent experts in the area of learning and teaching styles and brain behavior were invited to respond to the following questions: What are learning/cognitive styles? What recent insights do we have, based on experience and research, that support your varied approaches? The panel respondents included Anthony Gregory (educational consultant, phenomenological approach to learning styles), Gordon Lawrence (University of Florida; application of the Myers-Briggs Type Indicator to learning styles), Bernice McCarthy (Director of EXCEL, 4MAT system of learning styles), Bob Samples (a disciple of Jerome Bruner; brain behavior and creativity), and Rita Dunn (St. John's University; Director of the National Center for the Study of Teaching and Learning Styles). Counselors who are serious about investigating the differences among these varied approaches and the research base (or lack of it) are encouraged to send for the audiotape of this presentation.

The basic tenet of learning styles is that *there is no best way to teach or counsel students*. Instead, there are many different approaches—some of which are effective with some students and ineffective with others. Dr. Krumboltz cites an example of his daughter, Ann, who experienced difficulty in learning to read, and found the phonetic approach ineffective. If Ann's learning style preferences had been assessed, other approaches such as whole word recognition, linguistic decoding, or language-experience might have resulted in mastering reading sooner (Carbo, Dunn, & Dunn, 1986).

In his modesty, Krumboltz does us a disservice in not discussing his text on counseling methods (Krumboltz & Thoresen, 1976) in which he identifies common client problems, describes counseling techniques for altering maladaptive behavior, and summarizes research supporting the intervention. Many of the problem areas addressed are of critical importance to school counselors: delinquency, temper outbursts, child misbehavior, enuresis, test anxiety, school phobia, fear of social rejection, shyness, depression, and substance abuse.

Influence Changes in the System via Technology

"Computers . . . . have tremendous possibilities for adapting education and counseling to meet individual differences." In addition to the uses described, computer management systems can be used to monitor the learning process. If educators have a carefully defined system of learning goals and objectives, possibly implemented by a system such as Bloom's et al. (1971) taxonomy of educational objectives, ranging from basic knowledge and skill levels to higher-order critical thinking levels, each student can be assessed periodically and provided with individual feedback on the extent of achievement. Use of such systems recognizes the hierarchical nature of the learning process and would identify early on students who have not mastered the fundamentals, thereby halting the slippage that occurs in our educational system whereby, for example,

10th-grade students can't achieve in mathematics because they lack skill in the basic computational processes.

However, Bok (1986) cautions that educators should not expect too much from technology. He states that the best evidence is that media (including computers) are mere vehicles that deliver instruction but do not influence student achievement any more than the truck that delivers our groceries causes changes in our nutrition. Dr. Krumboltz seems to concur that such skepticism is necessary, particularly given the present state of the art in software.

Counselor Action to Promote Student Cooperation and Academic Achievement

The work of Johnson (1981) is cited as follows: "Cooperation promotes higher achievement than does interpersonal competition. These results hold for all subject areas, for all age groups, and for tasks involving concept attainment, verbal problem solving, categorizing, spatial problem solving, retention and memory, motor performance, and guessing-judging-predicting." The strong reservation that I have regarding Johnson's findings is that cooperation does *not* promote higher achievement than does interpersonal competition *for all individuals* nor *for all types of learning*. A number of studies reveal that, as a group, intellectually gifted students are self-learners who prefer large doses of independent study in contrast to cooperative learning for many tasks (Griggs & Price, 1980; Stewart, 1981; Wasson, 1980). The counselor's role as a consultant to teachers and parents can support the student's independence and help adults deal effectively with patterns of self-reliance (Griggs, 1984). It is important to recognize, however, that assessment of preferences should extend beyond group differences, for within the gifted group there are broad differences as well as similarities that affect the learning process.

Conclusions

"Counselors belong at the hub, not on the fringe, of the educational endeavor." In addition to facilitating student learning and achievement, counselors need to understand the politics of education and become visible student advocates. Collectively, counselors can influence the political process, not only in the area of counselor licensure but by ensuring that developmental counseling programs are mandated in every school system in kindergarten through grade 12, which has been the law in New York State since 1982.

Because of our intuitive concern for individuals, we as counselors must assume the leadership role required to focus teachers' emphasis away from class/group concerns and toward consideration of the unique strengths of each youngster. Indeed, we counselors have the key to improving education by applying our knowledge and skills to the instructional process as well as in the areas of human development and actualization.

References

Aronson, E. (1982). Modifying the environment of the desegregated classroom. In A.J. Stewart (Ed.), *Motivation and society: A volume in honor of David C. McClelland.* San Francisco: Jossey-Bass.

Association for Supervision and Curriculum Development. (1987). *Audiotape: Learning/ teaching styles and brain behavior.* Alexandria, VA: ASCD.

Blaney, N.T. (1977). Independence in the classroom: A field study. *Journal of Educational Psychology, 69,* 139–146.

Bloom, B.S. (1964). *Stability and change in human characteristics.* New York: John Wiley.

Bloom, B.S., Hastings, J.T., & Madaus, G.F. (1971). *Handbook on formative and summative evaluation of student learning.* New York: McGraw-Hill.

Bok, D. (1986). *Higher learning.* Cambridge, MA: Harvard University Press.

Carbo, M., Dunn, R., & Dunn, K. (1986). *Teaching students to read through their individual learning styles.* Englewood Cliffs, NJ: Prentice-Hall.

Dunn R., & Dunn, K. (1977). *Administrator's guide to new programs for faculty management and evaluation.* West Nyack, NY: Parker Publishing.

Dunn, R., & Dunn, K. (1978). *Teaching students through their individual learning styles.* Reston, VA: Reston Publishing.

Dunn, R., & Griggs, S.A. (in press). *Learning styles: The quiet revolution in American schools.* Reston, VA: National Association of Secondary School Principals.

Goodlad, J.I. (1984). *A place called school: Prospects for the future.* New York: McGraw-Hill.

Griggs, S.A. (1984). Counseling the gifted and talented based on learning styles. *Exceptional Children, 50,* 429–432.

Griggs, S.A., & Price, G.E. (1980). Comparison between the learning styles of gifted versus average surburban junior high school students. *Roeper Review, 3,* 7–9.

Johnson, D.S. (1981). Naturally acquired learned helplessness: The relationship of school failure to achievement behavior, attributes, and self-concept. *Journal of Educational Psychology, 73,* 174–180.

Johnson, E.W., & McClelland, D.C. (1984). *Learning to achieve: The basic.* Glenview, IL: Scott Foresman.

Krumboltz, J.D. (1986). Research is a very good thing. *The Counseling Psychologist, 14,* 159–163.

Krumboltz, J.D., & Thoresen, C.E. (1976). *Counseling methods.* New York: Holt, Rinehart & Winston.

McClelland, D.C. (1961). *The achieving society.* New York: Van Nostrand.

McClelland, D.C. (1965). Toward a theory of motive acquisition. *American Psychologist, 20,* 321–333.

McClelland, D.C. (1971). *Assessing human motivation.* Morristown, NJ: General Learning Press.

48

McClelland, D.C., & Winter, G. (1969). *Motivating economic achievement*. New York: Free Press.

NASSP. (1982). *Study skills program: Level I, grades 5–7; level II, grades 8–10; level III, grades 11–13*. Reston, VA: Author.

Pottebaum, S.M., Keith, T.Z., & Ehly, S.M. (1986). Is there a causal relation between self-concept and academic achievement? *Journal of Educational Research, 79*, 140–144.

Purkey, W.W. (1970). *Self-concept and school achievement*. Englewood Cliffs, NJ: Prentice-Hall.

Stewart, E.D. (1981). Learning styles among gifted/talented students: Instructional technique preferences. *Exceptional Children, 48*, 134–138.

Wasson, F.R. (1980). *A comparative analysis of learning styles and personality characteristics of achieving and underachieving gifted elementary students*. Ed. D. disseration, Florida State University, Tallahassee, FL.

Personal and Social Competency: Developing Skills for the Future

Dave Capuzzi

Professor and Coordinator, Counselor Education
Portland State University, Portland, Oregon

The major assumption of this paper is that counselors can do a better job of assisting students and counselees to develop coping skills for the future if they base their services on the research related to personal and social competency and coping. The preliminary ERIC computer searches (1967 to 1987) utilized to develop this paper identified nine areas that seem to be critical to the counselor's role in developing strong school counseling programs. These areas are: (1) self-esteem, (2) esting disorders, (3) child and adolescent suicide, (4) depression, (5) teenage pregnancy, (6) substance abuse, (7) physical and sexual abuse, (8) stress, and (9) children of divorce. More and more school counselors are being called upon to work with students experiencing problems connected with one or more of these nine areas, any of all of which present particular roadblocks to normal psychosocial development and current and future coping ability.

The purpose of this paper is to present the major research findings to date in these nine areas based on additional ERIC computer searches completed after identification of the aforementioned nine areas. In conjunction with each area, major research trends have been reviewed; in many instances, topics needing further explication have been identified. The concluding section of the paper identifies imperatives for future research in each of the nine areas.

Self-Esteem

During the last 20 years, extensive research has been done on the topic of self-esteem. Self-esteem and the school environment, self-esteem and school-related problems, self-esteem and the physically/mentally challenged, self-esteem and personality variables, self-esteem and family influences, self-esteem and gifted/talented students, self-esteem and muticultural perspectives, and self-esteem and measurement instruments are areas of emphasis that provide a rich data base to professionals interested in developing strong school counseling programs. Examining the highlights of the research on the topic of self-esteem provides a variety of implications for school counselors interested in facilitating the development of personal and social competency on the part of school-aged youth.

Self-Esteem and the School Environment

The impact of the classroom teacher on the self-esteem of the learner has been approached from a variety of perspectives. In a study by Derek Blease (1986) a significant and positive relationship between teacher perceptions of pupils and the pupils' views of themselves was demonstrated. The positive impact of teacher reinforcement on students' self-esteem was demonstrated in studies by Ledford and Ledford (1985), Phillips (1984) and Reynolds (1980). In addition, data suggest that teachers can contribute to enhanced levels of student self-esteem through emphasis on improving students' communication skills (Calsyn et al., 1980), physical fitness (Christie & Saccone, 1985), and assertiveness (Stake et al., 1983). Interestingly, a study that summarized 40 studies at the elementary level and 45 studies at the secondary level relating to the impact of inter-class ability grouping on self-esteem (Kulik, 1985) revealed that the average effect of grouping on self-esteem scores of students was near zero. The findings suggested that homogeneous grouping is often beneficial for talented students, may improve the self-esteem of slow learners, but has little effect on the self-esteem of average students. Interesting findings in view of the current emphasis on mainstreaming!

Self-esteem also has been investigated in relation to peer and significant other relationships (Walker & Greene, 1986; Curtis & Shaver, 1981; Openshaw & Thomas, 1981); computer-based reinforcement contingencies (Dalton & Hannafin, 1985a; Dalton & Hannafin, 1985b), the self-esteem of the counselor (Wiggins & Giles, 1984) and the role of school administrators (Sarokon, 1986). One thing seems clear: The school environment has a tremendous impact on the self-esteem of our young people.

Self-Esteem and School-Related Problems

A small number of studies between 1980 and 1986 explored the relationship between self-esteem and school-related "presenting" problems. The topics of truancy (Englander, 1986), substance abuse (Jones & Hartmann, 1985; Mitic, 1980), classroom management problems (Richman et al., 1984b), adolescent pregnancy (Hall & Taylor, 1984), delinquency (Zieman & Benson, 1983; Bynner et al., 1981), absenteeism (Reid, 1982), and interpersonal relationship problems (Kahle et al., 1980) all were studied in the context of self-esteem. Certainly all those connected with school counseling programs should be aware of this research as components for building-wide and district-wide guidance plans are developed. More research emphasis needs to be placed in this area.

Self-Esteem and the Physically/Mentally Challenged

Surprisingly little research has been focused on enhancing or assessing the self-esteem of the physically or mentally challenged individual. Most of the research that has been done has focused upon relationship between self-esteem and learning disabilities (Patten, 1983; Watts & Cushion, 1982; Pearl & Bryan, 1982; Rowley, 1981; Bingham, 1980; Tollefson et al., 1980). In general, results are inconclusive and implications for personal-social competency would be difficult to identify.

Only three studies (Brooks & Ellis, 1982; Meadow, 1980; Starr, 1980) explored self-esteem in connection with the physically challenged student. Again, results were inconclusive.

Self-Esteem and Personality Variables

Self-esteem has been examined in relation to a variety of personality traits exhibited by elementary and secondary school students. Self-esteem and locus of control (Dielman et al., 1984; Garner & Cole, 1984), sex, race, and social class (Richman et al., 1984a), socialization (Openshaw et al., 1983), self-concept (Blyth & Traeger, 1983), shyness (Lazarus, 1982), anxiety and extraversion (Kawash, 1982), self-presentation (Elliott, 1982), and depression (Battle, 1980) were the focus of a few scattered studies during the early and middle 1980s. The only definite pattern that emerged during the last few years related to studies and findings that linked self-esteem to sex-role identity (Cate & Sugawara, 1986; Hughes et al., 1985; Rust & McCraw, 1984; Lamke, 1982; Hurtig & Petersen, 1982). There is some, though not total, agreement that for both young men and young women an androgynous or masculine identity was associated with higher levels of self-esteem. If evidence continues to support such findings, there may be some rather definite implications for the helping professions about helping young people develop coping skills for the future.

Self-Esteem and Family Influences—Self-Esteem and the Gifted and Talented

Surprisingly little surfaced via the ERIC search investigating the impact of the family on self-esteem and analyzing the self-esteem of gifted and talented students. This seems worthy of notation because family dynamics has been related to areas such as youth suicide, physical and sexual abuse, and eating disorders. At times, both emphasis and controversy have been connected with funding and educational approaches for gifted and talented students. Family influences in terms of parental pressure (Eskilson et al., 1986), parental conflict (Amato,

1986), cohesion (Cooper et al., 1983), and parenting models (Loeb et al., 1980; Hinkle et al., 1980) have been examined resulting in scattered conclusions and limited generalizability. Counseling gifted and talented youth in relation to self-esteem issues has received limited attention (Hollinger & Fleming, 1985; Janos et al., 1985; Mills, 1984; Hollinger, 1983). No generalized conclusions are warranted in the context of the counseling needs of gifted and talented students.

Self-Esteem and Multicultural Perspectives

Self-esteem and multicultural perspectives have been studied from numerous points of view between 1981 and 1985. Higher self-esteem was correlated with positive perceptions of family and classroom in a study with Chinese adolescents (Cheung & Lau, 1985). Black-White differences as affected by response styles (Bachman & O'Malley, 1984), enhancing the creative potential and self-esteem of Nigerian students (Maqsud, 1983), self-esteem and self-evaluation of ethnic status by Black and Mexican-American youth (Jensen et al., 1982), levels of self-esteem among Filipino youth (Miller, 1982; Watkins & Astilla, 1980b; Watkins & Astilla, 1980a), the effect of self-esteem and locus of control in career decision making of adolescents in Fiji (Kishor, 1981), self-esteem and body build stereotypes among Japanese (Lerner et al., 1980) and Australian youth (Lawson, 1980), self-esteem and reading achievement of Mexican-American students (Curiel et al., 1980), the effects of assertiveness training on the self-esteem of Black high school students (Stewart & Lewis, 1986), and teacher behavior as related to the self-esteem of Mexican-American children (Gumbiner et al., 1981) are all examples of the kinds of multicultural perspectives that have been taken in recent research studies. Although the emphasis on multicultural perspectives and self-esteem is excellent and long overdue, not enough studies are focused on the same or related research questions to draw conclusions.

Self-Esteem and Measurement Instruments

Having surveyed dozens of research articles dealing with the self-esteem of our young people, an important question arose in the mind of this author. How good are current methods for investigating self-esteem? Do measurement instruments really reveal the factors on which a person's self-esteem rests? Rather than attempting to review the dozens (if not hundreds) of approaches and instrumentation to the measurement of self-esteem, let me leave you with this thought. Before we can be sure of the relationships between self-esteem and a variety of factors (e.g., parenting models, sex-role identity, academic achievement, etc.) or between self-esteem enhancement and approaches to counseling treatment, we, as a profession, must commit more energy to the development of more accurate assessment instruments. Before we can know whether counselors can effectively affect self-esteem (and, thus, facilitate better coping skills), we better make sure we can measure self-esteem and changes in self-esteem over time.

Eating Disorders

Once thought of as disorders exclusively afflicting young, upper-class women, more and more counselors are seeing clients with anorexia, bulimia, and other eating disorders who do not fit this original stereotype. Estimates show that one in every 100 teenage women has anorexia, and as many as one in every 50 women between the ages of 15 and 24 suffers from bulimia. About one in every 10 persons with eating disorders is male.

Counselors in almost every setting and almost every area of specialization must know about these illnesses, identify those who need assistance (which will be intensive and long-term), and assess whether they have the required expertise to offer counseling or whether they should refer clients to identified specialists for counseling and treatment of eating disorders.

The research in this area generally can be classified into three areas: (1) identification, (2) clinical or counseling approaches to treatment, and (3) school-based treatment approaches.

Identification of Eating Disorders

While many experts agree upon the descriptive features of anorexia nervosa and bulimia, early identification is more controversial. A number of studies (Eisele et al., 1986; Lundholm & Littrell, 1986; Smith, 1985; Post & Crowther, 1985; Carter & Duncan, 1984; Johnson et al., 1984) identified factors relating to eating disorders in young adolescent women. A predominant theme in this group of studies was that the adolescent eating disordered woman had "poor" attitudes about eating and dieting and was very influenced by images, often promoted via the media, of "ideal" body shape. In addition, a few studies (Gordon et al., 1983; Piazza et al., 1983; Strober, 1982) found correlations between eating disorders and depressive responses. Most studies, however, provided scattered and often conflicting predictive data. Eating disorders were related to feelings of failure (Kagan & Squires, 1984), locus of control (Strober, 1982; Hood et al., 1982), ego boundary disturbances (Strober & Goldenberg, 1981) and conformity, anxiety, emotionality, and stimulus avoidance. Although poor attitudes about eating and dieting, cognitive rigidity as related to ideal body shape, and depressive tendencies in young women may be used to identify those at risk for becoming eating disordered, there is a lack of conclusive evidence in the area of early identification.

Clinical or Counseling Approaches to Treatment

Clinical and counseling approaches to treating disordered clients are varied, often detailed, and definitely "required reading" for those interested in working with this type of client. Behavior modification, individual counseling, family counseling, group counseling, drug therapy, bibliotherapy, reality imaging, education, and hypnotherapy are discussed in a number of resources (Bayer &

Baker, 1986; Maine, 1985; Muuss, 1985; Harvill, 1984; Rittner, 1984). One observation is easy to make: Experts do not agree on a single approach to intervening with the eating disordered client.

School-Based Treatment Approach

Because anorexia nervosa and bulimia are major concerns for high school students, a number of research studies have been conducted in an attempt to provide guidelines for school faculty and staff. Class discussions on self-esteem, self-confidence, and coping with parents (McNab, 1983), diary keeping, tutoring and improved classroom management (Westerlage, 1980), psychoeducation (Cotugno, 1980), nutrition education (Thompson, 1985) and involvement of school psychologists for assessment (Peters et al., 1984) all have been addressed as possible school-based interventions. To date, data about the best school-based intervention(s) are inconclusive.

Child and Adolescent Suicide

Only 30 years ago, suicide among young people was rare. But since the mid-1950s something has reversed the picture. The adolescent suicide rate has tripled over the past 30 years and doubled since the 1960s, becoming, with 5,000 successful suicides a year, the second leading cause of death among the 11 to 24 age group. In addition, children of elementary school age are attempting or completing the act of suicide at escalating rates. Often, as is the case in many states, adolescents attempt or complete the act of suicide in "clusters" with one suicide triggering the next. Experts are uncertain about all the dynamics of "clustering," but one thing is clear: When there is one suicide in a school district or community, other students are immediately at risk. It is important for counselors to know what to do when a suicidal crisis arises. It is even more important to know how to intervene early in the lives of students at risk for suicide to facilitate the development of personal and social skills that enhance coping ability.

Suicide Among Children

Suicide among the young (Strother, 1986) has been approached from a variety of vantage points. Suicidal preoccupation in children (Bailey et al., 1985), environmental and personality similarities (Corder & Haizlip, 1984), imagined motion (Santostefano et al., 1984), and attraction and repulsion by life and death (Orbach et al., 1983) all have been studied in relation to suicide attempts among children. In addition, childhood suicidal behavior has been associated with the male sex, personal experiences of significant loss, academic underachievement, marital disintegration among parents, and past intrafamilial violence including physical abuse of the child (Kosky, 1983). Some studies of children who have attempted or threatened suicide discovered common characteristics including suicidal parents, a major family crisis, excessive parental demands, lack of satisfying relationships, paradoxical death attitudes, and lack of positive strivings to stay alive (Orbach et al., 1981; Pfeffer, 1981). In general, however, children's suicidal behavior is surrounded by controversy with no single theory to explain or assess vulnerable children.

Adolescent Suicide

Although the ERIC computer search identified a number of studies relating to adolescent suicide, surprisingly few studies focused on this topic given the fact that suicide is the second leading cause of death among the adolescent population. Studies detailing the profile of the adolescent attempter focused on suicidal preoccupation (Sharlin & Shenhar, 1986; Smith & Crawford, 1986; Simons & Murphy, 1985; Bailey et al., 1984; Schmidt et al., 1984; Bailey & Hernandez, 1982), stress (Maris, 1985; Gispert et al., 1985), loss (Crook & Raskin, 1975), depression (Spirito et al., 1985; Peck, 1982; Tishler et al., 1981), cognitive distortions (Peck, 1980), use and abuse of drugs (Wright, 1985; McKenry et al., 1983), achievement orientation (Smith, 1979), and social support (Topol & Reznikoff, 1982). Conspicuously absent was research relating the profile of the attempter to self-esteem, problem solving, communication skills, and guilt or self-blame. All of these latter areas are related to the profile of the attempter and have great implications for both personal-social competency and "coping."

A number of studies focused on interventions for prevention (Johnson, 1985; Congress of the U.S., 1985; New York State Education Department, 1984; Grob et al., 1983; Smith, E., 1981; Morgan, 1981; Hart, 1978) and postvention (Rudestam & Imbroll, 1983; Calhoun et al., 1981; Calhoun et al., 1980). A conspicuous gap in the area of crisis management was noted. No school-based program can deal effectively with the problem of adolescent suicide without a triadic approach to the problem: prevention, crisis management, and postvention.

An interesting group of studies examined adolescent suicide from a number of crosscultural perspectives. Adolescent suicide among members of the Native American population (Thurman et al., 1985; Dizmang et al., 1974), the Mexican American population (Domino, 1981), the European economic community (Diekstra, 1985) and the youth in Japan (Iga, 1981) provided valuable initial information. Much work needs to be done in this area because prevention, crisis management, and postvention efforts cannot, in the opinion of the writer, be approached crossculturally in the same way as they are approached with adolescents who are not members of minority groups.

Depression

Childhood Depression

Although most practitioners and researchers agree that childhood depression is an existing entity or syndrome (Pfeffer, 1984), there is considerable disagreement as to what signs and symptoms constitute a diagnosis of depression in children. Some researchers believe that childhood depression may manifest itself through a variety of symptoms that can be considered depressive equivalents or correlates (Glaser, 1967; Toolan, 1967). "Such symptoms include temper tantums, boredom, restlessness, hypochrondriasis, truancy, disobedience, delinquency, learning disabilities, hyperactivity, aggressive behavior, psychosomatic illness, and self-destructive behavior" (Pfeffer, 1984). Other researchers believe that depression in children can be diagnosed by the notation of depressive themes in fantasy, dreams, and verbal expression. Still others prefer to diagnose depression in children by identifying signs and symptoms similar to those observed in adult depression (Ctryn et al., 1980; Puig-Antich et al., 1978).

In keeping with this controversy, a number of studies examined the correlates of childhood depression such as cognitive and life event correlates (Mullins et al., 1982), conceptual tempo (Schwartz et al., 1982), motor hyperactivity (Staton & Brumback, 1981), locus of control and school achievement (Tesiny et al., 1980), behavior problems (Leon et al., 1980), and locus of control, self-esteem, and stimulus appraisal (Moyal, 1977). Self-reports (Leitenberg et al., 1986; Saylor et al., 1984b; Kazdin & Petti, 1982; Birleson, 1981), and parent/teacher observations (Korup, 1985; Lefkowitz & Tesiny, 1985) were also frequently reported approaches to diagnosing childhood depression. The research on instrumentation that can be used to diagnose childhood depression is substantial. Tests such as the Hopelessness Scale for Children (Kazdin et al., 1983), the Children's Depression Rating Scale (Poznanski et al., 1979), the Children's Depression Scale (Rotundo & Hensley, 1985), the Peer Nomination Inventory of Depression (Lefkowitz & Tesiny, 1980), and the Children's Depression Inventory (King et al., 1986; Finch et al., 1985; Campbell-Goymer, 1984; Saylor et al., 1984a) all were analyzed and evaluated. It would seem that all school counselors should become familiar with correlates, self-report and parent/teacher observation approaches, and the tests available for diagnostic purposes.

The "state-of-the-art" for the treatment of childhood depression, as reported in the literature, can be summarized as focusing upon one of the following seven treatment modalities: (1) psychoanalytic, (2) behavioral, (3) cognitive, (4) familial, (5) rational-emotive, (6) multimodal, and (7) medication (Clarizio, 1986; Clarizio, 1985; Schloss, 1983; Forrest, 1983; Staton et al., 1981; Golden, 1981; Butler et al., 1980; Brumback et al., 1980; Yahraes, 1978). There does not seem to be consensus about the most effective approach.

Adolescent Depression

There seem to be four major schools of thought concerning adolescent depression: (1) depression, as a clinical disorder, is not possible before late adolescence or early adulthood; (2) depression in children and adolescents is a unique clinical entity and different from adult depression; (3) adolescents manifest depression in the same way as adults; and (4) depression as a disorder rarely occurs in early or middle adolescence (Hartman, 1986). The current major issues in the study of adolescent depression involve conflicts concerning the diagnostic criteria for adolescent depression and its status as a valid clinical disorder. Although evidence derived from the research literature supporting the concept of adolescent depression as a clinical disorder is considerably stronger than it was a decade ago, uncertainty regarding a valid and reliable means of diagnosis and classification remains the major obstacle to its empirical verification (Hartman).

Interestingly, most of the research identified in the ERIC search analyzed either the correlates of adolescent depression or tests that could be used for diagnostic purposes. Adolescent depression was examined in relation to correlates such as attempted suicide (Harlow et al., 1986; Hodgman, 1985; Emery, 1983; Friedrich et al., 1982; Gibbs, 1981), activity (Carey et al., 1986), loneliness (Lapsley et al., 1984; Kaiser & Berndt, 1983; Siegel & Griffin, 1983), cognitive distortions (Stehouwer et al., 1985; Stehouwer & Bultsma, 1980), parental behavior (Colletta, 1982; Whiting, 1981) and psychosocial factors such as mother's occupation, geographical mobility, and self-reported problems (Gibbs, 1981). Tests such as the Beck Depression Inventory (Baron & Perron, 1986; Teri, 1982), the Depression Adjective Check Lists, Form E (Lubin & Levitt, 1979) and the Center for Epidemiological Studies Depression Scale (Schoenbach et al., 1983) have been widely used in research efforts to date.

Teenage Pregnancy

The social consequences of teenage child bearing are discussed on a consistent basis in the literature on this topic (Alan Guttmacher Institute, 1981; Presser, 1975; and Johnson, 1971). Statistics such as the following are typically reported in research studies.

- 40% of sexually active teenage women become pregnant by the time they reach 19.
- Teenagers bear nearly 20% of all babies born in the United States and 40% of these are born to single teenage women.
- More than 30% of all reported abortions are performed on young women 15 to 19 years of age.
- 25% of the teenagers who bear a child will become pregnant again within a year.
- Babies born to teenagers are two to three times more likely to die in their first year of life than are babies born to women in their early 20s.
- 80% of pregnant teenagers 17 or under never finish high school.

The majority of the research surveyed for this report can be categorized as focusing upon understanding the "profile" of the pregnant adolescent, prevention programs for schools and community agencies, and the counseling needs of pregnant teenagers.

The "Profile" of the Pregnant Teenager

The psychological correlates of teenage motherhood (Barth et al., 1983b) have been studied from a variety of perspectives. Feelings of loneliness and the desire to fill a void (Falk et al., 1981), self-concept (Zongker, 1977; Hall & Taylor, 1984) and mothers' decision-making ability (Black & De Blassie, 1985) are examples of such correlates. Considerable attention also has been given to the family histories of pregnant teenagers. Trends such as lower maternal educational levels, later sex education, poorer vocational adjustment, and poorer father/ daughter relationships (Ralph et al., 1984; Landy et al., 1983; Dixon, 1981; Miller et al., 1981) seem to be substantiated.

An interesting group of studies explored the attitudes of male adolescents toward adolescent pregnancy and fatherhood. Most studies indicated that male adolescents attempt to maintain positive relationships with their girl friends and the families of their girl friends, desire to participate in decision making, and try to make financial contributions. Problems seem to be focused upon parenting and parenting ability, employment opportunities, and earning power (Redmond, 1985; Sullivan, 1985; Gershenson, 1983; Robinson et al., 1983; Hendricks & Montgomery, 1983; Barret & Robinson, 1982; Hendricks, 1982; Hendricks, 1981).

Pregnancy Prevention Programs

Research on approaches to pregnancy prevention programs is varied but of high interest. Studies evaluating the effectiveness of interventions such as group counseling (Blythe et al., 1981), family planning with teenagers whose teenage sisters had become pregnant (Friede et al., 1986), educational programs emphasizing the importance of scholastic achievement and strong parent-child relationships (Olson & Worobey, 1984), involving the girls' sexual partners in counseling (Smith, P.B., 1981), expanding awareness of life options (Ortiz & Bassoff, 1984), developing more realistic expectations about the responsibilities of child care (Michaels & Brown, 1983), and providing teenagers support in combating the effects of peer influence and in defining career goals that might motivate them to avoid pregnancy (Morrison et al., 1981) all are available to the school counselor and all provide support for such efforts.

One final observation can be shared. There is a preponderance of research support for the effectiveness of sex education, continued and improved access to contraception, and safe legal abortion as answers to prevent children from having children (Newcomer, 1985; Vance, 1985; Goldstein, 1981; Jorgensen & Alexander, 1981; Potter & Smith, 1976).

Counseling Needs of Pregnant Teenagers

A complete review of the existing research on the counseling needs of the pregnant teenager is beyond the scope of this report. Hundreds and hundreds of studies have been completed. These studies generally can be described by stating that they identify the counseling needs of the pregnant teenager as focusing upon three areas: medical, educational, and emotional (Klerman, 1979). The importance of providing counseling and referral for prenatal and postpartum care cannot be overemphasized (Berg et al., 1979); some experts recommend that a comprehensive program of prenatal care be made available in public school settings (Berg et al.). Educational needs include information about adoption (Mech, 1986), infant and child development (Vukelich & Kliman, 1985), career options (Adler et al., 1985), parent-child interactions (McDonough, 1984), sexuality (Roosa, 1984), nutrition (Perkin, 1983), and continuing education options (Jackson, 1986). Counseling needs of the adolescent mother include self-esteem enhancement (Thompson, 1984), coping strategies (Barth et al., 1983a) and counseling for the family of origin (Furstenberg, 1980).

Substance Abuse

The foremost responsibility of any society is to nurture and protect its children; they are society's "tomorrow," its culture, its legacy. The most severe threat to the health and well-being of American children today is substance use and abuse.

A survey of the research on this topic revealed frequently made statements and conclusions such as the following:

- Drug use among children and adolescents is 10 times more prevalent than parents suspect.
- Many young people know that parents do not recognize the extent and the symptoms connected with substance use and abuse, and this knowledge leads them to believe they can use drugs with impunity.
- Although drug trafficking is controlled by adults, the immediate source of drugs for most students is other students.
- Drugs are a serious problem not only in high schools but also in middle and elementary schools.
- Many parents, teachers, counselors, and administrators believe that when a young person returns from a residential treatment program, he or she is "cured," when, in fact, "treatment" is just beginning.

How has research been focused in the area of prevention and intervention?

School-Based Intervention Efforts

There has been an accelerating interest in the creation and evaluation of school-based intervention efforts since the middle 1970s. The following types of programs are typical of what has been described in the literature to date (Michigan State Department of Education, 1975):

1. the introduction of basic substance abuse educational programs for student groups;
2. the provision of information and consultation to school faculty, students, and parent groups;
3. the creation of specific training programs geared to school staffs to improve in-school curricula and teaching formats relative to substance abuse prevention;
4. the creation of student service centers;
5. the training of paraprofessional citizen trainers to participate on school-based intervention teams;
6. the involvement of the entire family in substance abuse prevention; and
7. the development of school building and school district policies and procedures that facilitate a school climate conducive to substance abuse prevention.

In addition, classroom intervention programs (Austin Independent School District, 1985) have been reported and evaluated. These programs focused upon topics such as enhancing self-concept, providing positive alternatives to alcohol/drug use, education about alcohol and other drugs, personal concerns (e.g., depression and suicide), and school concerns (e.g., not liking school and conflicts with teachers). In general, studies such as these reported positive results with regard to student attitudes and student use and abuse of alcohol and other drugs.

Some examples of other types of school-based programs that have been evaluated include programs that linked drug counselors and police officers in teams to provide drug education (Blotner & Lilly, 1986), provided group counseling programs as part of an intervention effort (Fuhrmann & Washington, 1984), and attempted to clarify the relationship between psychological factors and drug use in the context of a school-based program (Paton & Kandel, 1978). A very interesting study (Nuttall & Nuttall, 1978) used variables such as academic failure indices, nervousness, parental lax discipline, test anxiety, sociability, poverty, earning money early in life, and hearing difficulties to predict heroin use. The prevention of alcohol use involved monitoring the following factors: sex, personality, parent-child relationships, academic performance, behavior patterns, financial status, and health.

Family-Based Intervention Efforts

Much research attests to the significance of the family perspective in the understanding, treatment, and prevention of substance use and abuse (Ellis, 1980). The effectiveness of conducting family therapy through one person (Szapocznik et al., 1986), targeted family problem-solving training (Bry et al., 1986), utilizing the principles of family involvement and peer pressure in family counseling (Iverson et al., 1978), and use of "Ecological Family Systems Therapy" as a model for family counseling (Szapocznik et al., 1976) are all examples of the varied family approaches reported in the literature. Tangentially related studies include those focused on psychological differentiation and locus of control among adolescent substance abusers, depressive moods and adolescent illicit drug use (Paton et al., 1977), outpatient treatment (Armstrong, 1983), prevalent and preferred styles in drug education (Antonow et al., 1976), and outreach programs in drug education (Sorensen & Joffe, 1975).

Physical and Sexual Abuse

The research on the long- and short-term effects of physical and sexual abuse on children and adolescents provides overwhelming evidence related to the impairment of personal and social competency and the development of coping skills for the future. The National Study on Child Neglect and Abuse Reporting was begun in 1973 (American Humane Association, 1978). By 1978, findings such as the following had been well substantiated: (1) families in which abuse occurs had a median annual family income well below the national average; (2) environmental stress factors played a greater relative importance in cases of neglect than in cases of abuse, where personal factors played a more important role; (3) natural parents composed 83% of the alleged perpetrators; and (4) there were little differences in the sex of the children involved. Also well substantiated were trends such as the following (Finkelhor, 1978): (1) although the problem of physical and sexual abuse cuts across all socioeconomic lines, it seems to be more prevalent in families of lower social class and rural backgrounds, indicating that social isolation may play a key role in victimization and family violence; (2) the role of mothers is crucial in protecting their daughters from sexual abuse; (3) girls whose mothers were absent, ill, poorly educated, or alcoholic were much more likely to be victimized; (4) children were most vulnerable prior to puberty, and most of them did not reveal the experience to anyone at the time it occurred, and (5) experiences involving more force were much more traumatic than those not involving force. Conspicuous gaps in the research to date seem to focus upon the sexual abuse of boys and male adolescents (Nielsen, 1983) and, to a surprising degree, the characteristics of parents who abuse their children (Oldershaw et al., 1986; Lahey et al., 1984; Sherrod et al., 1985).

Research pertinent to the topics of personal and social competency and building strong school counseling programs can be categorized into short-term effects, long-term effects, and the roles of teachers and counselors.

Short-Term Effects

The short-term effects of physical and sexual abuse are well documented. The following list of research findings is, by no means, exhaustive:

1. Abused children avoid social interaction and abused girls exhibit more avoidance than boys (Hecht et al., 1986).
2. Abused children manifest a greater number and frequency of behavior problems, have poor peer relationships and social skills, have less empathy, and manifest poor school adjustment and academic performance (Lamphear, 1985; Wolfe & Mosk, 1983; Jacobson & Straker, 1982).
3. Abused children test lower on verbal and memory scales of aptitude and achievement tests (Friedrich et al., 1983).
4. Reaction patterns of abused adolescents include acting-out, depression, generalized anxiety, extreme adolescent adjustment problems, emotional and thought disturbances, and feelings of helplessness and dependency (Farber & Joseph, 1985).
5. Maltreated adolescents experience low self-esteem, antisocial behavior, and suicidal tendencies (Galambos & Dixon, 1984).
6. Abused adolescents fare worse in family relations, emotional stability, psychopathology, impulse control, coping skills, and overall self-image (Hjorth & Ostrov, 1982).

The implications for social and personal competency should be apparent.

Long-Term Effects

Research on the long-term effects of physical and sexual abuse has uncovered more complicated repercussions than previously suspected. Multiple Personality Disorder, for example, is now associated with physical and sexual abuse during childhood (Coons, 1986). The most practical means of diagnosis is through interviews (Dalton, 1986). Amnesia, auditory hallucinations, unusual behavioral fluctuations, and imaginary companions may be preindications of the development of Multiple Personality Disorder (Dalton). Lifelong lowered self-concept also can be related to physical or sexual abuse during childhood (Ellsworth & Demos, 1981).

A number of noteworthy studies assessed the impact of physical or sexual abuse during childhood on adolescents. An Ohio study, for example, found that a significant percentage of adolescents arrested for violent crimes had been victims of severe child abuse and were likely to behave violently toward family members and caretakers (Kratcoski, 1982). Another study showed that female adolescents who were victimized during childhood tend to become runaways, and male adolescents are likely to commit violent crimes (Welsh, 1980). Hysterical seizures (Hysteroepilepsy) in adolescent women who had previously experienced incest (Goodwin et al., 1979) and adolescent prostitution (Seymour, 1977) are additional examples of longer term effects. Again, it should be apparent that all of these "effects" affect what I call the developmental process regulating the growth of personal and social competency.

Roles of Teachers and Counselors

The literature, during the last 10 years especially, provides more than enough documentation of the important role the classroom teacher plays in preventing, detecting, and reporting abuse (McIntyre, 1986; Molnar & Gliszczinski, 1983; Riggs, 1982; Thompson, 1979; and Wishon, 1979). The results of pre- and inservice education for teachers on the topic of physical and sexual abuse show that teachers who participate are more likely to (1) talk with individual students to determine whether abuse is occurring; (2) give a class preparation on child abuse; (3) be willing to avoid the use of physical punishment in the classroom; and (4) discuss child abuse with colleagues (Duhon, 1985; Ayers & Richey, 1984; Hazzard & Rupp, 1984).

Surprisingly, even though everyone in the counseling profession knows that school counselors are involved in prevention, detection, and reporting of child abuse, few studies on the counselor's role appeared in the ERIC computer literature search!

Stress

Definitions of stress usually imply that stress is a condition resulting from some change or imbalance that requires individual adjustment. When such an alteration or adjustment does not occur, stress becomes an adverse condition that eventually may cause serious harm. Numerous studies (McManus, 1984) have established a relationship between unrelieved stress and negative bodily reactions such as cardiovascular disorder, cancer, arthritis, respiratory ailments, and depression. The questioning of the traditional medical model in alleviating stress has given rise to other models of stress reduction focusing on wellness rather than the absence of disease. Individuals who maximize personal and social competency and develop high-level coping skills have learned to incorporate antistress practices into everyday routines.

Schools are sources of stress because they provide a context in which performance and relationship demands are made (Forman & O'Malley, 1984).

School counselors and, for that matter, entire school faculties can promote good stress management practices.

Research pertinent to this discussion can be categorized as follows: children in stress and stress management for children, adolescents in stress, educators and counselors in stress, and stress management for educators and counselors.

Children in Stress and Stress Management for Children

Pressures that may cause stress in children include shifting family patterns due to divorce or working parents, busy schedules, watching violence on television, moving, loss, illness, adoption, catastrophes, and demanding school schedules and expectations (Honig, 1986; Hodges et al., 1984; Rhiner, 1983; Duncan, 1983). Children who develop problems in response to stress are often victims of stress overload. Research shows that these children frequently lack strong coping skills or social support and quite often are "Type A" (coronary prone) personalities characterized by competitiveness, sense of time urgency, and higher than average levels of aggression and hostility (Duncan, 1983). Research substantiates that there are a variety of ways adults can help children in school to learn to manage stress.

A recent, interesting study (Zaichkowsky et al., 1986) demonstrated that young elementary school children can be taught approaches to stress management. Findings indicated that children could learn to control heart rate, respiration rate, and skin temperature responses by participating in a program that included instruction on proper breathing; modified, progressive muscle relaxation; and temperature biofeedback. Another study (Matthews & Casteel, 1984) showed that relaxation training can be successfully implemented in the classroom with limited teacher training and classroom disruption. Wrist temperature proved to be both a valid and reliable measure of the relaxation state. All students (N = 266) showed improvement though they varied greatly in their ability to elicit the relaxation response. The ability to relax was not significantly related to sex or race, but seemed to be related to cognitive abilities. Students receiving the training had fewer discipline problems and significantly higher self-concepts. The findings suggested that relaxation training for stress management purposes is beneficial and easily can be implemented in the regular school curriculum. The literature in this area has provided numerous documentations of similar results (Matthews, 1984; Matthews & Justice, 1983; Garside et al., 1987).

Adolescents in Stress

Research on the topic of adolescents in stress was less frequently listed in the ERIC search than research on children in stress; research on stress management approaches for adolescents was practically nonexistent. In the studies that were identified factors such as family structure, functioning in school, suicidal risk, depression, and stressful life events were examined (Gispert et al., 1985). Interstingly, one study (Gispert et al., 1985) correlated suicide risk with current stress and depression with both lifelong and current stress. In one study (Novy & Donohue, 1985) the relationship between adolescent stress events and delinquent conduct showed delinquent adolescents to be highly stressed. Some studies assessed the use of scales such as the Adolescent Life Change Event Scale (Forman et al., 1983) and The Hassles Scale, and Uplifts Scale (Miller et al., 1985) to predict stress levels. The few studies that examined approaches to teaching stress management to adolescents in schools (Hiebert & Eby 1985; Richardson et al., 1983) were similar to the one previously discussed in relation to childhood stress.

Educators and Counselors in Stress

One of the factors related to the stress levels of the children and adolescents in our schools is the stress level of our educators and counselors. Most studies of higher educator job stress focus on one of four categories (Farkas & Milstein, 1987): (1) lack of control with which to handle assigned responsibilities; (2) role conflict; (3) poor interpersonal work-place relations; and (4) time management difficulties. Numerous studies (Friesen, 1986; Jones, 1985; Ireland & Ireland, 1984; Hock, 1985; Klas et al., 1985; Gorrell et al., 1985; Triesen & Williams, 1985; Raquepaw & deHass, 1984; Saunders & Watkins, 1982; Belcastro & Gold, 1983) explore one, several, or all of the four categories listed above. Studies of teacher stress and teaching performance (Blase, 1986), stress and female teachers (Calabrese & Anderson, 1986), intrinsic and extrinsic stress factors of teachers (Evans et al., 1986), teacher stress as related to locus of control, sex, and age (Halpin et al., 1985), and stress-producing factors and their effects on learning disabilities specialists, regular educators, and other special educators (Faas, 1984) all have been investigated.

Studies of counselors in stress were less numerous and varied. Lack of decision-making authority, low wages, nonprofessional duties, job overload, and relationships with teachers and principals were major components of counselor stress in one relatively recent study (Moracco et al., 1984). In another study (Pierson & Archambault, 1984) school psychologists and school counselors were found to have higher levels of role-related stress than did classroom teachers. In one study (Butcke et al., 1984) involving 763 school counselors, age and school size were the variables that had the most influence on perceptions of stress. Counselor burnout (Morris, 1981) also has been the focus of limited study.

Stress Management for Educators and Counselors

The studies on the topic of stress management for educators and counselors, though available, are few and far between in comparison to the other categories of school-related stress studies previously reviewed. Although there are programs designed to teach stress management techniques to educators (Docking & Docking, 1984) there seems to be a great need for further investigation and implementation in this area.

Children of Divorce

Researchers agree that children of divorce are an at-risk population and that the effect of divorce interferes with personal-social competency and coping skills. There is disagreement, however, about how the divorce process affects children at different stages of psychosocial development. An analysis of the research to date shows that the preponderance of the research has focused on the effects of divorce on children (these effects have been approached from a variety of perspectives). Custody resolutions, the behavior of boys following a divorce, and school-related interventions with children of divorce all have received limited attention in comparison to the attention given to the effects of divorce on children.

Effects of Divorce on Children

The following list of effects documented by research may serve to illustrate the variety of perspectives from which such research has been approached:

1. Children of divorce assumed a confident role with their mothers. They also rated themselves lower in social competence (Devall et al., 1986).
2. Very definite age-related responses to parental separation may be observed, and denial that the divorce occurred will be seen most often in younger children (Wax, 1985).
3. Children from separated families showed significantly more school-related problems than did children from intact families (Hett, 1980).
4. Single-parent students scored lower than their two-parent counterparts on tests of academic achievement (Shreeve et al., 1985).
5. Children's post-separation adjustment was found to be related to their mother's adjustment rather than to their mother's work situation (Malley & Barenbaum, 1984).
6. Being from a divorced family predicted aggression, concentration problems, and acting out toward parents (Hodges et al., 1984).
7. Younger children were reported to exhibit more acting out whereas older children showed more depression (Hodges & Bloom, 1984).
8. Single-parent students were more often tardy, absent, and truant than were other students. They were also more often involved in disciplinary actions and dropped out more often (Institute for Development of Educational Activities, 1980).
9. Students who had experienced father loss through divorce and whose mothers had not remarried demonstrated significantly lower self-concepts than those who were from intact families (Parish & Taylor, 1979).

10. Patterns of family interaction changed dramatically in the 2 years following divorce, and the behavior of the divorced father became less important than that of the mother in the child's social and cognitive development (Hetherington et al., 1978).

In the opinion of this writer, effects such as those above may have a direct relationship to decreased personal-social competency and coping skills.

Custody Resolutions

Although divorcing parents have a variety of child custody arrangements from which to choose, opinions are mixed as to which children benefit from which arrangements (Shiller, 1985). Research findings do suggest some considerations, however. Continued involvement of the father, free or open access between father and child, and a mutually supportive and cooperative co-parental relationship are important factors to look for in deciding what custody decisions would be conducive to the child's psychological adjustment (Khoe, 1986). Joint custody is increasingly being awarded to divorcing parents because of a greater awareness of the importance of maintaining contact with both parents; more attention has been given to the child's needs and requests rather than just emphasizing parents' requests in determining custody decisions (Khoe, 1986).

The Behavior of Young Boys Following a Divorce

Most of the research that focused on the behavior of young boys following a divorce reported negative effects. A recently published study (Block et al., 1986), for example, reported the results of a longitudinal study showing that the behavior of boys, as early as 11 years prior to parental separation or formal dissolution of marriage, was consistently affected by predivorce marital stress. In a study by Peterson & Zill (1986), the negative effects of divorce were found to be lower if the child lived with the same-sex parent following divorce or maintained a good relationship with one or both parents. Some studies (Sack, 1985) have documented sex disturbance symptoms in boys (e.g., cross-dressing) as a regressive reaction to parental discord in divorce. Other findings of recent research indicated that: (1) boys whose parents engaged in less frequent negative interchanges and boys who saw their fathers often after separation were doing better in school than boys who witnessed overt marital hostility in the home prior to separation; (2) boys who scored lower on adaptive functioning tended to attribute more blame to themselves for their parents' breakup, to show a fear of abandonment by their families, and to report that the mother frequently made derogatory comments about the father; and, finally, (3) mothers whose sons were doing better at school reflected higher performance on a parental skills test and lower stress attributable to the restrictions of the parental role (Prinz et al., 1983). The well known Hetherington studies (Hetherington et al., 1978, 1979) also documented the adverse effects of divorce on young boys.

School-Related Interventions with Children of Divorce

Surprisingly little research has been done to evaluate outcomes connected with school-related interventions for children of divorce; yet, most school counselors have been involved with, or are aware of, children of divorce groups for children or units on the divorcing process that have been integrated into the school curriculum. Some studies have connected children of divorce groups with enhanced school performance (Freeman & Couchman, 1985; Freeman, 1984). Preliminary indications are that brief intervention through small group counseling may be as effective as long-term therapy. Some studies concerning young children of divorced parents recommended: (1) greater teacher awareness of the effects of divorce and appropriate modification of the curriculum (Schwertfeger, 1983); (2) placing very young children of recently divorced parents in preschool programs (Adams, 1982); (3) greater involvement of school personnel in the provision of educational and counseling services to children of divorce and their parents (Gay, 1981; Drake & Shellenberger, 1981); and (4) increasing awareness among all school personnel of the service needs of children of divorce (Benedek & Benedek, 1979).

Conclusions

The concluding section of this paper presents suggestions for continued research in each of the nine research areas previously critiqued. The implications for the practitioner interested in enhancing social and personal competency and skill development with respect to the younger generation should be obvious. I'm sure reactors' presentations and group discussions during this 20/20 conference will provide additional ideas for both research and application.

Self-Esteem

A number of suggestions can be made relative to directions research on this topic might take in the future:

1. There is a need for more emphasis on exploring the relationships between school climate and the self-esteem of students, and teacher behavior and the self-esteem of students.
2. Research on the relationships between counselor behavior and the self-esteem of counselees is needed.
3. The best methods of assisting teachers with approaches to enhancing the self-esteem of their students should be explored.
4. Because low self-esteem seems to put students at risk for any one of a number of problems (e.g., depression, suicide, eating disorders, substance abuse), more research on the relationship between self-esteem and school-related presenting problems needs to be done.

5. Although numerous studies have been completed on the relationships between low self-esteem and learning disabilities, little research has been undertaken focusing on evaluating the best interventions for enhancing the self-esteem of the physically or mentally challenged.

6. Some accumulating evidence supports the concept that, for both young women and young men, an androgynous or masculine identity is associated with higher levels of self-esteem. Certainly this trend needs to be further explored, along with implications for school counselors and other school faculty.

7. Self-esteem and family influence and self-esteem and the gifted and talented are topics on which much additional research is needed.

8. The research on self-esteem as it relates to multicultural perspectives is "scattered." More studies focused on the same or related research questions need to be undertaken.

9. As noted previously, there is some question about whether or not current measurement instruments accurately assess self-esteem.

Eating Disorders

1. There is a dearth of research on the topic of the male student or client with eating disorders.

2. There is a lack of conclusive research on early identification of individuals with eating disorders.

3. Experts do not agree on a single approach to intervening with clients who have eating disorders; more research is definitely warranted.

4. To date, data about the best school-based intervention(s) for clients with eating disorders are inconclusive.

Child and Adolescent Suicide

1. In general, children's suicidal behavior is surrounded by controversy with no single theory to explain or assess vulnerable children. More research is needed.

2. Conspicuously absent from much of the research relating to the profile of the adolescent attempter or completer was the relationship of this profile to self-esteem, problem solving, communication skills, and guilt or self-blame.

3. There is not enough research to date on the topic of interventions, especially school-based interventions for crisis management during a suicide crisis.

4. Because prevention, crisis-management and postvention cannot, in the opinion of the writer, be approached crossculturally in the same way as they are approached with adolescents who are not members of minority groups, more research is needed in regard to members of culturally different groups.

Depression

1. There is considerable disagreement as to what signs and symptoms constitute a diagnosis of depression in children.
2. Even though the tests available for use in the diagnosis of childhood depression are substantial, more research, especially as it relates to the item above, need to be initiated.
3. There is no consensus among professionals as to the efficacy to the following treatment modalities available for intervening with the depressed child: (a) psychoanalytic, (b) behavioral, (c) cognitive, (d) familial, (e) rational-emotive, (f) multimodal, and (g) medication.
4. Although evidence derived from research literature supporting the concept of adolescent depression as a clinical disorder is considerably stronger than it was a decade ago, uncertainty regarding a valid and reliable means of diagnosis and classsification remains the major obstacle to its empirical verification.

Teenage Pregnancy

1. The psychological correlates of teenage motherhood must be researched further.
2. The attitudes of male adolescents toward adolescent pregnancy and fatherhood merit additional attention.
3. Research on school-based pregnancy prevention programs, although impressive, needs additional refinement.
4. The counseling needs of pregnant teenagers, whether medical, educational, or emotional, must continue to be explored.

Substance Abuse

1. The accelerating interest in the creation and evaluation of school-based intervention efforts in the area of use and abuse of alcohol and other drugs by our young people is laudable. But which interventions have the most constructive effects?
2. Are classroom-based intervention programs more or less effective than building or district level programs?
3. How long must students be provided with after-care treatment through the schools once residential or outpatient treatment has been completed?
4. Which family-based intervention efforts are most effective, and is working with families in the context of the substance abuse of children and adolescents the best use of the school's resources?

Physical and Sexual Abuse

1. Conspicuous gaps in the research to date appear in the areas of sexual abuse of boys and male adolescents and, to a surprising degree, the characteristics of parents who abuse their children.

2. Continued exploration of the short-term effects of physical and sexual abuse seems warranted.
3. Much more effort and emphasis must be focused upon the long-term effects of physical and sexual abuse.
4. The roles of teachers and counselors in the prevention, detection, and reporting of all types of abuse must be further refined through the accumulation of a better data base.

Stress

1. The roles of all school faculty and personnel in the process of teaching stress management to children and adolescents must be further refined and evaluated.
2. Preliminary findings suggesting that stress management techniques should be taught through integration into the curricula of the schools should be extended.
3. Much more has been done relative to the topic of children in stress than to the topic of adolescents in stress.
4. Because one of the factors related to the stress levels of the children and adolescents in our schools is the stress level of our educators and counselors, more studies of the factors producing stress in school faculty must be completed.
5. Much more effort needs to be made to address stress burnout among school counselors.
6. Studies on the topic of stress management for educators and counselors, though available, are limited in number and scope.

Children of Divorce

1. Although studies of the effects of divorce on children frequently appear in academic journals, results are confusing and often contradictory.
2. Issues connected with custody resolution must become a more important component of research efforts.
3. The behavior of young boys following divorce must continue to receive increased attention by researchers.
4. Even though many school counselors have been involved with, or are aware of, children of divorce groups for children or units on the divorcing process that have been integrated into the school curriculum, surprisingly little research has been done to evaluate outcomes connected with school-related interventions for children of divorce.

Implications for School Counseling Programs

One way of approaching a brief consideration of the implications of this analysis of the research on the personal-social concerns of the young people in our schools is by sharing some observations and then posing some questions for the reader to consider. First, I can't help commenting on the fact that the reason areas connected with personal/social concerns are generating so much research is because the areas addressed in this paper represent many of the major presenting problems of the young of the 1980s. Second, it seems to me that if a professional counselor is interested in using the graduate education experience and what the research points to as the presenting problems of our young people to constructively intervene in the lives of students, teachers, and parents, such a counselor will seek a position as an elementary school counselor. Elementary counseling is new enough and viable enough to permit counselors to use their expertise to work with young people. If a counselor is not comfortable working with young people who are experiencing problems in areas such as the ones addressed in this paper, such a counselor may seek a counseling position in a secondary school. Even though there are exemplary secondary school counseling programs that provide a balanced constellation of services to constituent consumers, most secondary school counselors cannot help students with the personal problems they experience because they are "caught" in roles established over 25 years ago. Such traditional roles often emphasize educational advisement, scheduling, and a variety of nonguidance related quasi-administrative tasks.

My questions are these:

1. How can students benefit from an educational experience, no matter how excellent, if personal/social concerns make it impossible to participate?
2. Are problems such as low self-esteem, suicidal preoccupation, depression, and eating disorders likely to disappear suddenly from the lives of students in American schools?
3. How logical is it to continue to believe that only those employed *outside* the public school sector are to address directly the personal/social concerns of our youth?
4. Why are counselors so unassertive about refusing responsibilities that have little to do with their expertise and make it impossible to have the time to help students with their concerns?
5. Why aren't members of the profession adamant about expecting counselors to assist students to overcome personal/social issues that impinge on optimal coping by moving away from the roles of the past that no longer meet the needs of the students of the present?
6. Is it time for a complete reconceptualization of the role of the school counselor, especially the secondary school counselor?
7. How can such a reconceptualization of the role of the counselor be integrated into current educational structures so the counselor of the 1990s can *successfully* maintain, and periodically revise, a role that will make it possible to enhance the ability of students to cope with the issues of the day?

8. How will we elicit support for this reconceptualization from building principals, district superintendents, other school system administrators, school boards, teachers, and parent groups?

References

Adams, G.R. (1982). *The effects of divorce: Outcome of a preschool intervention program.* (ERIC Document Reproduction Service No. ED 214 667)

Adler, E.M., et al. (1985). Educational policies and programs for teenage parents and pregnant teenagers. *Family Relations, 34*(2), 183–187.

Alan Guttmacher Institute. (1981). *Teenage pregnancy: The problem that hasn't gone away.* New York: Author. (ERIC Document Reproduction Service No. ED 267 350)

Amato, P.R. (1986). Marital conflict, the parent-child relationship and child self-esteem. *Family Relations, 35*(3), 403–410.

American Humane Association. (1978). *National analysis of official child neglect and abuse reporting. Full report.* Washington, DC: National Center of Child Abuse and Neglect (DHEW/OHD). (ERIC Document Reproduction Service No. ED 155 840)

Antonow, W., et al. (1976). Prevalent and preferred styles in drug education. *Journal of Drug Education, 6*(2), 117–124.

Armstrong, B.A. (1983). Kairos: An out-patient progress report. *School Guidance Worker, 39*(1), 41–47.

Austin Independent School District. (1985). *Project connect: 1984–85 final technical report.* Austin, TX: Author, Office of Research and Evaluation. (ERIC Document Reproduction Service No. ED 265 180)

Ayers, J.B., & Richey, D.D. (1984). *Influencing teacher attitudes and knowledge about child maltreatment.* Washington, DC: American Association of Colleges for Teacher Education. (ERIC Document Reproduction Service No. ED 238 883)

Bachman, J.G., & O'Malley, P.M. (1984). Black-white differences in self-esteem: Are they affected by response styles? *American Journal of Sociology, 90*(3), 624–639.

Bailey, B.E., et al. (1982). *Projected suicidal ideation in regard to adverse life circumstances.* (ERIC Document Reproduction Service No. ED 232 072)

Bailey, B.E., et al. (1984). *Suicidal ideation across populations.* (ERIC Document Reproduction Service No. ED 251 778)

Bailey, B.E., et al. (1985). *Children's suicidal thinking: An empirical inquiry.* (ERIC Document Reproduction Service No. ED 263 470)

Baron, P., & Perron, L.M. (1986). Sex differences in the Beck depression inventory scores of adolescents. *Journal of Youth and Adolescence, 15*(2), 165–171.

Barret, R.L., & Robinson, B.E. (1982). A descriptive study of teenage expectant fathers. *Family Relations, 31*(3), 349–352.

Barth, R.P., et al. (1983a). Coping strategies of counselors and school-age mothers. *Journal of Counseling Psychology, 30*(3), 346–354.

Barth, R.P., et al. (1983b). Psychological correlates of teenage motherhood. *Journal of Youth and Adolescence, 12*(6), 471–487.

Battle, J. (1980). Relationship between self-esteem and depression among high school students. *Perceptual and Motor Skills, 51*(1), 157–158.

74

Bayer, A.E., & Baker, D.H. (1986). *Adolescent eating disorders: Anorexia and bulimia. Publication 352–044*. Blacksburg, VA: Virginia Cooperative Extension Service. (ERIC Document Reproduction Service No. ED 275 938)

Belcastro, P.A., & Gold, R.S. (1983). Teacher stress and burnout: Implications for school health personnel. *Journal of School Health, 53*(7), 404–407.

Benedek, R.S., & Benedek, E.P. (1979). Children of divorce: Can we meet their needs. *Journal of Social Issues, 35*(4), 155–169.

Berg, M., et al. (1979). Prenatal care for pregnant adolescents in a public high school. *Journal of School Health, 49*(1), 32–35.

Bingham, G. (1980). Self-esteem among boys with and without specific learning disabilities. *Child Study Journal, 10*(1), 41–47.

Birleson, P. (1981). The validity of depressive disorder in childhood and the development of self-rating scale: A research report. *Journal of Child Psychology and Psychiatry and Allied Disciplines, 22*(1), 73–88.

Black, C., & DeBlassie, R.R. (1985). Adolescent pregnancy: Contributing factors, consequences, treatment, and plausible solutions. *Adolescence, 20*(78), 281–290.

Blase, J.J. (1986). A qualitative analysis of sources of teacher stress: Consequences for performance. *American Educational Research Journal, 23*(1), 13–40.

Blease, D. (1986). Teachers' personal constructs and their pupils' self-images. *Educational Studies, 12*(3), 255–264.

Block, J.H., et al. (1986). The personality of children prior to divorce: A prospective study. *Child Development, 57*(4), 827–840.

Blotner, R., & Lilly, L. (1986). SPECDA—A comprehensive approach to the delivery of substance abuse prevention services in the New York City school systems. *Journal of Drug Education, 16*(1), 83–89.

Blyth, D.A., & Traeger, C.M. (1983). The self-concept and self-esteem of early adolescents. *Theory into Practice, 22*(2), 91–97.

Blythe, B.J., et al. (1981). Pregnancy-prevention groups for adolescents. *Social Work, 26*(6), 503–504.

Brooks, H.C., & Ellis, G.J. (1982). Self-esteem of hearing-impaired adolescents: Effects of labelling. *Youth and Society, 14*(1), 59–80.

Brumback, R.A., et al. (1980). Neuropsychological study of children during and after remission of endogenous depressive episodes. *Perceptual and Motor Skills, 50*(3), 1163–1167.

Bry, B.H., et al. (1986). Decreasing adolescent drug use and school failure: Long-term effects of targeted family problem-solving training. *Child and Family Behavior Therapy, 8*(1), 43–59.

Butcke, P., et al. (1984). Measuring occupational stress among counselors: A multidimensional concept. *Measurement and Evaluation in Guidance, 17*(1), 24–31.

Butler, L., et al. (1980). The effect of two school-based intervention programs on depressive symptoms in preadolescents. *American Educational Research Journal, 17*(1), 111–119.

Bynner, J.M., et al. (1981). Self-esteem and delinquency revisited. *Journal of Youth and Adolescence, 10*(6), 407–441.

Calabrese, R.L., & Anderson, R.E. (1986). The public school: A source of stress and alienation among female teachers. *Urban Education, 21*(1), 30–41.

Calhoun, L.G., et al. (1980). Reactions to the parents of the child suicide: A study of social impressions. *Journal of Consulting and Clinical Psychology, 48*(4), 535–536.

Calhoun, L.G., et al. (1981). *The aftermath of childhood suicide: Influences on the perception of the parent.* (ERIC Document Reproduction Service No. ED 204 700)

Calsyn, R.J., et al. (1980). Do improved communication skills lead to increased self-esteem? *Elementary School Guidance and Counseling, 15*(1), 48–55.

Campbell-Goymer, N.R. (1984). *Cognitive correlates of childhood depression.* (ERIC Document Reproduction Service No. ED 252 768)

Carey, M.P., et al. (1986). Relationship of activity to depression in adolescents: Development of the adolescent activities checklist. *Journal of Consulting and Clinical Psychology, 54*(3), 320–322.

Carter, J.A., & Duncan, P.A. (1984). Binge-eating and vomiting: A survey of a high school population. *Psychology in the Schools, 21*(2), 198–203.

Cate, R., & Sugawara, A. (1986). Sex role orientation and dimensions of self-esteem among middle adolescents. *Sex Roles, 15*(3–4), 145–158.

Cheung, P.C., & Lau, S. (1985). Self-esteem: Its relationship to the family and school social environments among Chinese adolescents. *Youth and Society, 16*(4), 438–456.

Christie, S.G., & Saccone, P.P. (1985). *An evaluation of the fitness, academic, and self-esteem training program at Meridian School, 1984–1985.* (ERIC Document Reproduction Service No. ED 267 053)

Clarizio, H.F. (1985). Cognitive-behavioral treatment of childhood depression. *Psychology in the Schools, 22*(3), 308–322.

Clarizio, H.F. (1986). Treatment of childhood depression: The state of the art. *Techniques, 2*(4), 322–332.

Colletta, N.D. (1982). *Depression and the maternal behavior of adolescent mothers.* (ERIC Document Reproduction Service No. ED 223 339)

Congress of the U.S. (1985). *Suicide and suicide prevention: A briefing by the Subcommittee on Human Services of the Select Committee on Aging. House of Representatives, Ninety-Eighth Congress, Second Session (November 1, 1984, San Francisco, CA).* (Report No. House-Comm-Pub-98-497). Washington, DC: House Select Committee on Aging. (ERIC Document Reproduction Service No. ED 259 261)

Coons, P.M. (1986). Child abuse and multiple personality disorders: Review of the literature and suggestions for treatment. *Child Abuse and Neglect: The International Journal, 10*(4), 455–462.

Cooper, J.E., et al. (1983). Self-esteem and family cohesion: The child's perspective and adjustment. *Journal of Marriage and the Family, 45*(1), 153–159.

Corder, B.F., & Haizlip, T.M. (1984). Environmental and personality similarities in case histories of suicide and self-poisoning by children under ten. *Suicide and Life-Threatening Behavior, 14*(1), 59–66.

Cotugno, A.J. (1980). A psychoeducational approach in the treatment of anorexia nervosa. *Psychology in the Schools, 17*(2), 222–240.

Crook, T., & Raskin, A. (1975). Association of childhood parental loss with attempted suicide and depression. *Journal of Consulting and Clinical Psychology*, *43*(2), 277.

Ctryn, L., McKnew, D.H., & Bunney. (1980). Diagnosis of depression in children: A reassessment. *American Journal of Psychiatry*, *137*, 22–25.

Curiel, H., et al. (1980). Achieved reading level, self-esteem, and grades as related to length of exposure to bilingual education. *Hispanic Journal of Behavioral Sciences*, *2*(4), 389–400.

Curtis, C.K., & Shaver, J.P. (1981). Improving slow learners' self-esteem in secondary social studies classes. *Journal of Educational Research*, *74*(4), 217–223.

Dalton, D.W., & Hannafin, M.J. (1985a). Examining the effects of varied computer-based reinforcement on self-esteem and achievement: An exploratory study. *AEDS Journal*, *18*(3), 172–182.

Dalton, D.W., & Hannafin, M. (1985b). Examining the effects of varied computer-based reinforcement on self-esteem and achievement: An exploratory study. (ERIC Document Reproduction Service No. ED 256 308)

Dalton, T.W. (1986). *Indicators of multiple personality disorder for the clinician*. Unpublished doctor of psychology research paper, Biola University, La Mirada, CA. (ERIC Document Reproduction Service No. ED 273 890)

Devall, E., et al. (1986). The impact of divorce and maternal employment on preadolescent children. *Family Relations*, *35*(1), 153–159.

Diekstra, R.F.W. (1985). Suicide and suicide attempts in the European economic community: An analysis of trends, with special emphasis upon trends among the young. *Suicide and Life-Threatening Behavior*, *15*(1), 27–42.

Dielman, T.E., et al. (1984). Health locus of control and self-esteem as related to adolescent health behavior and intentions. *Adolescence*, *19*(76), 935–950.

Dixon, R.D. (1981). The "illegitmacy runs in families" hypothesis reconsidered. *Journal of Black Studies*, *11*(3), 277–287.

Dizmang, L.H., et al. (1974). Adolescent suicide at an Indian reservation. *American Journal of Orthopsychiatry*, *44*(1), 43–49.

Docking, R.A. & Docking, E. (1984). Reducing teacher stress. *Unicorn, Bulletin of the Australian College of Education*, *10*(3), 261–274.

Domino, G. (1981). Attitudes toward suicide among Mexican American and Anglo youth. *Hispanic Journal of Behavioral Sciences*, *3*(4), 385–395.

Drake, E.A., & Shellenberger, S. (1981). Children of separation and divorce: A review of school programs and implications for the psychologist. *School Psychology Review*, *10*(1), 54–61.

Duhon, R.M. (1985). *Alleviate sexual abuse of children: Teachers can help*. (ERIC Document Reproduction Service No. ED 256 761)

Duncan, D.F. (1983). *Stress and children: A theoretical overview*. (ERIC Document Reproduction Service No. ED 230 542)

Eisele, J., et al. (1986). Factors related to eating disorders in young adolescent girls. *Adolescence*, *21*(82), 283–290.

Elliott, G.C. (1982). Self-esteem and self-presentation among the young as a function of age and gender. *Journal of Youth and Adolescence*, *11*(2), 135–153.

Ellis, B.G. (Ed.). (1980). *Drug abuse from the family perspective: Coping is a family affair*. (Report No. DHHS-ADM-80–910). Rockville, MD: National Institute on

Drug Abuse (DHEW/PHS). (ERIC Document Reproduction Service No. ED 205 849)

Ellsworth, S.K., & Demos, G. (1981). *A survey of the self-concept and intellect of girls who have been victims of incest.* (ERIC Document Reproduction Service No. ED 221 810)

Emery, P.E. (1983). Adolescent depression and suicide. *Adolescence, 18*(70), 245–258.

Englander, M.E. (1986). *Truancy/self-esteem.* (ERIC Document Reproduction Service No. ED 269 666)

Eskilson, A., et al. (1986). Parental pressure, self-esteem and adolescent reported deviance: Bending the twig too far. *Adolescence, 21*(83), 501–515.

Evans, V., et al. (1986). *Analysis of the intrinsic and extrinsic stress factors of K–12 physical education teachers.* (ERIC Document Reproduction Service No. ED 271 450)

Faas, L.A. (1984). *Stress producing factors and their effects on learning disabilities specialists, regular educators, and other special educators.* (ERIC Document Reproduction Service No. ED 249 706)

Falk, R., et al. (1981). Personality factors related to black teenage pregnancy and abortion. *Psychology of Women Quarterly, 5*(5), 737–746.

Farber, E.D., & Joseph, J.A. (1985). The maltreated adolescent: Patterns of physical abuse. *Child Abuse and Neglect: The International Journal, 9*(2), 201–206.

Farkas, J.P., & Milstein, M. (1987). *Educator stress: Myth or reality.* (ERIC Document Reproduction Service No. ED 275 062)

Finch, A.J., Jr., et al. (1985). Children's depression inventory: Sex and grade norms for normal children. *Journal of Consulting and Clinical Psychology, 53*(3), 424–425.

Finkelhor, D. (1978). *A survey of sexual abuse in the population at large: Some policy implications.* (ERIC Document Reproduction Service No. ED 169 462)

Forman, B.D., et al. (1983). Measuring perceived stress in adolescents: A cross validation. *Adolescence, 18*(71), 573–576.

Forman, S.G., & O'Malley, P.L. (1984). School stress and anxiety interventions. *School Psychology Review, 13*(2), 162–170.

Forrest, D.V. (1983). Depression: Information and interventions for school counselors. *School Counselor, 30*(4), 269–279.

Freeman, R. (1984). *Children in families experiencing separation and divorce: An investigation of the effects of planned brief intervention.* Ontario: Family Service Association of Metropolitan Toronto. (ERIC Document Reproduction Service No. ED 255 787)

Freeman, R., & Couchman, B. (1985). Coping with family change: A model for therapeutic group counseling with children and adolescents. *School Guidance Worker 40*(5), 44–50.

Friede, A., et al. (1986). Do the sisters of childbearing teenagers have increased rates of childbearing? *American Journal of Public Health, 76*(10), 1221–1224.

Friedrich, W., et al. (1982). Depression and suicidal ideation in early adolescents. *Journal of Youth and Adolescence, 11*(5), 403–407.

Friedrich, W.N., et al. (1983). Cognitive and behavioral characteristics of physically abused children. *Journal of Consulting and Clinical Psychology, 51*(2), 313–314.

Friesen, D. (1986). *Overall stress and job satisfaction as predictors of burnout. (ERIC Document Reproduction Service No. ED 274 698)*

Fuhrmann, B.S., & Washington, C.S., (Eds.). (1984). Substance abuse [Special issue]. *Journal for Specialists in Group Work, 9*(1).

Furstenberg, F.F., Jr. (1980). Burdens and benefits: The impact of early childbearing on the family. *Journal of Social Issues, 36*(1), 64–87.

Galambos, N.L., & Dixon, R.A. (1984). Adolescent abuse and the development of personal sense of control. *Child Abuse and Neglect: The International Journal, 8*(3), 285–293.

Garner, C.W., & Cole, E.G. (1984). *A pilot study on the congruency of locus of control and field dependence as related to self-esteem and academic achievement.* (ERIC Document Reproduction Service No. ED 241 492)

Garside, J.G., et al. (1987). *Mental health and adjustment: Symposium IV B.* (ERIC Document Reproduction Service No. ED 273 370)

Gay, V.B. (1981). *How the schools can meet the needs of the children of divorce.* (ERIC Document Reproduction Service No. ED 201 623)

Gershenson, H.P. (1983). Redefining fatherhood in families with white adolescent mothers. *Journal of Marriage and the Family, 45*(3), 591–599.

Gibbs, J.T. (1981). Depression and suicidal behavior among delinquent females. *Journal of Youth and Adolescence, 10*(2), 159–167.

Gispert, M., et al. (1985). Suicidal adolescents: Factors in evaluation. *Adolescence, 20*(80), 753–762.

Glaser, K. (1967). Masked depression in children and adolescents. *American Journal of Psychotherapy, 21*, 565–574.

Golden, J.M. (1981). Depression in middle and late childhood: Implications for intervention. *Child Welfare, 60*(7), 457–465.

Goldstein, P.J. (1981). Adolescent pregnancy. *Journal of the International Association of Pupil Personnel Workers, 25*(2), 124–129.

Goodwin, J., et al. (1979). Hysterical seizures: A sequel to incest. *American Journal of Orthopsychiatry, 49*(4), 698–703.

Gordon, D.P., et al. (1983). *A comparison of the psychological evaluation of adolescents with anorexia nervosa and of adolescents with conduct disorders.* (ERIC Document Reproduction Service No. ED 243 050)

Gorrell, J.J., et al. (1985). An analysis of perceived stress in elementary and secondary student teachers and full-time teachers. *Journal of Experimental Education, 54*(1), 11–14.

Grob, M.C., et al. (1983). The role of the high school professional in identifying and managing adolescent suicidal behavior. *Journal of Youth and Adolescence, 12*(2), 163–173.

Gumbiner, J., et al. (1981). Relations of classroom structures and teacher behaviors to social orientation, self-esteem, and classroom climate among Anglo American and Mexican American children. *Hispanic Journal of Behavioral Sciences, 3*(1), 19–40.

Hall, B., & Taylor, S. (1984). *Comparison of the self-concept and self-esteem among pregnant adolescent girls and their nullipara peers.* (ERIC Document Reproduction Service No. ED 272 810)

Halpin, G., et al. (1985). Teacher stress as related to locus of control, sex, and age. *Journal of Experimental Education, 53*(3), 136–140.

Harlow, L.L., et al. (1986). Depression, self-derogation, substance use, and suicide ideation: Lack of purpose in life as mediational factor. *Journal of Clinical Psychology, 42*(1), 5–21.

Hart, N.A. (1978). How teachers can help suicidal adolescents. *Clearing House, 51*(8), 369–373.

Hartman, D.D. (1986). *Adolescent depression: Issues of prevalence, phenomenology, and nosology.* (ERIC Document Reproduction Service No. ED 273 903)

Harvill, R. (1984). Bulimia: Treatment with systematic rational restructuring, response prevention, and cognitive modeling. *Journal of Counseling and Development, 63*(4), 250–251.

Hazzard, A., & Rupp, G. (1984). *Training teachers to identify and intervene with abused children.* (ERIC Document Reproduction Service No. ED 240 476)

Hecht, M., et al. (1986). Nonverbal behavior of young abused and neglected children. *Communication Education, 35*(2), 134–142.

Hendricks, L.E. (1981). *An analysis of two select populations of Black unmarried adolescent fathers. Volume I. Final report.* (Grant No. 1-R01-2555-07; 90CW637–01). Rockville, MD: National Institute of Mental Health (DHHS). (ERIC Document Reproduction Service No. ED 264 355)

Hendricks, L.E. (1982). *A comparative analysis of three select populations of Black unmarried adolescent fathers. Volume II. Final report.* (Grant No. 1R01-2555-07; 90CW637–01). Rockville, MD: National Institute of Mental Health (DHHS). (ERIC Document Reproduction Service No. ED 265 356)

Hendricks, L.E., & Montgomery, T. (1983). A limited population of unmarried adolescent fathers: A preliminary report of their views on fatherhood and the relationship with the mothers of their children. *Adolescence, 18*(69), 201–210.

Hetherington, E.M., et al. (1978, May). *Family interaction and the social, emotional and cognitive development of children following divorce.* Paper presented at the Symposium on The Family: Setting Priorities, sponsored by the Institute for Pediatric Service of the Johnson & Johnson Baby Company, Washington, DC. (ERIC Document Reproduction Service No. ED 156 328)

Hetherington, E.M., et al. (1979). Play and social interaction in children following divorce. *Journal of Social Issues, 35*(4), 26–49.

Hett, G.G. (1980). *Family separation: Its effects upon the education and social-emotional growth of children.* (ERIC Document Reproduction Service No. ED 262 347)

Hinkle, D.E., et al. (1980). Adlerian parent education: Changes in parents' attitudes and behaviors, and childrens' self-esteem. *Journal of Family Therapy, 8*(1), 32–43.

Hiebert, B., & Eby, W. (1985). The effects of relaxation training for grade 12 students. *School Counselor, 32*(3), 205–210.

Hjorth, C.W., & Ostrov, E. (1982). The self-image of physically abused adolescents. *Journal of Youth and Adolescence, 11*(2), 71–76.

Hock, R.R. (1985). *Professional burnout among public school teachers.* (ERIC Document Reproduction Service No. ED 204 219)

Hodges, W.F., et al. (1984). The cumulative effect of stress on preschool children of divorced and intact families. *Journal of Marriage and the Family, 46*(3), 611–617.

Hodges, W.F., & Bloom, B.L. (1984). Parent's report of children's adjustment to marital separation: A longitudinal study. *Journal of Divorce, 8*(1), 33–50.

Hodgman, C.H. (1985). Recent findings in adolescent depression and suicide. *Journal of Developmental and Behavioral Pediatrics, 6*(3), 162–170.

Hollinger, C.L. (1983). Counseling the gifted and talented female adolescent: The relationship between social self-esteem and traits of instrumentality and expressiveness. *Gifted Child Quarterly, 27*(4), 157–161.

Hollinger, C.L., & Fleming, E.S. (1985). Social orientation and the social self-esteem of gifted and talented female adolescents. *Journal of Youth and Adolescence, 14*(5), 389–399.

Honig, A.S. (1986). Research in review. Stress and coping in children (Part 1). *Young Children, 41*(4), 50–63.

Hood, J., et al. (1982). Locus of control as a measure of ineffectiveness in anorexia nervosa. *Journal of Consulting and Clinical Psychology, 50*(1), 3–13.

Hughes, C.M., et al. (1985). Sex role attitudes and career choices: The role of children's self-esteem. *Elementary School Guidance and Counseling, 20*(1), 57–66.

Hurtig, A.L., & Petersen, A.C. (1982, August). *The relationship of sex role identity to ego development and self esteem in adolescence.* Paper presented at the annual convention of the American Psychological Association, Washington, DC. (ERIC Document Reproduction Service No. ED 225 095)

Iga, M. (1981). Suicide of Japanese youth. *Suicide and Life-Threatening Behavior, 11*(1), 17–30.

Institute for Development of Educational Activities. (1980). *The most significant minority: One-parent children in the schools.* (ERIC Document Reproduction Service No. ED 192 438)

Ireland, L.W., & Ireland, R.R. (1984). *Identifying and handling stress in secondary education.* (ERIC Document Reproduction Service No. ED 266 091)

Iverson, D.C., et al. (1978). The effects of an education intervention program for juvenile drug abusers and their parents. *Journal of Drug Education, 8*(2), 101.

Jackson, R.B. (1986). *A study of Y.W.C.A. services performed for pregnant and parenting high school students of El Paso from 1982 to 1985.* El Paso, TX: SchoolCraft Consultants. (ERIC Document Reproduction Service No. ED 274 488)

Jacobson, R.S., & Straker, G. (1982). Peer group interaction of physically abused children. *Child Abuse and Neglect: The International Journal, 6*(3), 321–327.

Janos, P.M., et al. (1985). Self-concept, self-esteem, and peer relations among gifted children who feel "different." *Gifted Child Quarterly, 29*(2), 78–82.

Jensen, G.F., et al. (1982). Ethnic status and adolescent self-evaluations: An extension of research on minority self esteem. *Social Problems, 30*(2), 226–239.

Johnson, C., et al. (1984). Incidence and correlates of bulimic behavior in a female high school population. *Journal of Youth and Adolescence, 13*(1), 15–26.

Johnson, C.L. (1971, August). *Adolescent pregnancy and poverty: Implications for social policy.* Paper presented at annual meetings of The Society for the Study of Social Problems, Denver, CO. (ERIC Document Reproduction Service No. ED 056 356)

Johnson, W.Y. (1985). Classroom discussion of suicide: An intervention tool for the teacher. *Contemporary Education, 56*(2), 114–117.

Jones, J.R. (1985). *Differential stress levels in primary versus secondary classrooms.* (ERIC Document Reproduction Service No. ED 266 098)

Jones, R.M., & Hartmann, B.R. (1985). *Ego identity, self-esteem and substance use during adolescence.* (ERIC Document Reproduction Service No. ED 263 454)

Jorgensen, S.R., & Alexander, S. (1981). Reducing the risk of adolescent pregnancy: Toward certification of family life educators. *High School Journal, 64*(6), 257–268.

Kagan, D.M., & Squires, R.L. (1984). Eating disorders among adolescents: Patterns and prevalence. *Adolescence, 19*(73), 15–29.

Kahle, L.R., et al. (1980). Low adolescent self-esteem leads to multiple interpersonal problems: A test of social-adaption theory. *Journal of Personality and Social Psychology, 39*(3), 496–502.

Kaiser, C.F., & Berndt, D.J. (1983). *The lonely and gifted adolescent: Stress, depression and anger.* (ERIC Document Reproduction Service No. ED 236 495)

Kawash, G.F. (1982). A structural analysis of self-esteem from pre-adolescence through young adulthood: Anxiety and extraversion as agents in the development of self-esteem. *Journal of Clinical Psychology, 38*(2), 301–311.

Kazdin, A.E., et al. (1983). Hopelessness, depression, and suicidal intent among psychiatrically disturbed inpatient children. *Journal of Consulting and Clinical Psychology, 51*(4), 504–510.

Kazdin, A.E., & Petti, T.A. (1982). Self-report and interview measures of childhood and adolescent depression. *Journal of Child Psychology and Psychiatry and Allied Disciplines, 23*(4), 437–457.

Khoe, L. (1986). *The effects of divorce on children and implications for court custody cases.* (ERIC Document Reproduction Service No. ED 273 901)

King, R.B., et al. (1986). *Differentiating conduct disorder from depressive disorders in school age children.* (ERIC Document Reproduction Service No. ED 269 683)

Kishor, N. (1981). The effect of self-esteem and locus of control in career decision making of adolescents in Fiji. *Journal of Vocational Behavior, 19*(2), 227–232.

Klas, L.D., et al. (1985). Levels and specific causes of stress perceived by regular classroom teachers. *Canadian Counsellor, 19*(3–4), 115–127.

Klerman, L.V. (1979). Evaluating service programs for school-age parents: Design problems. *Evaluation and the Health Professions, 2*(1), 55–70.

Korup, U.L. (1985). Parent and teacher perception of depression in children. *Journal of School Health, 55*(9), 367–369.

Kosky, R. (1983). Childhood suicidal behaviour. *Child Psychology and Psychiatry and Allied Disciplines, 24*(3), 457–468.

Kratcoski, P.C. (1982). Child abuse and violence against the family. *Child Welfare, 61*(7), 435–444.

Kulik, C.C. (1985). *Effects of inter-class ability grouping on achievement and self-esteem.* (ERIC Document Reproduction Service No. ED 263 492)

Lahey, B.B., et al. (1984). Parenting behavior and emotional status of physically abusive mothers. *Journal of Consulting and Clinical Psychology, 52*(6), 1062–1071.

Lamke, L.K. (1982). The impact of sex-role orientation on self-esteem in early adolescence. *Child Development, 53*(6), 1530–1535.

Lamphear, V.S. (1985). The impact of maltreatment on children's psychosocial adjustment: A review of the research. *Child Abuse and Neglect: The International Journal, 9*(2), 251–263.

Landy, S., et al. (1983). Teenage pregnancy: Family syndrome? *Adolescence, 18*(71), 679–694.

Lapsley, D.K., et al. (1984). *Loneliness, depression, and epistemological relativity in early and late adolescence.* (ERIC Document Reproduction Service No. ED 248 431)

Lawson, M.C. (1980). Development of body build stereotypes, peer ratings, and self-esteem in Australian children. *Journal of Psychology, 104,* 111–118.

Lazarus, P.J. (1982). Correlation of shyness and self-esteem for elementary school children. *Perceptual and Motor Skills, 55*(1), 8–10.

Ledford, B.R., & Ledford, S.Y. (1985). *The effects of preconscious cues upon the automatic activation of self-esteem of selected middle school students.* (ERIC Document Reproduction Service No. ED 268 153)

Lefkowitz, M.M., & Tesiny, E.P. (1980). Assessment of childhood depression. *Journal of Consulting and Clinical Psychology, 48*(1), 43–50.

Lefkowitz, M.M., & Tesiny, E.P. (1985). Depression in children: Prevalence and correlates. *Journal of Consulting and Clinical Psychology, 53*(5), 647–656.

Leitenberg, H., et al. (1986). Negative cognitive errors in children: Questionnaire development, normative data, and comparisons between children with and without self-reported symptoms of depression, low self-esteem, and evaluation anxiety. *Journal of Consulting and Clinical Psychology, 54*(4), 528–536.

Leon, G.R., et al. (1980). Depression in children: Parent, teacher, and child perspectives. *Journal of Abnormal Child Psychology, 8*(2), 221–235.

Lerner, R.M., et al. (1980). Self-concept, self-esteem, and body attitudes among Japanese male and female adolescents. *Child Development, 51*(3), 847–855.

Loeb, R.C., et al. (1980). Family interaction patterns associated with self-esteem in preadolescent girls and boys. *Merrill-Palmer Quarterly, 26*(3), 205–218.

Lubin, B., & Levitt, E.E. (1979). Norms for the depression adjective check lists: Age group and sex. *Journal of Consulting and Clinical Psychology, 47*(1), 192.

Lundholm, J.K., & Littrell, J.M. (1986). Desire for thinness among high school cheerleaders: Relationship to disordered eating and weight control behaviors. *Adolescence, 21*(83), 573–579.

Maine, M.D. (1985). *Engaging the disengaged father in the treatment of eating disordered adolescents.* (ERIC Document Reproduction Service No. ED 267 360)

Malley, J.E., & Barenbaum, N.B. (1984). *Maternal employment patterns and mothers' and children's post-separation adjustment.* (ERIC Document Reproduction Service No. ED 256 478)

Maqsud, M. (1983). Relationships of locus of control to self esteem, academic achievement, and prediction of performance among Nigerian secondary school pupils. *British Journal of Educational Psychology, 53*(Pt. 2), 215–221.

Maris, R. (1985). The adolescent suicide problem. *Suicide and Life-Threatening Behavior, 15*(2), 91–109.

Matthews, D.B. (1984). *Academic and psychosocial effects of relaxation training on rural preadolescents. Research bulletin no. 34.* (ERIC Document Reproduction Service No. ED 252 801)

Matthews, D.B., & Casteel, J.F. (1984). *The effects of relaxation training using wrist temperature as biofeedback in an educational setting.* (ERIC Document Reproduction Service No. ED 244 199)

Matthews, D.B., & Justice, C. (1983). *Relaxation training: A stress management model for schools.* (ERIC Document Reproduction Service No. ED 232 110)

McDonough, S.C. (1984). Intervention programs for adolescent mothers and their off-spring. *Journal of Children in Contemporary Society, 17*(1), 67–78.

McIntyre, T. (1986). *Child abuse and the educator: A review of literature.* (ERIC Document Reproduction Service No. ED 276 181)

McKenry, P.C., et al. (1983). The role of drugs in adolescent suicide attempts. *Suicide and Life-Threatening Behavior, 13*(3), 166–175.

McManus, J.L. (1984). *Overview of stress effects on body and stress prevention techniques.* (ERIC Document Reproduction Service No. ED 248 428)

McNab, W.L. (1983). Anorexia and the adolescent. *Journal of School Health, 53*(7), 427–430.

Meadow, K.P. (1980). *Self-concept, self-esteem and deafness: Research problems and findings.* (ERIC Document Reproduction Service No. ED 199 603)

Mech, E.V. (1986). Pregnant adolescents: Communicating the adoption option. *Child Welfare, 45*(6), 555–567.

Michaels, G.Y., & Brown, R. (1983). *Values of children in adolescent mothers.* (ERIC Document Reproduction Service No. ED 237 865)

Michigan State Deapartment of Education. (1975). *Substance abuse prevention education program. 1974–75 evaluation report.* Lansing, MI: Author. (ERIC Document Reproduction Service No. ED 119 055)

Miller, B.C., et al. (1981). *Teenage pregnancy: A comparison of certain characteristics among Utah youth.* Salt Lake City, UT: Utah State Office of Education. (ERIC Document Reproduction Service No. ED 249 330)

Miller, E.B. (1982). *Levels of cultural knowledge and self-esteem of fourth, fifth, and sixth grade participants in a Philippine ethnic heritage curriculum conducted in Guam Catholic schools.* (Unpublished doctoral dissertation, University of Southern California). (ERIC Document Reproduction Service No. ED 232 764)

Miller, M.J., et al. (1985). Measuring hassles and uplifts among adolescents: A different approach to the study of stress. *School Counselor, 33*(2), 107–110.

Mills, C.J. (1984). *Sex differences in self-concept and self-esteem for mathematically precocious adolescents.* (ERIC Document Reproduction Service No. ED 245 983)

Mitic, W.R. (1980). Alcohol use and self-esteem of adolescents. *Journal of Drug Education, 10*(3), 197–208.

Molnar, A., & Gliszczinski, C. (1983). Child abuse: A curriculum issue in teacher education. *Journal of Teacher Education, 34*(5), 39–41.

Moracco, J.C., et al. (1984). Measuring stress in school counselors: Some research findings and implications. *School Counselor, 32*(2), 110–118.

Morgan, L.B. (1981). The counselor's role in suicide prevention. *Personnel and Guidance Journal*, *59*(5), 284–286.

Morris, J. (Ed.). (1981). Dimensions of counselor stress. *School Guidance Worker*, *37*(2), 5–57.

Morrison, P.A., et al. (1981). *Teenage parenthood: A review of risks and consequences*. Santa Monica, CA: Rand Corporation. (ERIC Document Reproduction Service No. ED 219 681)

Moyal, B.R. (1977). Locus of control, self-esteem, stimulus appraisal, and depressive symptoms in children. *Journal of Consulting and Clinical Psychology*, *45*(5), 951–952.

Mullins, L.L., et al. (1982). *Cognitive and life event correlates of depressive symptoms in children*. (ERIC Document Reproduction Service No. ED 224 581)

Muuss, R.E. (1985). Adolescent eating disorder: Anorexia nervosa. *Adolescence*, *20*(79), 525–536.

New York State Education Department. (1984). *Suicide among school age youth*. Albany, NY: Author. (ERIC Document Reproduction Service No. ED 253 813)

Newcomer, S.F. (1985). *Does sexuality education make a difference?* New York, NY: Planned Parenthood Federation of America, Inc. (ERIC Document Reproduction Service No. ED 269 673)

Nielsen, T. (1983). Sexual abuse of boys: Current perspectives. *Personnel and Guidance Journal*, *62*(3), 139–142.

Novy, D.M., & Donohue, S. (1985). The relationship between adolescent life stress events and delinquent conduct including conduct indicating a need for supervision. *Adolescence*, *20*(78), 313–321.

Nuttall, E.V., & Nuttall, R. (1978). *Implications for counseling practice of the Puerto Rican psycho-social precursors study*. (ERIC Document Reproduction Service No. ED 165 029)

Olson, C.F., & Worobey, J. (1984). Perceived mother-daughter relations in a pregnant and nonpregnant adolescent sample. *Adolescence*, *19*(76), 781–794.

Oldershaw, L., et al. (1986). Control strategies and noncompliance in abusive mother-child dyads: An observational study. *Child Development*, *57*(3), 722–732.

Openshaw, D.K., et al. (1983). Socialization and adolescent self-esteem: Symbolic interaction and social learning explanations. *Adolescence*, *18*(70), 317–329.

Openshaw, D.K., & Thomas, D.L. (1981). *Socialization and self-esteem: A test of symbolic interaction and social learning explanations*. (ERIC Document Reproduction Service No. ED 197 824)

Orbach, I., et al. (1981). Some common characteristics of latency-age suicidal children: A tentative model based on case study analyses. *Suicide and Life-Threatening Behavior*, *11*(3), 180–190.

Orbach, I., et al. (1983). Attraction and repulsion by life and death in suicidal and in normal children. *Journal of Consulting and Clinical Psychology*, *51*(5), 661–670.

Ortiz, E.T., & Bassoff, B.Z. (1984). *Adolescent pregnancy prevention: Strategies for the '80's*. (ERIC Document Reproduction Service No. ED 270 674)

Parish, T.S., & Taylor, J.C. (1979). The impact of divorce and subsequent father absence on children's and adolescents' self-concepts. *Journal of Youth and Adolescence*, *8*(4), 427–432.

Paton, S., et al. (1977). Depressive mood and adolescent illicit drug use: A longitudinal analysis. *Journal of Genetic Psychology, 131*(2), 267–290.

Paton, S.M., & Kandel, D.B. (1978). Psychological factors and adolescent illict drug use: Ethnicity and sex differences. *Adolescence, 13*(50), 187–200.

Patten, M.D. (1983). Relationships between self-esteem, anxiety, and achievement in young learning disabled students. *Journal of Learning Disabilities, 16*(1), 43–45.

Pearl, R., & Bryan, T. (1982). *Learning disabled children's self-esteem and desire for approval.* (ERIC Document Reproduction Service No. ED 222 022)

Peck, D.L. (1980). Towards a theory of suicide: The case for modern fatalism. *OMEGA: Journal of Death and Dying, 11*(1), 1–13.

Peck, M. (1982). Youth suicide. *Death Education, 6*(1) 29–47.

Perkin, J. (1983). Evaluating a nutrition education program for pregnant teen-agers: Cognitive vs. behavioral outcomes. *Journal of School Health, 53*(7), 420–422.

Peters, C., et al. (1984). Assessment and treatment of anorexia nervosa and bulimia in school age children. *School Psychology Review, 13*(2), 183–191.

Peterson, J.L., & Zill, N. (1986). Marital disruption, parent-child relationships, and behavior problems in children. *Journal of Marriage and the Family, 48*(2), 295–307.

Pfeffer, C.R. (1981). Parental suicide: An organizing event in the development of latency age children. *Suicide and Life-Threatening Behavior, 11*(1), 43–50.

Pfeffer, C.R. (1984). Suicide. In H. Wass & C.A. Corr (Eds.), *Childhood and death* (pp. 259–278). New York: Hemisphere.

Phillips, R.H. (1984). Increasing positive self-referent statements to improve self-esteem in low-income elementary school children. *Journal of School Psychology, 22*(2), 155–163.

Piazza, E., et al. (1983). Measuring severity and change in anorexia nervosa. *Adolescence, 18*(70), 293–305.

Pierson, D., & Archambault, F. (1984). *Predicting and comparing role stress and burnout for supportive service groups and classroom teachers.* (ERIC Document Reproduction Service No. ED 246 525)

Post, G., & Crowther, J.H. (1985). Variables that discriminate bulimic from nonbulimic adolescent females. *Journal of Youth and Adolescence, 14*(2), 85–98.

Potter, S.J., & Smith, H.L. (1976). Sex education as viewed by teenage unwed mothers. *Intellect, 104*(2374), 515–516.

Poznanski, E.O., et al. (1979). Depression rating scale for children. *Pediatrics, 64*(4), 442–450.

Presser, H.B. (1975). *Social consequences of teenage childbearing.* (ERIC Document Reproduction Service No. ED 192 189)

Prinz, R.J., et al. (1983). *Children of separating parents: They are not all alike.* (ERIC Document Reproduction Service No. ED 241 854)

Puig-Antich, J., Vlau, S., Marx, N., et al. (1978). Prepubertal major depressive disorder: A pilot study. *Journal of the American Academy of Child Psychiatry, 17*, 695–707.

Ralph. N., et al. (1984). Psychosocial characteristics of pregnant and nulliparous adolescents. *Adolescence, 19*(74), 283–294.

Raquepaw, J., & deHaas, P.A. (1984). *Factors influencing teacher burnout.* (ERIC Document Reproduction Service No. ED 256 980)

Redmond, M.A. (1985). Attitudes of adolescent males toward adolescent pregnancy and fatherhood. *Family Relations, 34*(3), 337–342.

Reid, K. (1982). The self-concept and persistent school absenteeism. *British Journal of Educational Psychology, 52*(Pt. 2), 179–187.

Reynolds, W.M. (1980). Self-esteem and classroom behavior in elementary school children. *Psychology in the Schools, 17*(2), 273–277.

Rhiner, P. (1983). The many pressures on children in today's world. *PTA Today, 8*(4), 5–8.

Richardson, G.E., et al. (1983). The efficacy of a three-week stress management unit for high school students. *Health Education, 14*(1), 12–15.

Richman, C.L., et al. (1984a). *General and specific self-esteem in late adolescent students: Race × Gender × SES effects.* (ERIC Document Reproduction Service No. ED 250 607)

Richman, C.L., et al. (1984b). The relationship between self-esteem and maladaptive behaviors in high school students. *Social Behavior and Personality, 12*(2), 177–185.

Riggs, R.S. (1982). Incest: The school's role. *Journal of School Health, 52*(8), 365–370.

Rittner, M. (1984). *Anorexia nervosa—A teacher's perspective.* (ERIC Document Reproduction Service No. ED 245 502)

Robinson, B.E., et al. (1983). Locus of control of unwed adolescent fathers versus adolescent nonfathers. *Perceptual and Motor Skills, 56*(2), 397–398.

Roosa, M.W. (1984). Short-term effects of teenage parenting programs on knowledge and attitudes. *Adolescence, 19*(75), 659–666.

Rotundo, N., & Hensley, V.R. (1985). The children's depression scale: A study of its validity. *Journal of Child Psychology and Psychiatry and Allied Disciplines, 26*(6), 917–927.

Rowley, J.E. (1981). *The relationship of self-esteem and learning disabilities.* (ERIC Document Reproduction Service No. ED 219 915)

Rudestam, K.E., & Imbroll, D. (1983). Societal reaction to a child's death by suicide. *Journal of Consulting and Clinical Psychology, 51*(3), 461–462.

Rust, J.O., & McCraw, A. (1984). Influence of masculinity-femininity on adolescent self-esteem and peer acceptance. *Adolescence, 19*(74), 359–366.

Sack, W.H. (1985). Gender identity conflict in young boys following divorce. *Journal of Divorce, 9*(1), 47–59.

Santostefano, S., et al. (1984). The structure of fantasied movement in suicidal children and adolescents. *Suicide and Life-Threatening Behavior, 14*(1), 3–16.

Sarokon, S.C. (1986). Student self-esteem: A goal administrators can help to achieve. *NASSP Bulletin, 70*(487), 1–5.

Saunders, R.R., & Watkins. J.F. (1982). *Teacher burnout/stress management: An exploratory look in an urban school system in Alabama.* (ERIC Document Reproduction Service No. ED 236 109)

Saylor, C.F., et al. (1984a). The children's depression inventory: A systematic evaluation of psychometric properties. *Journal of Consulting and Clinical Psychology, 52*(6), 955–967.

Saylor, C.F., et al. (1984b). Construct validity for measures of childhood depression: Application of multitrait-multimethod methodology. *Journal of Consulting and Clinical Psychology*, *52*(6), 977–985.

Schloss, P.J. (1983). Classroom-based intervention for student exhibiting depressive reactions. *Behavioral Disorders*, *8*(4), 231–236.

Schmidt, W.R., et al. (1984). *Adolescent suicidal thinking*. (ERIC Document Reproduction Service No. ED 253 783)

Schoenbach, V.J., et al. (1983). Prevalence of self-reported depressive symptoms in young adolescents. *American Journal of Public Health*, *73*(11), 1281–1287.

Schwartz, M., et al. (1982). The relationship between conceptual tempo and depression in children. *Journal of Consulting and Clinical Psychology*, *50*(4), 488–490.

Schwertfeger, J. (1983). *Research concerning young children of divorced parents and recommendations for teachers*. (ERIC Document Reproduction Service No. ED 242 409)

Seymour, V.L. (1977). *Teenage prostitution as a product of child abuse*. (ERIC Document Reproduction Service No. ED 154 564)

Sharlin. S.A., & Shenhar, A. (1986). The fusion of pressing situation and releasing writing: On adolescent suicide poetry. *Suicide and Life-Threatening Behavior*, *16*(3), 343–355.

Sherrod, K.B., et al. (1985). Child health and maltreatment. *Child Development*, *55*(4), 1174–1183.

Shiller, V. (1985). *Joint and maternal custody: The outcome for boys aged 6–11 and their parents*. (ERIC Document Reproduction Service No. ED 261 273)

Shreeve, W., et al. (1985). *Single parents and student achievement—A national tragedy*. (ERIC Document Reproduction Service No. ED 262 028)

Siegel, L.J., & Griffin, N.J. (1983). Adolescents' concepts of depression among their peers. *Adolescence*, *18*(72), 965–973.

Simons, R.L., & Murphy, P.I. (1985). Sex differences in the causes of adolescent suicide ideation. *Journal of Youth and Adolescence*, *14*(5), 423–434.

Smith, E. (1981). Adolescent suicide: A growing problem for the school and family. *Urban Education*, *16*(3), 279–296.

Smith, K., & Crawford, S. (1986). Suicidal behavior among "normal" high school students. *Suicide and Life-Threatening Behavior*, *16*(3), 313–325.

Smith, L.L. (1985). *Media images and ideal body shapes: A perspective on women with emphasis on anorexics*. (ERIC Document Reproduction Service No. ED 257 109)

Smith, P.B. (1981). The pregnant adolescent: Counseling issues in school settings. *School Counselor*, *29*(2), 111–116.

Smith, R.M. (1979). *Adolescent suicide and intervention in perspective*. (ERIC Document Reproduction Service No. ED 184 017)

Sorensen, J.L., & Joffe, S.J. (1975). An outreach program in drug education: Teaching a rational approach to drug use. *Journal of Drug Education*, *5*(2), 87–95.

Spirito, A., et al. (1985). *The relationship between social skills and depression in adolescent suicide attempters*. (ERIC Document Reproduction Service No. ED 269 656)

Stake, J.E., et al. (1983). The effects of assertive training on the performance self-esteem of adolescent girls. *Journal of Youth and Adolescence, 12*(5), 435–442.

Starr, P. (1980). Cleft type, age, and sex differences in teen-agers' ratings of their own behavior, self-esteem, and attitude toward clefting. *Rehabilitation Literature, 41*(7–8), 177–179.

Staton, R.D., et al. (1981). Cognitive improvement associated with tricyclic antidepressant treatment of childhood major depressive illness. *Perceptual and Motor Skills, 53*(1), 219–234.

Staton, R.D., & Brumback, R.A. (1981). Non-specificity of motor hyperactivity as a diagnostic criterion. *Perceptual and Motor Skills, 52*(1), 323–332.

Stehouwer, R.S., et al. (1985). Developmental differences in depression: Cognitive-perceptual distortion in adolescent versus adult female depressives. *Adolescence, 20*(78), 291–299.

Stehouwer, R.S., & Bultsma, C.A. (1980). *Cognitive-perceptual distortion in depression as a function of generational differences.* (ERIC Document Reproduction Service No. ED 198 436)

Stewart, C.G., & Lewis, W.A. (1986). Effects of assertiveness training on the self-esteem of black high school students. *Journal of Counseling & Development, 64*(10), 638–641.

Stober, M. (1982). Locus of control, psychopathology, and weight gain in juvenile anorexia nervosa. *Journal of Abnormal Child Psychology, 10*(1), 97–106.

Strober, M., & Goldenberg, I. (1981). Ego boundary disturbance in juvenile anorexia nervosa. *Journal of Clinical Psychology, 37*(2), 433–438.

Strother, D.B. (1986). Suicide among the young. *Phi Delta Kappan, 67*(10), 756–759.

Sullivan, M.L. (1985). *Teen fathers in the inner city: An exploratory ethnographic study. A report to the Ford Foundation urban poverty program.* New York, NY: Vera Institute of Justice. (ERIC Document Reproduction Service No. ED 264 316)

Szapocznik, J., et al. (1976). *Culture specific approaches to the treatment of Latin multiple substance abusers: Family and ecological intervention models.* Coral Gables, FL: Miami University. (ERIC Document Reproduction Service No. ED 193 371)

Szapocznik, J., et al. (1986). Conjoint versus one-person family therapy: Further evidence of the effectiveness of conducting family therapy through one person with drug-abusing adolescents. *Journal of Consulting and Clinical Psychology, 54*(3), 395–397.

Teri, L. (1982). The use of the Beck Depression Inventory with adolescents. *Journal of Abnormal Child Psychology, 10*(2), 277–284.

Tesiny, E.P., et al. (1980). Childhood depression, locus of control, and school achievement. *Journal of Educational Psychology, 72*(4), 506–510.

Thompson, G.S. (1985). *Anorexia nervosa/bulimia: The teenager's dilemma.* (ERIC Document Reproduction Service No. ED 270 708)

Thompson, J.V. (1979). The social worker, the teacher, the school counsellor and child abuse. *School Guidance Worker, 34*(5), 21–25.

Thompson, R.A. (1984). The critical needs of the adolescent unwed mother. *School Counselor, 31*(5), 460–466.

Thurman, P.J., et al. (1985). An assessment of attempted suicides among adolescent Cherokee Indians. *Journal of Multicultural Counseling and Development, 13*(4), 176–182.

Tishler, C.L., et al. (1981). Adolescent suicide attempts: Some significant factors. *Suicide and Life-Threatening Behavior, 11*(2), 86–92.

Tollefson, N., et al. (1980). *An application of attribution theory to developing self-esteem in learning disabled adolescents.* Lawrence, KS: Kansas University, Institute for Research in Learning Disabilities. (ERIC Document Reproduction Service No. ED 217 637)

Toolan, J.M. (1967). Depression in children and adolescents. *American Journal of Orthopsychiatry, 32,* 404–415.

Topol, P., & Reznikoff, M. (1982). Perceived peer and family relationships, hopelessness and locus of control as factors in adolescent suicide attempts. *Suicide and Life-Threatening Behavior, 12*(3), 141–150.

Triesen, D., & Williams, M. (1985). Organizational stress among teachers. *Canadian Journal of Education, 10*(1), 13–34.

Vance, P.C. (1985). Love and sex: Can we talk about that in school? *Childhood Education, 61*(4), 272–276.

Vukelich, C., & Kliman, D.S. (1985). Mature and teenage mothers' infant growth expectations and use of child development information sources. *Family Relations, 34*(2), 189–196.

Walker, L.S., & Greene, J.W. (1986). The social context of adolescent self-esteem. *Journal of Youth and Adolescence, 15*(4), 315–322.

Watkins, D., & Astilla, E. (1980a). Birth order, family size, and self-esteem: A Filipino study. *Journal of Genetic Psychology, 137*(2), 297–298.

Watkins, D., & Astilla, E. (1980b). Self-esteem and school achievement of Filipino girls. *Journal of Psychology, 105*(1), 3–6.

Watts, W.J., & Cushion, M.B. (1982). Enhancing self-concept of LD adolescents: One approach. *Academic Therapy, 18*(1), 95–101.

Wax, S.M. (1985). *Children's reliance on denial in fantasy in response to parental separation and divorce.* (ERIC Document Reproduction Service No. ED 263 475)

Welsh, R.S. (1980). *The belt theory of discipline and delinquency: Critical issues presentation.* (ERIC Document Reproduction Service No. ED 196 149)

Westerlage, P.A. (1980). *Anorexia nervosa.* (ERIC Document Reproduction Service No. ED 195 109)

Whiting, S. (1981). The problem of depression in adolescence. *Adolescence, 16*(61), 67–89.

Wiggins, J.D., & Giles, T.A. (1984). The relationship between counselors' and students' self-esteem as related to counseling outcomes. *School Counselor, 32*(1), 18–22.

Wishon, P.M. (1979). *School-aged victims of sexual abuse: Implications for educators.* (ERIC Document Reproduction Service No. ED 181 373)

Wolfe, D.A., & Mosk, M.D. (1983). Behavioral comparisons of children from abusive and distressed families. *Journal of Consulting and Clinical Psychology, 51*(5), 702–708.

Wright, L.S. (1985). Suicidal thoughts and their relationship to family stress and personal problems among high school seniors and college undergraduates. *Adolescence, 20*(79), 575–580.

Yahraes, H. (1978). *Causes, detection and treatment of childhood depression.* Rockville, MD: National Institute of Mental Health (DHEW), Division of Scientific and Public Information. (ERIC Document Reproduction Service No. ED 154 587).

Zaichkowsky, L.B., et al. (1986). Biofeedback—Assisted relaxation training in the elementary classroom. *Elementary School Guidance and Counseling, 20*(4), 261–267.

Zieman, G.L., & Benson, G.P. (1983). Delinquency: The role of self-esteem and social values. *Journal of Youth and Adolescence, 12*(6), 489–500.

Zongker, C.E. (1977). The self-concept of pregnant adolescent girls. *Adolescence, 12*(48), 477–488.

Counseling for Personal and Social Competency:
Linking Research to the School Counseling Program

Thelma Jones Vriend

Educational Coordinator, Detroit, Michigan

School counselors generally are able to devote a relatively small percentage of an overall developmental counseling program to the personal and social counseling component (ERIC/CAPS Brief, 1984). Therefore, personal and social counseling in public school counseling programs tends to be sparse and superficial. A large percentage of the youngsters in America are enrolled in public urban schools. Many large, urban school counseling programs are crisis oriented and demand that counselor time be spent meeting immediate needs with quick solutions. Students in these schools, however, are in great need of a retreat from the violence, confusion, and chaos that threaten their communities. They require assistance to get a clear picture of the world in which they must live and struggle for survival, beginning with completing or dropping out of school (Stroud, 1987).

Counseling for social and personal coping is in great demand by our students despite the inability of the school counselor to give the assistance requested. Students writing in their own school newspapers report, from student opinion polls and other student journalistic research ("We the students," 1987), the same areas for attention in personal/social problem solving as raised in the Capuzzi paper (Capuzzi, 1988). Counselors in a variety of settings can find research and the scientific approach helpful to them in solving the problems they encounter as practitioners, although research is often perceived as irrelevant, time consuming, and impractical (Anderson & Heppner, 1986).

While accepting the basic assumption of the Capuzzi paper that if school counseling programs are based on research they will be more effective, another observation seems important. If counseling research is to be more effectively utilized in planning school programs, it must reflect current student needs and local school and community concerns. Thorough examination of the nine areas identified reveals that they lead to larger, more inclusive societal ills. We must, however, start to address solvable issues while remaining aware of their interconnectedness to major societal pressures. In addressing these concerns, we can begin to assist our students to develop coping skills for present and future life styles.

The Use of Major Research Findings by Practitioners

The need for counselors to assist students to develop personal and social competency has been established not only by the review of research cited by Dave Capuzzi. Student needs are reflected in the findings of experimental research, local action research, observations of environmental conditions, and what students themselves tell us, or more importantly, show us.

The nine critical areas identified in the Capuzzi paper can be related to three major developmental success skills: (1) social skills, or learning effective interpersonal relationship behaviors; (2) personal problem-solving or decision-making skills; and (3) life problem skills or anxiety management (Cisek & George, 1985). To be successful, students require counselor assistance that frees them to think and to learn. Help is required to feel safe and to deal with environmental conditions; to cope with peer and parental pressures; to seek wellness and wholeness; to survive unstable school conditions; to make major personal and moral decisions; and to repair and build self-esteem. The nine crisis-oriented social/personal counseling issues identified by the Capuzzi research review address prevention and postvention as well as crisis intervention. This points to the developmental nature of the school counseling program and the desirability of basing interventions on developmental concerns and approaches within a total school guidance program (Gysbers, et al., 1984).

A time lag exists between research identification, conducting the research, and its availability to the practitioner. This presents a problem in basing the response to immediate, new student needs on research findings. The current social crisis in youth violence is a case in point. Local and regional student concerns may require program flexibility that precedes experimental research. These needs may suggest programs of local research. Practitioners can conduct their own research individually or in teams. Applied research and evaluation such as needs assessment, interviews, and questionnaires, and action research whether diagnostic or participant-based, are more available for current problem solving (Goldman, 1986).

Research on the effectiveness of school or community team approaches to counseling for catastrophic situations is indicated. The team approach also has been investigated in preparing a total district or local school plan for social behaviors that reach epidemic proportions such as youth suicide, youth violence, teen pregnancy, and substance abuse (Collison et al., 1987).

Generally major problems of a personal/social nature persist over time so that traditional research can be beneficial in building a developmental counseling component. Counseling interventions that are difficult to evaluate, that do not produce immediate results, and that require updated counselor skills often are given low priority in school counseling programs. Many school counselors have responded to student needs in these areas by identifying the personal/social concerns of the student, preparing the student for referral to other mental health professionals such as the school social worker or community social agencies, developing a liaison with referral sources and agencies, and providing some follow-up on the student's progress.

Implications for Counseling Preservice and Inservice Training

The belief that research related to personal and social competency and coping can be used to improve the delivery of services to students must convincingly be conveyed to school counselors. If, in fact, there exist ample opportunities for the practitioner to use research, and the need to address many counseling questions through research, an examination of counselor readiness and competency seems to be indicated (Anderson & Heppner, 1986). How can school counselors be helped to evaluate the need for and the utilization of counseling research?

1. An examination of the counselor preservice training model is indicated as it relates to research courses, research projects, and applied practitioner training such as theory, practicums, and internships (Heppner & Anderson, 1985). Counselor educators must find better ways of using research in the education of counselors.

2. Consortiums of community agencies, counselor education institutions, local school districts, counselor supervisors, and local school counseling departments can be powerful allies for the generation and dissemination of applied and action research that responds to urgent social concerns such as substance abuse and youth violence.

3. We need preservice and inservice training in new modalities that teach self-help techniques to students and counselors. Counseling practices that reflect new age consciousness and techniques from the popular culture abound through media technology and convey the excitement and accessibility of personal change strategies such as assertiveness training, self-talk, subliminal communication, and many others (Lucas, 1985).

4. Counselor inservice requires ongoing cooperative efforts between local school districts and supervisors of school counselors to provide opportunities for the practitioner to continually update research skills and identify research needs.

5. Research-based information must be made more readily available to the school counselor both while in training and while counseling in the schools. More systematic linkages between ERIC/CAPS, local school programs, intermediate school districts, and counselor training institutions should be promoted for the dissemination of research-based information and its use.

6. Counselor educators need to examine ways to keep themselves involved and current in research information, and to teach counselors to apply research findings and research methods in the schools.

7. Local school district counselor supervisors could coordinate efforts to make counseling research findings systematically available to the practicing school counselor through inservice activities and articulation programs with community and counselor education institutions. Community referral and support sources also need to be carefully and clearly identified, kept current, and utilized.

Implications for Future Research Imperatives

Dave Capuzzi identified imperatives for future research in each of the nine personal/social research areas specified as critical to the school counseling program. I support these listings and offer a few others for the reader's consideration.

Youth Violence

In 1986, 15 of every 100,000 Detroit youth were killed in violent confrontation (Detroit Free Press, April 28, 1987). There are indications that counseling research on youth violence will be valuable. The role of the school counselor in providing interventions is under examination (Nuttall & Kalesnik, 1987). There are questions to be answered about youth violence as it relates to environmental and family violence, the media and entertainment, and unemployment. Students need skills in conflict mediation, decision making, and values clarification. The effects of competitiveness, failure, communication, and relationships on youth violence are not clear.

School Counseling Program Models

Cooperative school counseling program models designed to teach developmental skills in interpersonal relationships, self-esteem, values clarification, problem solving, and decision making need to be examined and disseminated. New and inspirational techniques and interventions that build on adult community models for social problems could be integral parts of such models. The use of group counseling, peer counseling, and other group methods would be part of such a model (Vriend, 1969). The mental health team concept for the delivery of services in the personal/social areas may prove to be feasible.

Self-Esteem

Additional research is indicated on the relationship of self-esteem to youth violence, the effects of student transciency and relocation on self-esteem, and methods for the short-term treatment of temporary loss of self-esteem (McClure, 1986). Action research models that have not been reported are in use in local school districts. In Detroit public schools pilot programs are under way that focus on school truants and students who are failing academically (Vriend, 1985), community sponsored group counseling programs of peer support (Twelve Together), and student efficacy programs based on national research and specific subject matter. Short-term results and reports should be made available.

Eating Disorders

Obesity and poor diet remain problems of an addictive nature for many children and youth. Research on holistic health treatment models, school-based health clinics, and wellness models is needed.

Child and Adolescent Suicide

Further research is indicated on the effects of early independence of children (taking care of self), isolation, and the lack of supervision on youth suicide.

Depression

Specific research on social conditions that cause feelings of powerlessness such as poverty, transiency, cultural background, and fear of annihilation through nuclear war is needed for relationships to depression and its treatment.

Physical and Sexual Abuse

A school model for the identification and reporting of child abuse as mandated by local laws could be researched. The team approach to treatment and referral for child abuse victims in schools requires study.

Teen Pregnancy and Substance Abuse

A study of community and school linkages for family and teen programs of education, prevention, and postvention seems especially relevant in these areas. Community agencies and counseling departments form parts of a team focus.

Stress

Further study is indicated on the effects of teaching life skills at early ages as an intervention strategy for stressful conditions. Stress reduction programs for counselors and teachers need to be widely reported (Dwyer, 1986).

Summary

A successful student must cope with personal/social conditions on the way to learning. In addressing the "whole" student, counselors must recognize and assist the student-at-risk whether identified by the nine critical areas of the Capuzzi paper, or by other methods accessible to the counselor.

Effective developmental school counseling programs must focus on prevention and postvention as well as crisis intervention. The school team approach to student interventions, utilizing community consortiums, referrals, and parent education, is an essential step as we seek partners in meeting the needs outlined in the research. Counselor availability to provide parent education on all personal/social issues is a consideration in establishing school counseling programs. In-service and preservice training for counselors seems to be at least as crucial to counselor effectiveness as the research itself.

References

Anderson, W., & Heppner, P.P. (1986). Counselor applications of research findings to practice: Learning to stay current. *Journal of Counseling and Development, 65*, 152–155.

Capuzzi, D. (1988). Personal and social competency: Developing skills for the future. In G.R. Walz (Ed.), *Research and counseling: Building strong school counseling programs*. Alexandria, VA: American Association for Counseling and Development.

Cisek, J., & George, A. (1985, Nov.–Dec.). Teaching success skills to young people. *New Designs*.

Collison, B., Bowden, S., Patterson, M., Snyder, J., Sandall, S., & Wellman, P. (1987). After the shooting stops. *Journal of Counseling and Development, 65*, 389–390.

Dwyer, M.L. (1986). *Creating personal wellness*. Unpublished manuscript.

ERIC/CAPS Information Digest. (1984). *The role of the school counselor: Secondary level* (Contract No. 400–83–0014). Ann Arbor, MI: University of Michigan.

Goldman, L. (1986). Research and evaluation. In M.D. Lewis, R.L. Hayes, & J.A. Lewis. *An Introduction to the counseling profession* (pp. 278–300). Itasea, IL: F.E. Peacock Publishers.

Gysbers, N.C., & Associates. (1984). *Designing careers*. San Francisco: Jossey-Bass.

Gysbers, N.C., & Henderson, P. (1988). *Developing and managing your school guidance program*. Alexandria, VA: American Association for Counseling and Development.

Heppner, P., & Anderson, W. (1985). On the perceived non-utility of research in counseling. *Journal of Counseling and Development, 65*, 545–547.

Lucas, C. (1985). Out at the edge: Notes on a paradigm shift. *Journal of Counseling and Development, 64*, 165–171.

McClure, J.J. (1986). *A Model for the improvement of self-esteem to minimize the short-term effects of retention in third, fourth, and fifth graders using a group counseling approach and participation in the creative arts*. Unpublished master's project. Wayne State University, Detroit, MI.

Nuttall, E.V., & Kalesnik, J. (1987). Personal violence in the schools: The role of the counselor. *Journal of Counseling and Development, 65*, 372–375.

Stroud, J.H. (1987, September 6). Youth violence: We must start somewhere. *Detroit Free Press*, p. 7A.

Together: The schools begin to seek help from parents on youth violence (1987, April 28). *Detroit Free Press*, p. 8A.

Vriend, T.J. (1985, October). *A Goal-directed group counseling approach to the improvement of student performance: High school intervention centers.* Michigan Association for Counseling and Development Conference, Boyne Mt., MI.

Vriend, T.J. (1969). High-performing inner-city adolescents assist low-performing peers in counseling groups. *Personnel and Guidance Journal*, May, 897–904.

We the students: A special report to the city (1987, April 2). *Detroit Free Press*, pp. 1–16B.

Career Guidance: A Professional Heritage and Future Challenge

Norman C. Gysbers

Professor, Educational and Counseling Psychology
University of Missouri, Columbia, Missouri

Since the early 1900s, the guidance and counseling profession has been influenced and shaped by various political, social, and economic events and conditions. In addition, the guidance and counseling profession has been influenced and shaped as it responded to changing individual and societal needs. Although these forces continue to cause changes in the profession, the evolving concept of career guidance has served and continues to serve as a link connecting our past to the present; as an anchor providing stability and continuity to our professional mission and practices in the schools. Thus, this concept is part of our professional heritage, but at the same time provides stability and continuity for our professional program of work today and into the foreseeable future.

To help us understand how the evolving concept of career guidance has served and continues to serve as an anchor for our profession and as a link from the past to the present, discussion in the first part of the paper focuses on the historical aspects of this concept, *A Professional Heritage*. Then, based on this discussion, the second part of the paper presents an overview of developments and trends in career guidance, *The Contemporary Scene*. Finally, the last part of the paper examines the meanings and importance that these trends may have for our schools in general and school counselors in particular, *A Professional Commitment*.

A Professional Heritage

The Early Years: Selection and Placement

During the early part of the 20th century, many countries, including the United States, were involved directly and deeply in the industrial revolution. It was a period of rapid industrial growth, social protest, social reform, and utopian

99

idealism. Social protest and social reform were being carried out under the banner of the Progressive Movement, a movement that sought to change negative social conditions associated with industrial growth. Vocational guidance (later, the name was changed to career guidance and was the process that, in part, gave birth to school counseling as we know it today) was born, at last in a modern sense, during the height of this movement (Stephens, 1970).

Vocational guidance during this period had, as one focus, occupational selection and placement. The emphasis was on the transition from school to work, with special attention on occupational choice. Parsons (1909), the originator of the term *vocational guidance* (Davis, 1969), saw it as a means whereby individuals would come to a better understanding of themselves and the work world; individuals would choose appropriate occupations and then prepare and progress in them. The process of vocational guidance was seen as unfolding through the now familiar three steps here paraphrased: know yourself, know the work world, and bring the two together through a process of "true reasoning" (Parsons, 1909).

Almost immediately, whether by direct connection or by independent discovery, schools in different parts of the country were initiating vocational guidance activities. According to Ryan (1919, p. 26) "by April, 1914, approximately 100 public high schools, representing some 40 cities, were reported. . .as having definitely organized conscious plans of vocational guidance, through vocation bureaus, consultation committees, trial vocational courses, or regular courses in vocations." In Grand Rapids, Davis (1914) inaugurated a plan of teaching vocational guidance through the English curriculum.

The Middle Years: Guidance for Personal Adjustment

By the 1920s, changes were occurring in the theory and practice of vocational guidance. There was less emphasis on guidance for vocation and more on educational and personal-social guidance. The focus shifted to more attention to personal adjustment. More specifically, at least within the school setting, there apparently was a "displacement of the traditional vocational, socioeconomic and political concerns from the culture at large to the student of the educational subculture whose vocational socialization problems were reinterpreted as educational and psychological problems of personal adjustment" (Johnson, 1972, p. 221).

By the 1930s, the term *guidance* was seen as an all-inclusive term including "problems of adjustment to health, religion, recreation, to family and friends, to schools and to work" (Campbell, 1932, p. 4). Vocational guidance, on the other hand, had a more specific meaning and was defined as "the process of assisting the individual to choose an occupation, prepare for it, enter upon and progress in it. As preparation for an occupation involves decision in the choice of studies, choice of curriculums, and the choice of schools and colleges, it becomes evident that vocational guidance cannot be separated from educational guidance'' (Campbell, 1932, p. 4). Thus, whereas previously vocational guidance was guidance, now there was vocational guidance, educational guidance and personal-social guidance. In addition, the clinical-services model of guidance was coming into focus so that the terms *counseling*, *assessment*, *information*, *placement*, and *follow-up* were used increasingly to describe the components of guidance in the schools.

While educational and personnel-services guidance in the schools gained strength during the 1930s, the vocational emphasis also continued to show strength. For example, in 1938, a national advisory committee on education issued a report that pointed to the need for an occupational information service at the national level. As a result of these recommendations and the George Dean Act, the Occupational Information and Guidance Service was established in 1938 in the Vocational Division of the U.S. Office of Education (Wellman, 1978).

As the 1930s ended, the clinical-services model of guidance and counseling continued to evolve, assisted by a growing interest in psychotherapy. Of particular importance to guidance and counseling in the schools was the work of Carl Rogers, beginning with the publication of his book *Counseling and Psychotherapy* in 1942. This was important in the 1940s but it was even more important during the late 1950s and the 1960s when thousands of school counselors were educated using the client-centered approach of Carl Rogers. Aubrey (1982) used the expression ''steamroller impact'' to describe the effect that Carl Rogers had on guidance and counseling in the schools.

In 1946, the George-Barden Act was passed. As a result of that Act, funds could be used to support guidance activities in a variety of settings and situations. One outcome was that attention was given to the preparation of counselors. A number of reports were prepared including one titled ''Counselor Competencies in Occupational Information'' (Office of Education, 1949). The group that prepared the report was chaired by Edward C. Roeber and the report was published in March, 1949.

In 1958, Public Law 85–864, the National Defense Education Act, was passed. Under Part B of Title V, funds were provided for training institutes to prepare individuals to become counselors in secondary schools. In the 1960s, provisions were added to support training for elementary and junior high counselors. What was the nature of the training these prospective counselors were to receive? Not much attention was given to role definition because, as Pierson (1965, p. 39) pointed out, ''The adequately trained school counselor develops his own role, a role that tends to be unique with him and unique to the situation in which the role developed.'' Another aspect of the role dilemma was identified by Tyler in her review of the first 50 NDEA Institutes. She stated the following:

Before one can really define the role of the counselor, it will be necessary to clarify the roles of all workers who make up guidance staffs. It may be desirable to replace the ambiguous word "guidance" with the clearer term "pupil personnel work." (Tyler, 1960, p. 77)

Further analysis of NDEA Institutes also makes it clear that there was a heavy emphasis on individual and group counseling. Placement and traditional educational and occupational information procedures (including vocational planning and decision making as it was called then) received relatively less attention. Pierson (1965, p. 46) summarized curriculum offering in Institutes by pointing out that:

[T]he curricular in regular session institutes has placed great stress upon practicum; about one-third of an enrollee's time has been spent in supervised practice in counseling. At the same time, institutes have strengthened their instruction in psychology, particularly in the areas of personality, learning, growth and development, and mental health.

Note that no mention was made of strengthening instruction in career development. Hence, during this period, many professionals did not give high priority to career development theory and its practice, career guidance in the schools.

Concurrent with the influence of NDEA on the development of guidance in the schools was the influence of the pupil personnel services movement in the 1960s. What were those services? The Council of Chief State School Officers stated in 1960 that pupil personnel services included the following: "guidance, health, psychological services, school social work, and attendance" (p. 3).

As the 1960s continued to unfold, the effect of the pupil personnel services movement on guidance became increasingly apparent. Many state departments of education and local school districts placed guidance administratively under the pupil personnel services umbrella. Also, textbooks written in the 1960s on the organization and administration of guidance adapted the pupil personnel service model as the way to organize guidance in the schools. This fit nicely with the services model of guidance that had been evolving since the 1920s. As a result, guidance became a subset of services to be delivered within the broader framework of pupil personnel services. The number of these services varied depending upon the authority quoted, but usually there were six, including orientation, individual inventory, counseling, information (career development/ career guidance) placement, and follow-up. Thus, the clinical model of guidance with counseling as the central service became dominant.

In a chapter titled "Guidance Services," Stripling and Lane (1966) stressed the centrality of counseling—both individual and group. A second priority was consultation. Other guidance functions such as appraisal, information, and placement were seen as supplementary and supportive to counseling, group procedures, and consultation. The same theme of counseling as the core service was emphasized by Ferguson (1963).

> No longer is it viewed merely as a technique and limited to vocational and educational matters; counseling is regarded as the central service in the guidance program (p. 40).

As the decade of the 1960s began to draw to a close, it was apparent that career guidance was not a high priority in the education of school counselors or the practice of guidance and counseling in the schools. That is not to say that activities were not being conducted. What it does mean, however, is that the attention of both counselor educators and school counselors was elsewhere, at least for the time being.

The Maturing Years: Guidance for Development

Beginning in the 1960s, the concept of guidance for development began to emerge. Mathewson (1962), in discussing future trends for guidance, suggested that although adjustive guidance was popular, a long-term movement toward the developmental focus of guidance would probably prevail.

> In spite of present tendencies, a long-term movement toward educative and developmental forms of guidance in schools may yet prevail for these reasons: the need to develop all human potentialities, the persistence and power of human individuality, the effects of dynamic educative experience, the necessity for educational adaptability, the comparative costs, and the urge to preserve human freedom. (p. 375)

The call came in the late 1960s to reorient guidance in the schools from what had become an auxiliary, crisis-oriented service to that of a comprehensive, developmental program. The call for reorientation came from diverse sources, including a renewed interest in vocational-career guidance and its theoretical base in career development, concern about the efficacy of the prevailing approach to guidance in the schools, concern about accountability and evaluation, and from a renewed interest in developmental guidance. During the 1970s the accountability movement intensified. It was joined by increasing interest in career development theory, research, and practice and its educational manifestations, career guidance and career education.

Additional support was provided by the development in a number of states in the early 1970s of state guides for integrating career development into the school curriculum (Drier, 1971; California State Department of Education, 1971). This was followed by a national effort to assist all states, the District of Columbia, and Puerto Rico in developing models or guides for implementing career guidance, counseling, and placement programs in local schools (Gysbers & Moore, 1974).

Thus, by the 1970s, the movement toward developing and implementing comprehensive, developmental guidance programs K–12 was under way. Career development theory offered the content, the knowledge base; the emphasis on accountability evaluation provided the knowledge to plan, structure, implement, and judge guidance programs; and systems thinking provided a way to systematically organize evaluation.

During the same period career education became a national priority, offering an alternate but closely related way to implement career development concepts into the schools' educational program. The career development process was used as a philosophical/research basis for conceptual and implementation efforts; career guidance, for example, was defined as a set of services designed in part to assist individuals in the career decision-making process and to implement decisions that have been made. In this way career guidance and career education are very similar.

Federal funds and state and local funds became available in the 1970s to develop, implement, and evaluate career education. Because career education was not defined in the beginning in the belief that the federal role was to provide leadership, not definitions, it remained for definitions to evolve at the local, state, and national levels. And evolve they did.

An analysis of these definitions reveals three recurrent themes common to all. Most if not all stressed the need for attention to self-understanding and the development of interpersonal skills. Another common theme was the concern for assisting individuals in understanding the decision-making process and in developing decision-making skills. Finally, a third common theme was the need for individuals to gain an understanding of current and potential life roles, settings, and events. Some definitions stressed the work role and the related worker maturity skills involved. Others focused on the work role but in the context of other life roles such as student, parent, or spouse.

During the late 1960s and the 1970s professional guidance and counseling organizations once again began to take an active role in encouraging the application of career development concepts in the schools. In 1966, NCDA (the NVGA) sponsored a conference entitled "Implementing Career Development Theory and Research Through the Curriculum." Later, Ohio State University's Center for Research and Leadership Development in Vocational and Technical Education conducted several conferences to discuss the vocational aspects of guidance (as it was called for years). Concurrently, conferences were jointly sponsored by AACD (then APGA) and AVA—one in 1966 and one in 1967. In May 1975 a special issue of the *Personnel and Guidance Journal* was published, entitled "Career Development: Guidance and Education."

Then in 1973, two associations joined together to adopt a position paper. NCDA and AVA sought to bring the elements of career development together in a single statement and to examine its relationship to education, K–12. This position statement stated that career guidance programs should assist individuals in:

1. self-understanding, which includes a person's relationship to his or her own characteristics and perceptions, as well as to others and to the environment;
2. understanding of the work society and those factors that affect its constant change, including worker attitudes and discipline;
3. awareness of the part that leisure time may play in a person's life;
4. understanding of the necessity for and the multiplicity of factors to be considered in career planning; and
5. understanding of the information and skills necessary to achieve self-fulfillment in work and leisure.

Then in 1975, AACD developed a position paper entitled "Career Guidance: Role and Functions of Counseling and Guidance Personnel Practitioners in Career Education." A number of desirable counselor roles were endorsed, including to provide leadership in the assimilation and application of career decision-making methods and materials. Another related to the identification, classification, and use of self, educational, and occupational information.

Later, in 1976, ACES published a position paper designed to improve pre-service and inservice training in career development, career guidance, and career education. In that paper ACES's position was that all students and adults must be provided with career guidance opportunities to ensure that they:

1. understand that career development is a lifelong process based on an interwoven and sequential series of educational, occupational, leisure, and family choices;
2. examine their own interests, values, aptitudes, and aspirations in an effort to increase self-awareness and self-understanding;
3. develop a personally satisfying set of work values that leads them to believe that work, in some form, can be desirable to them;
4. recognize that the act of paid and unpaid work has dignity;
5. understand the role of leisure in career development;
6. understand the process of reasoned decision-making and the ownership of those decisions in terms of their consequences;
7. recognize that educational and occupational decisions are interrelated with family, work, and leisure;
8. gather the kinds of data necessary to make well-informed career decisions;
9. become aware of and explore a wide variety of occupational alternatives;
10. explore possible rewards, satisfactions, life styles, and negative aspects associated with various occupational options;
11. consider the probability of success and failure for various occupations;

12. understand the important roles of interpersonal and basic employability skills in occupational success;
13. identify and use a wide variety of resources in the school and community to maximize career development potential;
14. know and understand the entrance, transition, and decision points in education and the problems of adjustment that might occur in relation to these points;
15. obtain chosen vocational skills and use available placement services to gain satisfactory entrance into employment in relation to occupational aspirations and beginning competencies; and
16. know and understand the value of continuing education to upgrade or acquire additional occupational skills or leisure pursuits. (ACES, 1976, pp. 8–9)

The "ACES Position Paper: Commission on Counselor Preparation for Career Development/Career Education" (1976) was an important document for a number of reasons. First it was important because the major organization dealing with counselor education felt the need in the late 1970s to make a statement about career development and its importance in the work of counseling and guidance. Did ACES feel that not enough attention was being given to career development? Based on my brief review of the history of attention to career development, I suspect that this was the case. Second, the ACES Position Paper was important because it recognized the central role that career development concepts play in the work of counselors, especially school counselors. Third, it was important because it was in tune with the times. As I pointed out earlier, career guidance was once again being seen as a priority.

In 1979, the National Career Development Association, drawing on its historic commitment to career development, published a systems approach to developing, implementing, and evaluating career guidance programs. This was followed by the identification of counselor competencies in career guidance. Six broad areas were identified including general counseling skills, information, individual and group assessment, management and administration, implementation, and consultations.

Then in 1981, the American School Counselors Association published the "ASCA Role Statement: The Practice of Guidance and Counseling by School Counselors." Four role statements germane to the topic of career development were included:

1. Organize and implement through interested teachers guidance curricula interventions that focus upon important developmental concerns of adolescents (identity, career choice and planning, social relationships, and so forth).

2. Organize and make available comprehensive information systems (print, computer-based, audiovisual) necessary for educational-vocational planning and decision making.

3. Assist students with assessment of personal characteristics (e.g., competencies, interests, aptitudes, needs, career maturity) for personal use in such areas as course selection, post-high school planning, and career choices.

4. Provide remedial interventions or alternative programs for those students showing in-school adjustment problems, vocational immaturity, or general negative attitudes toward personal growth (p. 10).

Later in 1984, ASCA adopted the following policy statement on career guidance:

> Career guidance is a delivery system which systematically helps students reach the career development outcomes of self-awareness and assessment, career awareness and exploration, career decision making, career planning and placement. The school counselor's role covers many areas within a school setting and career guidance is one of the counselor's most important contributions to a student's lifelong development.

Also in 1984, the Carl D. Perkins Vocational Education Act (P.L. 98–524) (U.S. Congress, 1984) was signed into law. It mandated that career guidance and counseling programs shall be designed to assist individuals to acquire among other skills self-assessment, career planning, career decision-making, and employability skills. It authorized guidance and counseling programs that included instructional activities along with other services to assist individuals to acquire the above skills.

Many states using Perkins's monies or state monies are focusing on the importance of career guidance for young people and adults. Wisconsin, for example, developed the concept of "Education for Employment" to provide each student with both the skills needed for productive entry into the work force and the academic knowledge needed for further education and training. One part of this program is entitled career exploration, planning, and decision making. The Educator from Employment program in Wisconsin provides for career exploration, planning, and decision making using the competencies included in the new Wisconsin Developmental K–12 Guidance Program. The states of Iowa, Missouri, and New Jersey also are involved in establishing either comprehensive career guidance and counseling programs or comprehensive guidance programs K–12. Each of these programs in part focuses on the development of career planning and decision-making skills in students K–12.

In 1986, the National Occupational Information Coordinating Committee, aware of the need to identify outcomes for quality career development, guidance, and counseling programs, awarded a grant to the North Dakota State Occupational

Information Coordinating Committee. This committee is developing validated guidelines from which states and local schools can set standards for comprehensive competency-based programs so that during the later part of 1987 and the first part of 1988, a number of states can demonstrate the use of the guidelines.

The Contemporary Scene: Developments and Trends

As the re-emergence of career guidance continues to take place in the 1980s, it is imperative that we examine more closely what our heritage is in today's terms. This is important because the nature of our professional commitment rests squarely on what career development and career guidance mean today, not on what they meant yesterday. To help us toward a clearer understanding of what career development and career guidance mean today let me share with you, in broad brush strokes, several major trends in the literature. (Gysbers & Associates, 1984).

Evolving Meanings of Career Development

Modern theories of career development began appearing in literature during the 1950s. At that time the occupational choice focus of the first 40 years of career development began to give way to a broader, more comprehensive view of individuals and their occupational development over the life span. Occupational choice was beginning to be seen as a developmental process. It was during this time that the term *vocational development* became popular as a way of describing the broadening view of occupational choice.

By the 1960s, knowledge about occupational choices as a developmental process had increased dramatically. At the same time, the terms *career* and *career development* became popular. Today, many people prefer them to the terms *vocation* and *vocational development*. This expanded view of career and career development was more useful than the earlier view of career development as occupational choice because it broke the time barrier that had previously restricted the vision of career development to only a cross-sectional view of an individual's life.

In the 1970s, the definitions of *career* and *career development* used by some writers became broader and more encompassing. Jones, Hamilton, Ganschow, Helliwell, and Wolff (1972) defined career as encompassing a variety of possible patterns of personal choice related to an individual's total life style, including occupation, education, personal and social behaviors, learning how to learn, social responsibility, and leisure time activities.

Gysbers and Moore (1975; 1981) proposed the concept of life career development in an effort to expand and extend career development from an occupational perspective to a life perspective in which occupation (and work) has place and meaning. They defined life career development as self-development over the life span through the integration of the roles, settings, and events of a person's life. The word *life* in the definition means that the focus is on the total person—the human career. The word *career* identifies and relates the roles in which individuals are involved (worker, learner, family, citizen); the settings where individuals find themselves (home, school, community, work place); and the events that occur over their lifetimes (entry job, marriage, divorce, retirement). Finally, the word *development* is used to indicate that individuals are always in the process of becoming. When used in sequence, the words *life career development* bring these separate meanings together, but at the same time a greater meaning emerges. Life career development describes unique people with their own life styles.

Similarly, Super (1975; 1981) proposed a definition of career that involved the interaction of various life roles over the life span. He called it the career rainbow. "Super emphasizes that people, as they mature, normally play a variety of roles in many different theaters. . . .For Super, the term *career* refers to the combination and sequence of all the roles you may play during your lifetime and the pattern in which they fit together at any point in time" (Harris-Bowlsbey, Spivack, & Lisansky, 1982, p. 17–18).

Wolfe and Kolb (1980, p. 1–2) summed up the life view of career development when they defined career development as involving one's whole life.

> Career development involves one's whole life, not just occupation. As such, it concerns the whole person, needs and wants, capacities and potentials, excitements and anxieties, insights and blindspots, warts and all. More than that, it concerns him or her in the ever-changing contexts of his or her life. The environmental pressures and constraints, the bonds that tie him or her to significant others, responsibilities to children and aging parents, the total structure of one's circumstances are also factors that must be understood and reckoned with. In these terms, career development and personal development converge. Self and circumstances—evolving, changing, unfolding in mutual interaction—constitute the focus and the drama of career development.

Increasing Numbers, Diversity, and Quality of Programs, Tools, and Techniques

In the National Career Development Association's third decennial volume, *Designing Careers* (Gysbers & Associates, 1984), the authors documented the rapid expansion in and the almost bewildering diversity of career development programs, tools, and techniques available today to help individuals with their career development. These same authors projected that this expansion will continue into the foreseeable future. Also, it was pointed out that these programs, tools, and techniques are better organized, are more frequently theory-based, and are used more systematically than ever before. Finally, it was projected that these emphases will continue into the future.

Let us look more specifically at what is involved in this major trend. The theory and research base of counseling psychology has been expanded and extended substantially during the past 20 years but particularly during the past 10 years. The growth in the theory and research base for career psychology has been an interesting convergence of ideas in counseling and career psychology concerning human growth and development, and the interventions to facilitate it. This convergence of ideas has stimulated a new array of counseling programs, tools, and techniques. These new programs, tools, and techniques are emerging from this convergence through the application of marriage and family counseling concepts (Zingaro, 1983) and cognitive-behavioral psychology (Keller, Biggs, & Gysbers, 1982). We also are seeing it in the application of contemporary thinking about our personal styles (Pinkney, 1983), learning styles (Wolfe & Kolb, 1980), and hemispheric functioning.

A publication by the National Career Development Association also documents this trend from another perspective. The publication is titled "A Counselor's Guide to Vocational Guidance Instruments" edited by Kapes and Mastie (1982). In it are reviews of career counseling instruments. A number of them have been around for a long time. Some have been developed more recently, and they represent new directions for the field. There are new instruments in the traditional category of interest inventories, but the new directions for the field are in the category of work values, career development and maturity, and card sorts.

Finally, it is clear that career development programs, tools, and techniques are more frequently theory-based. Matthews (1975) pointed out that there were some missing links between materials and people; and that one of the missing links was the lack of an organizing philosophy. "In essence," she stated, "we are now confronted with random materials in search of philosophy" (Matthews, 1975, p. 652). According to a number of authors of decennial volume chapters, this point has been recognized; now, theorists, researchers, and practitioners are devoting more time and energy to organizing and using career programs, tools, and techniques in comprehensive, systematic ways that are theory-based.

Expanding Populations and Settings

At the turn of the century, one focus for counseling was to help young people in the transition from school to work; to make occupational choices in line with their understandings about themselves and the work world through a process called true reasoning (Parsons, 1909). Today, young people still are the recipients of counseling and will be in the future. Additional populations to be served by counseling have been added over the years and have included such groups as individuals with handicapping conditions, college students, the disadvantaged, and unemployed individuals. As the world in which we live and work continues to become more complex, the needs of people in these populations for counseling will increase, not decrease.

As new concepts about career development began to appear and evolve, it became obvious that people of all ages and circumstances had career development needs and concerns, and that they and society could and would benefit from career development programs, services, and counseling. Two such concepts, in particular, had an effect. First was the shift from a point-in-time focus to the life-span focus for career development. And second was the personalization of the concept of career (the human career) relating it to life roles, settings, and events. By introducing these two concepts, the door opened for counseling personnel to provide programs to a wide range of people of all ages in many different kinds of settings.

The newer concept of career development emerged as a result of and in response to the continuing changes that are taking place in our social, industrial, economic, and occupational environments and structures. Because of these changes, adults and adult career development became a focal point for an increasing number of career development theorists and practitioners in the 1970s (Campbell & Cellini, 1981). This focus continued into the 1980s and, in all probability, will continue into the future. As a result, institutions and agencies that serve adults traditionally have added career development components, including counseling. And, new agencies and organizations have been established to provide adults with career development programs, services, and counseling where none had existed.

Career development programs, services, and counseling in business and industry also became a focal point in the 1970s and 1980s. This trend, too, will continue and probably be intensified in the foreseeable future. More businesses and industries as well as many other organizations are realizing the benefits of these activities for their employees. And, if employees benefit, then the organizations benefit also.

Increasing Evidence of Impact

Two studies completed by the National Center for Research in Vocational Education provide documentation of the increasing evidence available concerning the impact of career guidance. The first study was published in 1983 (Campbell, Connell, Kinnel-Boyle, & Bhaerman, 1983). To be included in this review of research, the studies had to be conducted since 1970, focused on grades 9–12 with a sample size of 25 or more, have an educational agency or community service base, and be an empirical study.

In terms of the outcomes, the following summaries indicate the major findings of the empirical studies.

Improved school involvement and performance

A total of forty-one studies focused on one or more of the five dimensions of this theme. The majority of the studies reported gains in student behaviors. The gains were attributed primarily to interventions involving individualized student learning experiences such as Experience-Based Career Education, special classroom activities, career exploration, and counseling.

Personal and interpersonal work skills

A total of thirty studies dealt collectively with this multiple objective—nineteen with self-awareness, five with interpersonal and life skills, and six with work values. The overwhelming majority of studies in this outcome category reported positive effects, i.e., twenty-six out of the total thirty. In summary, the various interventions utilized—particularly EBCE, career education, and career and vocational exploration—led to favorable results.

Preparation for careers

Fourteen studies focused on this theme. Twelve studies demonstrated positive gains. The gains were attributed to four types of interventions: (1) counseling, (2) classroom instruction, (3) EBCE, and (4) career exploration activities.

Career planning skills

In general, career guidance interventions seem to have a beneficial impact on acquiring career planning skills. Of the thirty-four studies reporting evidence on this theme, twenty-seven found a positive outcome. Although many different interventions were used to achieve the outcomes, two were mentioned in over half the studies—ECBE and counseling. Other interventions ranged from computer-based programs to classroom activities.

Career awareness and exploration

Forty-four studies reported data in this area. Of the total, thirty-one studies showed positive results in various aspects of this objective. The remaining thirteen indicated either no significant differences between the groups studied, mixed results, or minor differences. In terms of interventions that showed more positive effects, the following were most prevalent: career and vocational exploration, experienced-based career education, counseling activities, and career education activities. (pp. vii–ix).

Based on the major findings in their review Campbell, Connell, Kinnel-Boyle, and Bhaerman (1983), offered the following conclusions:

The preponderance of evidence suggests that career guidance interventions achieve their intended objectives if guidance personnel are given the opportunity to provide structured guidance interventions in a systematic, developmental sequence.

Career guidance has demonstrated its effectiveness in influencing the career development and adjustment of individuals in the five broad outcome areas.

Career guidance has been successful in assisting individuals representing a wide range of subpopulations and settings, such as in correctional institutions, vocational training centers, community colleges, and rehabilitation centers.

The number of variety of career interventions has greatly increased, giving researchers and practitioners a large pool of treatments from which to draw. For example, due to significant progress in computer applications for career exploration and choice, there are several dozen models from which to choose. (p. x)

The second study is titled "Outcomes of Career Guidance and Counseling" (Hotchkiss & Vetter, 1987). The following paragraphs are taken from the executive summary to the study.

The goal of this project was to estimate effects of career guidance and counseling on intermediate outcomes measured while respondents remained in high school and on employment and educational outcomes measured after respondents left high school. Data from the 1980 sophomore and senior cohorts of the High School and Beyond (HSB) database were used in multivariate analyses.

The analyses strongly replicated findings of past research regarding the impact of status background and personal characteristics (gender, race, ethnicity) on career expectations and performance measures (tests, grades). These variables also affected college-going behavior and exhibited smaller and more erratic patterns of effects on early labor market variables (hours worked, weeks worked, unemployment, but not wage). The career expectation variables (educational and occupational expectation) and perceived ability to complete college also exhibited strong positive effects on college attendance measures and tended to have negative effects on the work variables. In contrast, general attitudes such as self-esteem and locus of control did not have strong effects on post-high school job or education outcomes.

The analyses did not attempt to answer the question regarding interdependence of college and work and the effect this dependence may have on the influence of background and lagged career expectations on college and work after high school. In all cases, total effects of background on work and college were estimated. For example, the coefficient indexing the effect of educational expectation in high school on time spent in college since high school is the sum of the direct effect plus indirect effects operating through the work variables.

In contrast to the strong and consistent effects of background and attitudes, effects of guidance program variables are rather small and exhibit some erratic patterns. Several limitations of the data must be considered, however. First, the data describing guidance describe features of the school a youth attended, not guidance activities to which each youth was exposed during high school. Second, the guidance data were collected in 1984, 2 years after the 1980 sophomore cohort (normally) finished high school and 4 years after the senior cohort finished. Third, program features of guidance were described for each school by a single person, the head of the guidance and counseling department or comparable person.

Within these limitations in mind, the analyses revealed some interesting results. First, youth who attended schools that emphasize counseling (as indicated by student exposure reported by guidance personnel) tended to have higher career goals and attend college more than other youth. Second, youth who attended schools for which the counselor respondent expressed positive attitudes about the guidance program also tended to have higher career goals and college attendance. Anomalously, youth who attended schools that emphasized occupational information had lower growth on test scores than other youth. Several interesting interactions were found, though none were large. A "strong" guidance program (as indicated by a summary index of many of the guidance program variables) increased the effect of base year occupational expectations on first follow-up educational expectations. The guidance index also decreased the influence of educational expectations on tests, tended to destabilize perceived college ability, and reduced the influence of test scores on perceived college ability. None of these results were strong, however. Thus, confidence in these results must await replication.

The pattern of effects involving the nonguidance variable probably provides more useful insight regarding guidance policy than the analyses of the effect of guidance programs, though the two types of effects must be combined to arrive at informed policy. The fact that status background, race, and gender influence career outcomes is a salient finding for guidance programs. There was limited evidence that guidance program variables do affect educational and occupational plans and perceived college ability, but the effects are much smaller than they would have to be in order to reduce the effects of background to a substantial degree. (pp. vii–viii)

Another study, completed by the American College Testing Program, provides additional evidence of impact (Prediger & Sawyer, 1986). They compared indicators of student career development collected in 1973 and again in 1983. This is an important comparison because career guidance and career education were receiving renewed interest in 1973 and this provides a 10-year period to see possible impact. The comparisons were made on nationally representative samples of junior and high school students (N = 18, 129 in 1973 and 15,432 in 1983). The indicators included career-related concerns, career planning involvement, and reactions to career planning services. The major trends identified included:

[A] 32% increase in the proportion of 11th graders who reported receiving some or a lot of career planning help from their schools. Moreover, the proportion of students involved in typical career exploration activities increased significantly over the 10 years of the study. In general, the 10-year trends indicate that schools are having a greater impact on student career development than they were in 1973. (Prediger & Sawyer, 1986, p. 45)

In the same study, Prediger and Sawyer (1986) reported selected results of the 1985 Gallup Poll of teachers' attitudes toward the public school. The Gallup Poll, they reported, found that when parents were asked to rank 25 goals of education, the goal that ranked third highest was "To develop an understanding about different kinds of jobs and careers including their requirements and rewards." Tied for sixth was "To help students make realistic plans for what they will do after high school graduation" (Gallup, 1985, p. 327).

In summary, what is the answer to the question, "Do career guidance interventions have an impact?" The answer is yes. That yes is qualified, however, by Campbell, Connell, Kinnel-Boyle, and Bhaerman (1983). They pointed out that career guidance does have an impact "*if* guidance personnel are given the opportunity to provide structured guidance interventions in a systematic, developmental sequence'' (p. x). That is an important *if!* Thus, the next section of the paper focuses on a recommended professional program of work that provides a structured, systematic, developmental program of guidance K–12.

A Professional Commitment: A Professional Program of Work

The behavior of individuals is, in part, determined by their thought processes. The language people use represents their underlying conceptual schemes, and, in turn, their conceptual schemata determines their behavior (Gerber, 1983). As definitions of career and career development have evolved, and become broader and more encompassing, particularly during the past 20 years, there has been a corresponding broadening and expansion of career guidance programs and services to children and young people in our schools. And, they do have an impact (Campbell, Connell, Kinnel-Boyle, & Bhaerman, 1983; Hotchkiss & Vetter, 1987; Prediger & Sawyer, 1986).

Although it is clear that a broad definition of career and career development opens up more possibilities and opportunities for programs and services for children, young people, and adults than a narrow definition, it is equally clear that other variables are involved. The changing economic, occupational, industrial, and social environments and structures in which people live and work have created conditions and needs not previously present. Individuals must now give more attention to their career development. In addition, a more complete understanding of human growth and development from counseling and career psychology, and the corresponding improvement of intervention strategies and resources, have helped in the expansion and extension of career guidance programs in the elementary and secondary schools as well as other educational and agency settings.

As these trends converge they have begun to shape a new focus for career guidance programs for the future. What will be the focus of career guidance programs in the future? Will future programs be remedial, emphasize crises, and deal with immediate concerns and issues in people's lives? Will they be developmental and emphasize growth experiences and long-range planning activities? Or, will they do both? The sense of the trends discussed in *Designing Careers* (Gysbers & Associates, 1984) and in the literature in general clearly indicate that career guidance programs of the future will respond to the developmental, long-term career needs of students as well as to their more immediate career crises needs.

Traditionally, career guidance programs have focused on immediate problems and concerns of people. Personal crises, lack of information, a specific occupational choice, and ineffective relationships with others are examples of the immediate problems and concerns to which school counselors are asked to respond. This focus for career guidance programs will continue, and new and more effective ways of helping children and young people with their problems and concerns will continue to emerge. To help counselors meet the challenges they may face in the future, however, this focus for career guidance is not sufficient. What is needed is a developmental focus.

Based on this premise, a primary goal of career guidance is to assist all persons (children, young people, and adults) to become competent achieving individuals; to maximize their potential through the effective use or management of their own talents and their environment. As a result career guidance should focus on assisting all individuals in the development of self-knowledge and interpersonal skills, in obtaining life career planning competencies, in identifying and using placement resources, and in gaining knowledge and understanding of life roles, settings, and events, specifically those associated with family, education, work, and leisure. Individuals' feelings of control over their environment and their own destiny, and their relations with others and with institutions are of prime importance.

Career Development Needs of Students

To accomplish this primary goal just discussed it is first necessary to identify the career development needs of students. What are some of those needs?

1. Students need improved and expanded opportunities to become aware of and develop their career (self) identity. Many students are disadvantaged when it comes to opportunities for career development. They have an inadequate sampling of work world models on which to base their emerging career identity. It is not that they don't have any, but those they have generally are inadequate. A lack of such opportunity, however, does not result in an occupational knowledge and value vacuum. Opinions are formed, judgments are made, and many times these result in premature educational and occupational foreclosure. An opportunity unknown is not an opportunity at all.

2. Students need improved and expanded opportunities to conceptualize their emerging career identity through continuous and sequential career exploration activities. Students need a chance to explore and test out some of their notions about the work world. Possible career options require continuous testing to help them evaluate what such options may mean to them. Students need opportunities to ask themselves the question, "What do these options mean to me as I'm developing and growing in my career identity?"

3. Students need improved and expanded opportunities to generalize their emerging career identities through effective placement and follow-through adjustment activities. They need help in translating their emerging career identities into reality. Students need the opportunity to continuously and systematically explore and test out from an internal frame of reference their personal attributes in relation to the wide range of educational and career opportunities that may be available to them. It should be clearly understood that the primary goal is not to have students choose careers to fit jobs but rather to enlarge students' capacities and vision to make decisions about themselves and their career development in the context of the society in which they live, go to school, and work.

Meeting the Career Development Needs of Students

If we are fully to meet the career development needs of students, it is my contention that what is required is a comprehensive, developmental guidance program K–12 that has a career emphasis/dimension firmly and identifiably embedded in it. I say this because I am convinced that to assist students with their career development requires that the total, overall program of guidance in the schools (K–12) be restructured and reformulated. If we don't attend to the overall structure and formulation of all of guidance in the schools, then whatever is popular for the time will be emphasized. Although guidance programs must be sensitive to the times, there also must be continuity and stability of purpose and program.

What are some basic assumptions that undergird the organization and management of a comprehensive, developmental guidance program (Gysbers & Henderson, 1988)?

First, guidance is a program. As a program it has characteristics similar to other programs in education, including:

1. learner outcomes (student competencies) in such areas as self-knowledge and interpersonal relations, decision making and planning, and knowledge of life roles;
2. activities and processes to assist learners in achieving these outcomes;
3. professionally recognized personnel; and
4. materials and resources.

Second, guidance programs are developmental and comprehensive. They are developmental in that guidance activities are conducted on a regular and planned basis to assist young people and adults to achieve specified competencies. Although immediate and crisis needs of individuals are to be met, a major focus of a developmental program is to provide all individuals with experiences to help them grow and develop. Guidance programs are comprehensive in that a full range of activities and services is provided, including assessment, information, counseling, placement, follow-up, and follow-through.

Third, guidance programs focus on the development of individuals' competencies as well as the remediation of their deficits. To some, a major focus in guidance is on the problems individuals have and the obstacles they may face. This emphasis is important, but it should not be dominant. If it is emphasized in isolation, attention often focuses on what is wrong with individuals, not what is right. Obviously, problems and obstacles need to be identified and remediated, but they should not overshadow the existing or potential competencies of individuals. A major emphasis in guidance programs should be on helping individuals identify the competencies they already have and assisting them to develop new ones.

Finally, guidance programs are built on a team approach. A comprehensive, developmental program of guidance is based on the assumption that all staff are involved. At the same time, it should be understood that professionally certified counselors are central to the program as coordinators. In this role, they provide direct service to individuals, as well as work in consultative relations with other members of the guidance team.

What does a comprehensive, developmental program look like that is based on these assumptions? What are its components? Gysbers and Henderson (1988) recommend the following components:

Definition. The program definition identifies the centrality of guidance within the educational process and delineates in outcome terms the competencies individuals will possess as a result of their involvement in the program.

> Guidance is an integral part of each school's total educational program. It is developmental by design and includes sequential activities organized and implemented by certified school counselors with the support of teachers, administrators, students and parents. The Guidance Program includes:
>
> 1. a guidance curriculum;
> 2. individualized planning with students and their parents;
> 3. responsive counseling, consultation and referral; and
> 4. program management.
>
> It is designed to address the needs of all students by helping them to acquire competencies in career planning and exploration, knowledge of self and others, and educational and vocational development. (Missouri Department of Elementary and Secondary Education, 1986)

Rationale. The rationale discusses the importance of guidance as an equal partner in the educational process and provides reasons why individuals in our society need to acquire the competencies that will accrue to them as a result of their involvement in a comprehensive, developmental guidance program.

Assumptions. Assumptions are principles that shape and guide the program.

Guidance Curriculum. The guidance curriculum contains the majority of guidance activities K–12. The curriculum contains goals, lists of competencies to be developed by students, and activities to assist students to achieve the competencies. The curriculum is organized by grade levels and sequenced K–12. It is designed to serve all students.

Individual Planning. Included in this component are guidance activities that assist students to understand and monitor their growth and development and to take action on their next step educationally, occupationally, with placement and follow-through assistance. It is designed to serve all students.

Responsive Services. This component includes such guidance activities as crisis-personal counseling, consulting with administration, staff, and parents, and referral. Small group counseling is a frequently used strategy along with individual counseling. It is designed to serve all students.

System Support. Included in this component are the management activities necessary to support the activities in the other three components as well as activities used to support other programs in the school.

Concluding Thoughts

What began at the turn of the century with a selection and placement focus, and then shifted in the 1920s and 1930s to a focus on personal adjustment, has now assumed a developmental focus. Guidance for selection, placement, and adjustment remains, but now these emphases are encompassed within guidance for development, including career development, over the life span. Societal conditions, interacting with our more complete knowledge of human growth and development in career terms, as well as the broader array of tools and techniques, have brought us to the realization that career development is a life-span phenomenon and that all individuals can benefit from participating in a comprehensive guidance program K–12 that firmly but identifiably imbeds career development in it. The future face for guidance programs in the schools will indeed have a career profile. It is our professional heritage and future challenge.

References

American School Counselor Association. (1981). ASCA role statement: The practice of guidance and counseling by school counselors. *School Counselor*, 7–10.

American School Counselor Association. (1984). *Role statement: The school counselor in career guidance: Expectations and responsibilities.* Alexandria, VA: Author.

Association for Counselor Education and Supervision. (1976). *ACES position paper: Commission on counselor preparation for career development/career education.* Alexandria, VA: American Association for Counseling and Development.

Aubrey, R.F. (1982). A house divided: Guidance and counseling in 20th century America. *Personnel and Guidance Journal, 61*(4), 198–204.

California State Department of Education. (1971). *Career guidance: A California model for career development k–adult.* Sacramento, CA: Author.

Campbell, M.E. (1932). *Vocational guidance-committee on vocational guidance and child labor section III. Education and training. White House Conference on Child Health and Protection.* New York: Century.

Campbell, R.E., & Cellini, J.V. (1981). A diagnostic taxonomy of adult career problems. *Journal of Vocational Behavior, 19*, 175–190.

Campbell, R.E., Connell, J.B., Kinnel-Boyle, K., & Bhaerman, R.D. (1983). *Enhancing career development: Recommendations for action*. Columbus, OH: The National Center for Research in Vocational Education.

Council of Chief State School Officers. (1960). *Responsibilities of state departments of education for pupil personnel services*. Washington, DC: Author.

Davis, H.V. (1969). *Frank Parsons: Prophet, innovator, counselor*. Carbondale: Southern Illinois University Press.

Davis, J.B. (1914). *Vocational and moral guidance*. Boston: Ginn.

Drier, H.N. (Ed.). (1971). *Guide to the integration of career development into local curriculum—Grades k–12*. Madison: Wisconsin Department of Public Instruction.

Ferguson, D.G. (1963). *Pupil personnel services*. Washington, DC: The Center for Applied Research in Education.

Gallup, A. (1985). The Gallup Poll of teachers' attitudes toward the public schools, Part 2. *Phi Delta Kappan, 66*, 323–330.

Gerber, A., Jr. (1983). Finding the car in career. *Journal of Career Education, 9*, 181–183.

Gysbers, N.C., & Henderson, P. (1988). *Developing and managing your school guidance program*. Alexandria, VA: American Association for Counseling and Development.

Gysbers, N.C., & Moore, E.J. (Eds.). (1974). *Career guidance counseling and placement: Elements of an illustrative program guide*. Columbia: University of Missouri.

Gysbers, N.C., & Moore, E.J. (1975). Beyond career development—Life career development. *Personnel and Guidance Journal, 53*, 647–652.

Gysbers, N.C., & Moore, E.J. (1981). *Improving guidance programs*. Englewood Cliffs, NJ: Prentice-Hall.

Gysbers, N.C., & Associates. (1984). *Designing Careers*. San Francisco: Jossey-Bass.

Harris-Bowlsbey, J., Spivack, J.D., & Lisansky, R.S. (1982). *Take hold of your future*. Iowa City, IA: American College Testing Program.

Hotchkiss. L., & Vetter, L. (1987). *Outcomes of career guidance and counseling*. Columbus, OH: The National Center for Research in Vocational Education.

Johnson, A.H. (1972). *Changing conceptions of vocational guidance and concomitant value-orientations 1920–1930*. Doctoral dissertation, Indiana State University.

Jones, G.B., Hamilton, J.A., Ganschow, L.H., Helliwell, C.B., & Wolff, J.M. (1972). *Planning, developing and field testing career guidance programs: A manual and report*. Palo Alto, CA: American Institutes for Research.

Kapes, J.T., & Mastie, M.M. (Eds.). (1982). *A counselor's guide to vocational guidance instruments*. Washington, DC: National Vocational Guidance Association.

Keller, K.E., Biggs, D.A., & Gysbers, N.C. (1982). Career counseling from a cognitive perspective. *Personnel and Guidance Journal, 60*, 367–371.

Mathewson, R.H. (1962). *Guidance policy and practice* (3rd ed.). New York: Harper & Row.

Matthews, E. (1975). Comment. *Personnel and Guidance Journal, 53*, 652.

Missouri Department of Elementary and Secondary Education. (1986). *Missouri comprehensive guidance: A model for program development and implementation*. Jefferson City, MO: Author.

National Career Development Association. (1973). *Position paper on career development*. Washington, DC: American Association for Counseling and Development.

Office of Education. (1949). *Counselor competencies in occupational information.* Washington, DC: Federal Security Agency, Division of Vocational Education.

Parsons, F. (1909). Choosing a vocation. Boston: Houghton Mifflin.

Pierson, G.A. (1965). *An evaluation—Counselor education in regular session institutes.* Washington, DC: U.S. Department of Health, Education, and Welfare, Office of Education, U.S. Government Printing Office.

Pinkney, J.W. (1983). The Myers-Briggs type indicator as an alternative in career counseling. *Personnel and Guidance Journal, 62,* 173–177.

Prediger, D.J., & Sawyer, R.L. (1986). Ten years of career development: A nationwide study of high school students. *Journal of Counseling and Development, 65,* 45–49.

Rogers, C.R. (1942). *Counseling and psychotherapy.* Boston: Houghton Mifflin.

Ryan, W.C., Jr. (1919). *Vocational guidance and the public schools.* Washington, DC: Department of the Interior, Bureau of Education, Bulletin, 1918, No. 24, Government Printing Office.

Stephens, W.R. (1970). *Social reform and the origins of vocational guidance.* Washington, DC: National Vocational Guidance Association.

Stripling, R.O., & Lane, D. (1966). Guidance services. In L.O. Eckerson & H.M. Smith (Eds.), *Scope of pupil personnel services.* Washington, DC: U.S. Government Printing Office.

Super, D.E. (1975). Vocational guidance: Emergent decision making in a changing society. *Bulletin-International Association of Educational and Vocational Guidance, 29,* 16–23.

Super, D.E. (1981). The relative importance of work. *Bulletin-International Association of Educational and Vocational Guidance, 37,* 26–36.

Tyler, L.E. (1960). *The vocational defense counseling and guidance training institutes program: A report of the first 50 institutes.* Washington, DC: U.S. Department of Health, Education, and Welfare, Office of Education, U.S. Government Printing Office.

Wellman, F. (1978). U.S. Office of Education Administrative Unit: Past, present, and future. In, *Report, current state of the art, guidance and counseling services, U.S. Office of Education, Region Seven.* Developed under the auspices of the Division of Pupil Personnel Services, Missouri State Department of Elementary and Secondary Education, American Personnel and Guidance Association, and the U.S. Office of Education.

Wolfe, D.M., & Kolb, D.A. (1980). Career development, personal growth, and experimental learning. In J. Springer (Eds.), *Issues in career and human resource development.* Madison, WI: American Society for Training and Development.

Zingaro, J.C. (1983). A family systems approach for the career counselor. *Personnel and Guidance Journal, 62,* 24–27.

Response to Career Guidance: A Professional Heritage and Future Challenge

Lee Richmond

Professor, Counselor Education, Loyola College, Baltimore, Maryland

The paper that Norm Gysbers presented contains not only a history of the career guidance movement, documentation of its effectiveness, and a future agenda. More than that, it is a paper that portrays a profession at the crossroads.

Dr. Gysbers cited research that indicates that life-span career guidance is a growing public priority in the United States. He also stated that increasing numbers, diversity, and quality characterize career guidance programs that utilize new tools and new techniques. Furthermore, he cited research that strongly documents that programs of career guidance work, provided they are systematically and vigorously applied.

Embedded in these findings, however, is another somewhat more disturbing finding, and that is that sex, race, ethnicity, and, implicitly, socioeconomic status, affect career expectations, and that guidance efforts thus far have not effectively mediated for these factors. That is to say, there is a difference between the haves and the have-nots in our society with regard to technologies, programs, and opportunities.

The purpose of my response to Dr. Gysbers's paper is to identify issues that the paper raises regarding the use of major research findings for practitioners, the implications for counseling preservice and inservice training, and implications for future research.

First, I would like to discuss the use of major findings for practitioners.

Because life-span career guidance is a growing public priority, we who practice career guidance are important people. I think it is necessary to make this point at the outset, simply because counselor image is still at issue. We are not "just a's," we are not just counselors, we are not just career counselors. We are people who have the knowledge and skills to help others with what they consider most important: developing competencies in the career area so that they will have come control over their own environments and their own destinies. Because we have these skills, we must unabashedly and assertively recruit other people to work with us in the career guidance effort. In the schools, this means recruiting teachers, administrators, and other staff to help with the development and implementation of systematic and structured developmental programs of guidance K–12. In other work settings, whether they be educational or mental health settings, it also means that we must educate other agency personnel to the importance of the career guidance effort. Furthermore, we must give increased attention, even priority, to the needs of women, particularly pregnant adolescents, Blacks, Hispanics, and other minorities, especially those from low socioeconomic status. We must also pay increased attention to the disabled. This attention cannot be merely lip service. Just as we must use appropriate programs, tools, and techniques utilizing the latest technologies to work with the general population, so we must learn to use appropriate programs, tools, and techniques with those who have the greatest needs.

I would like to suggest at this point that we may not yet know how to counteract for the effects of sex, race, ethnicity, and disability, but I would also suggest that we had better learn and that it play a major part in our research agenda.

All of this argues for increased dialogue and increased professionalization. As counselors, it is important that we familiarize ourselves with the competency statements and ethical standards of the National Career Development Association, and also those of NBCC.

It is important that we become informed of the standards set by the National Board for the Certification of Counselors as they pertain to career counselors. Most of us know that such standards exist and that we *can* become certified career counselors. If we are serious about our image and serious about our practice and believe that we not only have a statement to make, but can seriously assist people with the ongoing human task of becoming increasingly competent and achieving individuals, then we are serious about our own professional development.

This leads me to a discussion of the implications of Dr. Gysbers's paper for preservice and inservice training. In both of these areas, it is important that programmatic approaches that are student-outcome driven are stressed. Counselor training traditionally emphasizes the area of counseling. Without diminishing the importance of skills leading to personal empowerment and counseling per se, we must stress equally the importance of program planning and development, program implementation, and program evaluation. Counselors and counselor education programs are unique in their emphasis on individual development. It is time that they become equally unique in their emphasis on program development. Inservice training also must be geared to this area because it is the area of greatest lack among people presently practicing counseling.

Also important for preservice and inservice training is greater emphasis on the whole area of career development itself, and the tools and techniques that are used to assist individuals in this effort, including the placement of these within the curriculum. It is heartening to note that in the new CACREP Standards, career development and career counseling are stressed. Preservice programs accredited by CACREP are now guaranteed to pay attention to this area. Furthermore, we are beginning to see that one's life work and one's mental health and attitudes toward living are not really distinct and separate domains. What we do and how we spend our time is part and parcel of who we are and how we feel about ourselves.

I had mentioned before that career guidance and career counseling are presently at a crossroads. Dr. Gysbers emphasized the point in his paper that we are talking about life career development, that when we talk about career guidance, we are speaking about a person's whole life and not a decision made at one specific point in time.

Implicitly, human history is also at a crossroads. This is a time when we are going to have to learn from the future and not merely from the past because the future is more rapidly upon us than it has ever been in the history of the world. Generations of computers die in less than 18 months. Information travels around the world instantaneously, and the occupations of the past will not hold for the future. As all of us know, fewer and fewer human beings are being used in the production of capital goods. Farming and manufacturing are driven by automated and computerized machinery, not by persons.

What this has to do with preservice and inservice training is that other disciplines, such as economics, political science, philosophy, ethics, and futurism itself have things to say to us as counselors. Counselor educators need to discern where these disciplines interface with counseling curriculums and what place they have in them. Conversely, we have things to say to other disciplines, such as sociology and psychology and, perhaps, even to religion and theology. We need to think of counselor education not as 36- or even a 48-hour curriculum, but as a lifelong process for us if our approaches to systematic programming of lifelong career guidance are to be effective for others.

Furthermore, with regard to preservice and inservice training, we need programmatic approaches that are outcome driven not only for students, but also for counselors and counselor education programs themselves.

For the past several years, we have talked rather consistently about "the counselor of tomorrow." It is our counselor education programs that define this entity. It is time for us, as counselor educators, to turn toward the future, uncloud our minds, and address totally new approaches to training the person who will be "tomorrow's counselor."

Lastly, the area of research. Previously mentioned is the fact that we need to know what works with whom and under what specific conditions and circumstances. This is particularly true with regard to the minorities and special interest groups previously mentioned, but also with the population at large in view of the plethora of new programs emerging on the scene. We need new methods of assessing needs and evaluating programs and, it goes without saying that in order to do this, we must learn much more about adults and their decision-making patterns. This implies further alliances with other disciplines, such as adult education, gerontology, and also with the various other human service specialties. Much work has been done with the handicapped and prosthetic devices, but do we know what helps whom to interface better with work? Do we have a system of vocational education for the future—travel from one country to another? Do we have the assessment instruments to evaluate not only past success but future potential? But, perhaps, our greatest research agenda is our need to learn how to read the future. It is not enough to evaluate our old tools and our old techniques. For a new age, new thoughts, new tools, and new techniques will have to be developed.

Furthermore, we will not only have to evaluate the structured systematic developmental programs of guidance as Dr. Gysbers suggests, but, as previously stated, we also have to evaluate counselor education programs and even our research agenda itself. Pressing issues face us, and we know them: the future of work, equalization of opportunity, technology in work, the humanization of work, work and family roles, and minorities in the work place. All of these issues we must address if we are to become a world partner for productivity and peace. Touch a child, and you touch a life. Touch a life, and you touch the community. Touch a community, and you touch the nation. Touch the nation, and you touch the world. This is the work we are doing. This is the profession at the crossroads that Norm Gysbers presented to us. We are important people with a new concept.

Long ago, we were taught two axioms: to value old wine, but not to put old wine in new wineskins. Thank you, Norm, for presenting to us the old wine and a vision of the new. Thanks to each of us for helping to create the new wineskins.

The School Counselor: Image and Impact, Counselor Role and Function, 1960s to 1980s and Beyond

Claire G. Cole

Director of Secondary Education (Acting)
Montgomery County Public Schools, Christiansberg, Virginia

Scenario I—May in the 1960s

Miss Lillian poured her first cup of coffee of the workday and surveyed her small office with satisfaction. She glanced proudly at the shelf of books that she could use to help students: there were *The Occupational Outloook Handbook*, a thick volume listing many colleges, and a really fine display of information given her by those nice military people. She was careful how she used that, though, what with the unpopularity of the Vietnam War; counselors had to be careful about making waves on controversial issues, and she was glad her principal was so protective of her that she never got into trouble about that.

Sharpening two pencils, Miss Lillian found a yellow legal pad and opened her calendar. She would meet with the scholarship committee, check with the valedictorian about how her speech was going, and write two recommendations for students going to college after she'd copied out their transcripts and embossed them with that distinguished school seal. With a little luck, no student would stop in to interrupt her today; she was a little frazzled because she had her graduate examination tonight. The other teachers just did not understand how hard this graduate school stuff was; well, at least she had her permanent certificate because she had her bachelor's degree. A lot of teachers still did not have their college degrees. Miss Lillian had gone to that NDEA Institute last summer and was trying to get some more courses to learn more about this guidance business.

The bell summoned Miss Lillian to her first period English class. This school was lucky to have a counselor with three whole periods a day to work with kids who wanted to go to college. Miss Lillian had heard that

127

there were schools where guidance teachers worked with students who had problems—were pregnant or something bad like that. She was also a little worried because she'd recently heard somebody say a master's degree might be required for this guidance job. Well, that was in the future, and right now she was grateful to be able to escape the classroom for three periods a day. Let them say she was put there just because she was a bad teacher; Miss Lillian did not care! Three periods away from the students was payment enough for whatever they wanted to say.

Historical Development of School Guidance and Counseling

The role of the school counselor in the 1950s and 1960s was very different from the current position, yet contained the seeds of the job of today's counselor. The school guidance and counseling movement historically emerged from a number of societal forces (Miles, 1976) in the first half of the 20th century. Among the most influential were these:

1. A philanthropic and humanitarian movement in the early part of the 20th century that resulted in the development of settlement houses and an early counseling interest that stressed vocational guidance for young wage earners.

2. A mental hygiene emphasis that called for more humane treatment for mental patients, leading to the present-day mental health movement and subsequent emphasis on counseling both for persons with adjustment problems and for those with normal developmental counseling needs.

3. Social changes affecting education, such as technological unemployment and economic depression between the world wars, laws reducing child labor, and compulsory school attendance that sent into the secondary schools large numbers of youngsters who were not interested in public school as preparation for professionals (Traxler & North, 1966). More recent changes such as the technology race instigated by Sputnik's launch; the Vietnamese conflict; civil rights of women, minorities, and the handicapped; an emphasis on vocational education and a quality education and graduation for all students; and other influences continued to shape the role of education in general and school counselors in particular.

4. Industrialization, urbanization, and perceived depersonalization of American society, with a resultant emphasis in schools on the individual, giving rise to counseling emphasis (Barry & Wolf, 1963).

5. Measurement, accountability, and a call for quality education for all students, requiring much attention to the individual in a school, as well as to the system of schooling.

Probably the single strongest impetus for the role of the school counselor was the National Defense Education Act of 1958. This legislation, a response to the Russian launch of Sputnik in 1957, emphasized guidance with substantial funding for the purpose of retooling science education and discovering more scientific talent through testing and counseling (Borow, 1964). Almost 20,000 school counselors were prepared through NDEA Institutes by the mid-60s, at a cost of $58 million (Hoyt, 1974). The number of counselors in secondary schools increased from about 12,000 in the late 1950s to almost 30,000 in the early 1960s (Odell, 1973).

Another influential piece of legislation was the Vocational Education Act of 1963 (Miles, 1976), which strengthened previous vocational education legislation that had fostered vocational guidance. This act required vocational guidance and counseling for all students enrolled in vocational courses; later versions of the act expanded counseling for disadvantaged and handicapped students and for elementary school youngsters. This act and its later amendments instituted state and national vocational guidance conferences and funded innovative projects in career guidance and counseling (Hoyt, 1974).

Professional organizations have been very influential in the development of the role of the school counselor, primarily those associated with the Association for Counseling and Development (AACD). Formerly called the American Personnel and Guidance Association (APGA), AACD traces its development from several organizations interested in guidance and counseling, the earliest being the National Vocational Guidance Association beginning about 1910. In 1951, the organization now known as AACD was formally approved. AACD, composed of numerous different branches, anointed the American School Counselor Association (ASCA) its fifth division in 1953 (McDaniels, 1964). From the 315 charter members, ASCA grew to become the largest division of AACD. This organization, along with the parent AACD, has been one of the single greatest influences on school counseling in America. ASCA has developed role statements, drafted position papers, funded research projects, supported various kinds of publications, lobbied for legislation favorable to school counseling, and emerged as collective spokesperson for school counselors on a variety of issues. One of the most important ways ASCA has shaped the counseling profession is through its two journals, *The School Counselor*, published bimonthly during the school year, and *Elementary School Guidance and Counseling*, a quarterly publication.

Following the 1962 publication of the influential book *The Counselor in a Changing World* by C. Gilbert Wrenn, commissioned by the APGA and the Fund for the Advancement of Education (Beale, 1986), the role of the modern school counselor became even more recognizable. In 1964 ASCA published a *Statement of Policy for Secondary School Counselors* (Odell, 1973), advocating a 2-year training program that contained a practicum.

Important social issues of the 1960s and 1970s continued to influence the development of the school counselor's role (Blum, 1987). Unemployment of some segments of society juxtaposed against relative affluence for a large proportion of Americans created much unrest. Sit-ins, boycotts, protest marches, and other demonstrations by civil rights workers dramatized the social, political, and economic situation of Black Americans. Protests against the Vietnam War and the draft characterized many high school and college campuses. Drugs became more available and sex more acceptable for high school students. From the original role of helping students find vocational programs and colleges, school counselors found themselves with students in the 1960s struggling with issues such as evading the draft, school officials concerned about drugs, and parents lamenting pregnant or runaway flower children. School officials and communities looked to counselors with their presumed "expert" knowledge of human behavior for assistance in easing racial tensions as races encountered each other in many school classrooms for the first time.

Also in the 1960s and 1970s more women entered the work force, the divorce rate went up, and traditional family units became decidedly less traditional as mobile families scattered around the country. School counselors in the 1960s and 1970s began to be concerned with latchkey children, youngsters in divorce, step-parenting and legal custody, and other such family-related matters. Although many contended that these were not issues within the purview of schools, counselors saw the results of children's lacking proper attention and heard the concerns of frustrated, frightened, confused single parents. And counselors were moved to react, to intervene on behalf of their young clients.

The part-time school counselors of the 1950s tried to help scholars into prestigious universities and other youngsters into vocational courses. Counselors of the next decades found themselves overwhelmed fighting the tide of social woes in an age of divorce, affluent substance abuse, sexual permissiveness, and fashionable depression when everyone was suddenly "stressed out." And still they were expected to do the vocational and educational counseling tasks originally assigned. Many school counselors were reluctant to tackle many of the issues, uncertain of their own feelings on some of the subjects, and patently unprepared for the complexity of therapy required to change youngsters' behavior and alleviate their anxieties.

Scenario II—May in the 1980s

Mr. Reynolds walked through the career resource room, noting with approval that several students were working with the paraprofessional before their first-hour class. He greeted his secretary, picked up a photocopy of his messages, and switched on the terminal on his desk as he entered his office. Calling up his calendar as he sipped his decaffeinated coffee, he noted meetings with the gifted advisory committee and the task force to create a community-based crisis intervention plan. Lunch today would be his speech at Rotary on dropout intervention efforts at the middle school. He had appointments with Lula—had she decided to go to the pregnant teens school?—and with John to go over test scores.

A couple of others would drop in for their morning care-taking chat, and there was the last meeting of the group of students with divorcing parents. At 3:00 he and the others would meet with parents of incoming elementary school students, and he really should schedule a departmental meeting with the other counselors today, check with the secretary to make sure all transcripts had been sent, the program to print final grades was up and running, etc., etc.

He was feeling a little frazzled today, because he had his final oral examination coming up for his education specialist certificate. With all there was to do, studying certainly came tough. And he really should make a decision about deciding to become a licensed professional counselor—some said one might soon even have to have a doctorate to stay in school counseling, able to do family therapy and all that stuff. Well, it was tough enough keeping up as it was—Mr. Reynolds was glad he wouldn't have to get a doctorate. But if they could only get another secretary and a couple more terminals for the office, the job would surely be easier.

Techniques and Theories, Technology and Topics

New demands on the school counselor in the 1970s and 1980s meant different techniques and approaches. No longer were a reasonable information base, some testing knowledge, and the ability to communicate well sufficient preparation to be a school counselor. Different techniques, approaches, and theories, aided by technology, emerged to equip school counselors with skills needed to help students, with new topics deemed appropriate for school counselors.

Techniques

Consultation and coordination, focused on developmental programs for all students, evolved as major dimensions of the school counselor's role in the late 1960s and 1970s. Consultation emerged as an attempt to maximize counselor effectiveness by enabling adults other than the counselor to work better with students (Patouillet, 1968). Wrenn (1965) suggested that working with adults involved in students' lives might be time better spent than counseling with the students themselves.

Dinkmeyer (1968) emphasized the consultation role for elementary counselors, as did a 1966 joint committee report from the Association for Counselor Education and Supervision (ACES) and ASCA on the role of the elementary guidance counselor. This ACES-ASCA committee concluded that counselors have three major responsibilities: counseling, consulting, and coordination, defining consultation as:

> The process of sharing with another or group of persons information and ideas, of combining knowledge into new patterns, and of making mutually agreed upon decisions about the next step needed. (Miles, 1987, p. 105)

Consultation was also listed as a responsibility of the secondary school counselor (ASCA, 1977), a need in Standards for the Preparation of Counselors (ACES, 1977), a requirement when working with handicapped youth (Humes, 1978), and a function for middle school counselors (Cole & Anderson, 1979).

Coordination is typically viewed as a part of the school counselor's role (ACES-ASCA, 1966; ASCA, 1977; Cole & Anderson, 1979), but is less well described than is consultation. Coordination became more important to the school counselor as services for students proliferated within the school and as referral resources outside the school became more available. Although coordination was rarely emphasized in textbooks or taught in counselor preparation, the task became a very time-consuming part of the school counselor's job, particularly if the counselor was assigned to be the manager of resources for students in special programs, such as special education.

Referral and working collaboratively with other professionals became much more a part of the school counselor's role for at least three reasons.

1. More outside sources of help were available to the general population, with the advent of community mental health centers, licensed professional counselors, and other resources.
2. It became more acceptable to seek help, and more affordable, with sliding-scale clinic fees and more insurance coverage for mental health care.
3. Professionals outside the school were willing and often eager to work with school counselors, recognizing the tremendous impact of the school culture on their school-aged clients.

Coordination has emerged as an important part of the school counselor's job. The counselor is now often seen as the person in the school who knows the most about students and about available resources, and therefore the professional to identify, refer, and link resources on behalf of the student (Cole, 1987).

Another major shift in technique for school counselors was the inclusion of group counseling in the school counselor's repertoire of skills. Formerly the domain of the therapist, group counseling became an accepted part of the school counselor's training in the early 1970s, although there still is concern about the quality of that training in many programs (Corey, 1983). School counselors themselves still often feel inadequately prepared to do group counseling. In some schools, counselors are constrained by scheduling problems when teachers and administrators are uncooperative about students missing class for group meetings. In other schools, group counseling is an accepted part of the counseling program for many students. In some middle schools, for example, all students participate in a growth group as a part of the developmental counseling program. Some counselors have been creative in scheduling groups at lunchtime, during study hall, before or after school, or at other non-class times.

Group counseling to attack specific problems has become an accepted part of the secondary school counseling program. Myrick and Dixon (1985) reviewed past attempts to change negative student attitudes and behavior through group counseling. Others have looked at self-concept development (Cangelosi, Gressard, & Hines, 1980), conflict resolution (Hutchins & Cole, 1977), grief counseling (Krysiak, 1985) and other specific problem areas. For a 10-year time span in the 1970s and 1980s, group counseling was one of the most-published topics in *The School Counselor* (Carroll & Gladding, 1984).

Depending on the training and orientation of the school counselor, many techniques formerly found in the therapist's office began to be seen in schools. Although some school counselors contented themselves with individual counseling consisting of questions, answers, and testing, others were learning to use new individual and group strategies. Some of these were behavioral contracting, bibliotherapy, structured writing, guided fantasy, relaxation training, role-playing, and many others (Hutchins & Cole, 1986). School counseling in the 1970s and 1980s became much more a matter of personal style and training, with diverse preparation and approaches to professional concerns.

Theories and Approaches

School counselors trained in the 1950s and 1960s learned about the influence of Sigmund Freud and Alfred Adler and heard about Frank Parsons's and E.G. Williamson's trait-factor approaches. Probably they were thoroughly grounded in Carl Rogers's client-centered approach and likely practiced being genuine, warm, empathic, unconditionally positively regarding, and nondirective (Hutchins & Meo, 1987). Although many counselors enjoyed being Rogerian, they discovered that the counseling process took far too long for the traditional school setting. Or they found the nondirective approach to be unproductive with nonverbal, reluctant youngsters who were often involuntary clients of the school counselor.

In the 1960s, up-to-date programs included behavioral counseling, based on B.F. Skinner's work and translated into a practical counseling approach by John Krumboltz and Carl Thoresen (1969). The behavioral approach made it easier in an era of accountability for counselors to demonstrate to their supervisors behavior change that resulted from counseling. Other counselors embraced the work of Albert Ellis (1967) and became proponents of rational emotive therapy, or followed the Gestalt theory of Frederick Perls (1973).

Several thinker/practitioners became popular in the 1970s and 1980s in counselor training programs and as speakers at counselor seminars and conferences.

1. William Glasser (1965) with his combination of school-based experience and his counseling approach of reality therapy has many current followers.

2. William Purkey has adapted his invitational education message (1978) for school counselors.
3. David Hutchins (1986) is attracting converts to his Thinking/Feeling/Acting approach to interaction of behavior in clients.
4. Maxie Maultsby, Jr., (1984) teaches rational behavior therapy to school counselors who see this as an efficient, effective way of helping students change their behavior.

Several other approaches to working with clients have found their way into school counselors' offices, including these.

1. **Primary prevention** assumes that many problems can be prevented if youngsters are taught coping strategies before problems occur. *The Personnel and Guidance Journal* (1984) published a two-issue series of articles on primary prevention, with one issue dedicated to K–12 programs.
2. **Multimodal therapy** uses a variety of techniques and resources to change students' behavior (Gerler, 1977; Seligman, 1981).
3. **Holistic counseling** looks at students in their environment from a total health perspective (Dinkmeyer & Dinkmeyer, 1979).
4. **Crosscultural or multicultural counseling** (Arciniega & Newlon, 1981) considers minority cultures and the acculturation process, with implications for counselors who are not from those cultures.

Other theories and approaches will doubtless emerge in the 1980s as counselors search for structure and meaning in their jobs.

Technology

A number of technological advances dramatically have changed the role of the school counselor in the past 20 to 30 years. Probably the two most used pieces of technology are so familiar that one might not consider them counseling tools: the telephone and the copying machine. A school counselor who conscientiously logs telephone calls will probably find that a great deal of work is done over the telephone. Some consider the telephone an interrupter and a nuisance, but the thoughtful counselor recognizes the value of the telephone as an efficient communications device. Though not a new technology, the telephone, with many school counseling offices having private phone numbers and separate phone lines from the rest of the school, surely has increased the counselor's range of communication in the past 20 years.

Likewise, the photocopier has decreased the time necessary for exchanging records of students. Those who have been counselors for 20 years probably remember hand-copying students' grade sheets and test scores for colleges and prospective employers, then embossing them with the school seal to ensure their sanctity. Countless hours were spent by early school counselors—probably without secretarial help—in simply copying information about students for others to use.

More dramatic examples of technology that has changed school counseling in the past 20 years include instructional television and the VCR, microfiche and microfilm, and, most dramatically, computers—minis, micros, and mainframes.

Probably the most widespread uses of these devices in the late 1970s and the 1980s have been in giving information to students. Frequently several different kinds of technology were combined into an information system (McDaniels, 1987). A career resource center, for example, in the 1960s—if one existed—probably contained almost entirely printed material. Much of the career and educational information was in the counselor's head. An affluent school district might have had a few films or filmstrips, with maybe some audiotapes, played on a huge reel-to-reel tape recorder. The career resource center in the 1970s would have had many more filmstrips, perhaps a key-sort information search, and maybe some microfilm. Educational television programs on career guidance may have been used in classrooms or with counseling groups. The same career resource center by the mid-1980s probably had career and educational information available through either a micro- or a mainframe computer system. Students could learn about careers and colleges by viewing videotapes on a VCR system. A microfiche reader may have made even more information available to students. And through the use of a computer printer and a photocopier, students could have their own copies of career and educational information. The shelves of college catalogs accessible to students in the 1960s had been reduced to a small bundle of microfiche or a floppy disk by the 1980s—and the information was much more cheaply and easily updated.

Although computers are relatively new in schools, their use was foretold by many leaders in the counseling field in the 1960s and 1970s, including C. Gilbert Wrenn (1962) and Donald Super (1970). Computers met with mixed reactions from school counselors. From some who thought computers would solve all ills, to others who believed computers were anti-human and had no place in the counseling office (Kennedy, 1987), counselors enthusiastically, painfully, or matter-of-factly incorporated the technology into their work. Primary use of microcomputers in the 1980s counseling office include these:

1. **Word processing.** Counselors and their clerical assistants have learned the efficiencies of producing personalized letters, mailing lists, and other written documents.
2. **Database sorting.** Counselors have learned through tedious experience how long it takes to sort and resort information, unless they use a computer that greatly simplifies the task—and increases accuracy.
3. **Spreadsheet calculating.** Though used less than the first two, counselors have learned that data can be manipulated through a spreadsheet in much

more efficient fashion than by manual calculation. This computer function is especially useful for a task such as calculation of students' class rank.

4. **Testing.** Many tests counselors use are now available on microcomputers. Counselors and students get almost instant scoring and reporting. Larger computers can be used to manipulate test data, generate test reports, analyze scores, regroup data, and do a variety of other tasks associated with testing that are sometimes assigned to counselors.

5. **Completing administrative tasks.** Although not properly in the realm of the counselor, all too often the guidance professional has been saddled with tasks such as scheduling, arranging for grade reporting, attendance accounting, and other truly administrative assignments. All of these are done much more efficiently by small or large computer systems.

6. **Preparing documents.** Computers can be used to design and print newsletters, brochures, recognition certificates, overhead transparencies, and other documents counselors use to explain their programs or give information to their publics.

7. **Information giving.** Surely no counselor can begin to remember information as well as the smallest computer. Easy to use and easy to update, the computer is used most often in counseling offices to give career and educational information to students.

8. **Teaching.** Students can use computer programs to learn things counselors consider important, such as information for a new student's orientation or tips on how to study.

9. **Collecting information.** Counselors can use a computer to collect information, such as having a student complete open-ended sentences or take a study skills inventory.

10. **Organizing and accounting for time.** The calendar feature of many computers allows counselors to keep dates in mind. Logging activities enables generating quick and clear accountability reports.

Professional literature has begun to give much attention to technology, particularly to the computer. In 1983, Joseph Rotter edited a special issue on computers for *Elementary School Guidance and Counseling*. Charles E. Kennedy, II, began a new column, "Techniques and Technology," in *The School Counselor* in 1987 to discuss computer applications to the tasks of the school counselor. ASCA maintains a computer applications committee and AACD has established a technology committee. Walz (1984) sees the computer as a device of unparalleled significance in counseling. As one counseling computer expert, Lee Richmond, says regarding computers, ". . . the counseling profession cannot afford ignorance" (1987, p. 232).

It is important for counselors to remember, however, that technology needs people. Technology makes tools that free counselors to work, but does not replace counselors.

Topics

An examination of topics of importance to the school counselor for the last 20 years is somewhat puzzling to one searching for themes and trends in counseling. Although there are some topics that seem to receive more attention at times than others, generally the same topics have been discussed in the literature for the last 20 or so years.

Looking at *The School Counselor*, the major journal for practicing counseling professionals in schools, one can discern some directions, at the same time realizing that the interests and expertise of the editors and editorial board members surely shape the content to some degree. The publication of a special issue typically signaled significant interest in a particular topic; a number of special issues already have been cited in this paper.

These trends seem important, as divined by scanning tables of contents of *The School Counselor* of the past 20 years.

1. A major change in school counseling in the past 20 years has been the increasing emphasis on work with parents and other family members. Counselors began teaching parent education groups, offering counseling groups for single parents, providing information on developmental stages of children and financial aid for college, and doing any of a host of other activities aimed specifically at parents or other family members. A special issue of *Elementary School Guidance and Counseling* (McComb, 1981) was devoted to family counseling, with articles on family therapy, single-parent families, the dual-career family, and other such topics. Dave Capuzzi (1981) offered a special issue of *The School Counselor* that featured articles on stepfamily and family therapy, marriage and premarital counseling, and substance and emotional abuse. This journal issue explored the increasing role of school counselors in changing family and educational systems.

One of the biggest changes in school counseling, and one of the more controversial, is the movement toward family therapy. As counselors began to realize that many problems stemmed from the home and could not be resolved adequately without involving other family members, the school counseling profession faced a dilemma that has not yet been solved. Should school counselors become family therapists, or is their role to work only with a youngster in the school setting? How much should counselors involve themselves with family workings, regardless of how much family stress and symptoms affect the youngster at school? Who is the client: the student, the troubled family, or both? Many more articles are appearing in the professional literature today on the topic of the school counselor's role in family therapy (Wilcoxon & Comas, 1987).

2. There seemed to be more interest in career counseling in the late 1960s and 1970s than there has been in recent years. One might speculate that counselors may currently receive better training in the use of educational and occupational information and in principles of career counseling, so they need and have interest in fewer articles on career counseling. Or is it that an "old" topic such as this simply receives less attention, particularly as newer topics related to aspects of personal counseling occupy more of counselors' thinking?

3. Substance abuse has been an area of concern to school counselors since the 1960s. The terminology and focus changed from drugs to substances sometime in the 1970s, usually including alcohol and maybe tobacco. Focus also has shifted from individual to group plus individual approaches, and from the individual as counseling client to a much broader consultation and coordination role where counselors work with teachers, administrators, private therapists, parents, and community mental health—especially substance abuse—agencies. The emphasis also has expanded from the student at school as client to a family systems approach (Davis, Johnston, DiCicco, & Orenstein, 1985) in many counseling offices. The addition of tobacco use to the school counselor's list of concerns is relatively recent (Smith & Brown, 1986), surely a reflection of society's concern with wellness in general and also a response to a trend banning all tobacco use in many schools.

4. Another continuing theme from the 1960s through the 1980s is teenage pregnancy. The focus has shifted somewhat in the 2 decades, however, from unwed motherhood to teenage pregnancy. The concern seems no longer to be the out-of-wedlock aspect of the pregnancy but rather the inability of the teen parent dropout to support herself and a child financially and emotionally (Rousseve, 1985). Abortion also is seen as a counseling concern associated with teen pregnancies. This new emphasis is consistent with society's sexual permissiveness, to the point of birth control clinics in some schools. There probably are counselors who were forbidden to mention sexual issues in earlier years who now refer students to birth control clinics located within their own schools! Other sexual issues, such as homosexuality (Krysiak, 1987; Powell, 1987), AIDS, and sexual abuse (Devoss & Newlon, 1986) are becoming more common in school counseling literature. Clearly, sexual issues currently are being discussed by school counselors and students.

5. Concern for members of minority groups has been constant throughout the sixties, seventies, and eighties, though a definition of who is a minority or which group receives emphasis has changed from decade to decade. In the 1960s and 1970s, publication interest centered on Blacks. In later years, terminology evolved to non-White and to multicultural. The change in name of the AACD division perhaps best illustrates this as it emerged from the Association for Non-White Concerns (ANWC) to the Association for Multi-Cultural Counseling and Development (AMCD). Journal articles turned their attention to other minority

groups in America, including the American Indian (Gade, Hurlburt, & Fuqua, 1986), as well as continuing to consider concerns of Black students (Rousseve, 1985). Two significant groups of newcomers to the ranks of minorities are women and persons with handicapping conditions (Petrusic & Celotta, 1985). Gifted and creative children also have received some attention in the counseling literature in recent years.

6. Child abuse has been in the literature throughout the 20 years, but much more so in the later 1970s and 1980s. Legislation requiring school personnel to report child abuse, media attention to the topic, and programs presenting information to youngsters in the schools have galvanized attention on the school's role, usually with the counselor as the designated school person to handle child abuse concerns (Alford, Martin, & Martin, 1985).

7. Articles on methods and techniques used in school counseling are among the most-published topics. Discussions of group counseling have been in the literature at a fairly consistent rate for the 20 years, with the focus of the articles shifting from how to do group counseling in the earlier years to a more recent emphasis on types and topics of group work, a shift from technique to topic. Peer counseling emerged in the 1970s and continues to receive some attention in more recent journal issues (Bowman, 1986). Bibliotherapy (Pardeck & Pardeck, 1985) has received occasional mention in school counseling journals, as have relaxation techniques (Ragan & Hiebert, 1987).

8. A big shift in interest in the literature has been to techniques and topics of interest to elementary and middle school counselors. ASCA publishes a separate journal for elementary counselors, *Elementary School Guidance and Counseling*, which also considers the middle school years. *The School Counselor* offered a theme issue in January 1986 on middle school counseling, edited by A. Michael Dougherty.

9. In the 1970s accountability emerged as an urgent theme as budget cuts forced elimination of some counseling positions and concrete justification of others; this continues to be a topic of interest (Lombana, 1985). Closely related to accountability is evaluation of counselors' work, a topic that receives intermittent attention in the literature (Gorton & Ohlemacher, 1987). Along with accountability came public relations, as school counselors realized that much of their work was invisible to persons making economic decisions for them. Thus, articles on public relations (Shields, 1986) and an ASCA response for public relations materials, spearheaded by Louise Forsyth, a past-president of ASCA and AACD, helped school counselors plan a program to inform their publics better about their jobs.

10. The topics of separation and loss have emerged as very important for school counselors. Weaker family units meant that, in many cases, school counselors offered assistance that might have come from family members a few decades ago. Death (Krysiak, 1985), divorce (Pardeck & Pardeck, 1985), and

the modern mobile family meant grief of separation for students as they experienced not only deaths in families but also loss of a parent through divorce and loss of friends and family through moves to a new locality.

11. Added to these areas of grief and loss was the spectre of suicide (Martin & Dixon, 1986), when counselors suddenly found themselves with a whole school—adults as well as students—plunged into shock and grief following the suicide of a student. And increasingly, school counselors are becoming not only self-critical for failing to prevent a suicide, but also the target of angry bereaved parents or communities for not rendering sufficient assistance to youngsters in need.

12. Counseling handicapped youngsters and their families has been one of the most dramatic role changes for school counselors in the past 2 decades. With the passage of PL 94–142 and similar legislation, school counselors, as did all other school professionals, found an ever-increasing expectation of service with few added resources as students needing much counseling and personal attention entered the public schools. Counselors, special educators, and administrators formed a team to work with students and their parents. Counselors in many schools became, by default, case managers who began to spend enormous amounts of time handling special education paperwork, attending endless numbers of meetings, and trying to keep up with strict regulations and procedures. Although not properly in the counselor's domain, this responsibility often was assigned to the counselor. Articles on the counselor's role in special education began to appear regularly in *The School Counselor* in the 1970s and remain a topic of interest at present (Levinson, 1985, and Omizo & Omizo, 1987, for example).

13. Counselors have become concerned with eating disorders, as more students exhibit symptoms of bulimia and anorexia nervosa (Hendrick, 1985), although counselors' role in working with youngsters with eating disorders is unclear.

Trends in Theories, Techniques, Technology, and Topics

In terms of theories, techniques, technology, and topics, these changes seem apparent over the last 20 years.

1. Counseling literature indicates a search for more efficient, time-saving, effective theoretical approaches and techniques. These approaches must be applicable to a program for all students, not just one elite group or those with profound problems or special needs. School counseling has emerged as a service for all students. Even though counselor/student ratios have decreased substantially during the past 2 decades, the scope of counseling services has increased so dramatically that more useful theories and techniques are sought by school counselors.

2. Counselors have been somewhat slow to use available technology but realize the time-saving, efficient qualities of technology, especially the computer. Computer use by counselors is a current topic of great interest.

3. Generally, the concerns counselors have today have appeared in the literature for the past 2 decades. Journals emphasize different topics more at different times, but most of the concerns—drug abuse, dropouts, teenage pregnancy, child abuse, effects of family stress—have been prominent throughout the past 20 years. There seem to be few new concerns, but rather periodic new approaches to or new interest in ongoing problems.

4. Role confusion of counselors seems apparent from the literature. For more than 20 years, there have been numerous articles on the role and function of the school counselor. Even considering that the profession is relatively new, this seems a long time for an identity search. One does not see articles in a computer journal, for example, on the role and function of the systems analyst, nor on becoming more assertive about what one's role is. Yet counselors themselves still seem confused about just what their mission is—and that confusion is indeed mirrored in the differences in tasks performed from school to school. One professional may tend the school clinic and issue attendance slips and change schedules whereas a colleague may do extensive family therapy. Although both might be providing valuable service to their school, it is difficult to conclude that both fullfill the same role in the school structure. Perhaps the uncertainty of the role also led to the call a few years back for assertiveness training for counselors so they could quit being, in many cases, apologists and instead become more active definers of their roles in the schools.

5. It is clear that there is more interest in, and presumably more emphasis on, counseling and less on guidance, although classroom guidance is alive and well in elementary, middle, and high schools. There are many more articles in the journals on counseling topics than on guidance areas.

In a 1980 article in *The School Counselor*, Donald Hays compared the school counselor to the buffalo, the dodo bird, and the whooping crane. A more apt comparison today might be to the slide rule. Remember what an instrument of technology the slide rule was 20 years ago? Budding scientists, mathematicians, and engineers owned one or more models and generally wore one on their belts. A slide rule was a symbol of technical capability, a mark of education and intellect.

School counselors have been the mark of progressive, caring schools sporting highly trained individuals in sometimes somewhat elitist roles. Just as slide rules were replaced by considerably more efficient, easier-to-use pocket claculators available to all at a low cost, so can school counselors be replaced by cheaper technology or people if counselors fail to define and perform their roles well. A Macintosh computer is lots cheaper than a counselor, can sort and give information faster and better, takes up much less space, doesn't get sued by angry parents, and can print in many different type styles. Counselors must take care to use the technology and not be replaced by it through lack of understanding of what the counselor can uniquely contribute. Counselors must not let themselves become slide rules.

Implications for the Present and Future

The counseling profession has been shaped by what is happening in society, probably much more so than any other profession represented in the school. Those entering the profession must be capable of and willing to acquire new sets of skills as their client demands change. Whereas a teacher can remain perhaps marginally effective with little change from year to year, the school counselor cannot. Counselors are probably the resident sociologists in their schools, thus the most likely school persons to know about societal trends and mores in their community. A good counselor probably knows, for example, these things:

- what the drug of choice is for youngsters;
- how acceptable unmarried teen pregnancy is in town; and
- which prominent family may well be harboring a child abuser.

The counselor can probably name 10 families considered stable by the community who are in fact on the verge of disintegration, and can probably predict which senior would go to jail for his beliefs if the draft for military service returns.

Perhaps as a result of this dynamic nature of the school counseling role, the issue of role identity persists and must be addressed. Despite role statements, research, and countless articles, much diversity and confusion continue. There are several ways of approaching this issue.

1. Counselors, counselor educators, and state departments of education can continue to educate others who supervise and assign counselors tasks on the appropriate role for the school counselor. The counselor must then be held accountable for that role and evaluated on the performance of the role.

2. Legislation and accreditation standards can be set that define the counselor's role, with true accountability for those standards. In Virginia, for example, there is a requirement that school counselors spend 60% of their time counseling individuals or groups. Although that is not a practical requirement, given the current assignment of tasks for most counselors and that the monitoring of that requirement is nonexistent in many school divisions, the mandate is an example of an attempt to define the school counselor's role as a professional. State accreditation standards often also set maximum student/counselor ratios that help to define expectations.

3. Counselors themselves must understand that role confusion may remain because of the responsive nature of the position. If suicide rates go up in a community, most likely crisis intervention counseling will increase and career counseling or some other developmental area counseling will inevitably decrease, by community demand. Counselors will likely continue to be the school people most sensitive to societal changes, with a degree of ambiguity implicit in this role. Acceptance of this ambiguity may be necessary for those in the counseling profession.

Partly due to the diversity of the school counselor's role, much more research needs to be done on what works, for whom, and under what conditions in counseling. We again advocate the school-university counselor educator partnership as the strongest team to conduct such research (Cole, 1986). Too much of our literature consists of reportedly successful practices, with little or no data to establish the validity of the program of action being described.

Indeed, the whole issue of just what is the school counselor's responsibility needs more debate. How far does the school professional's role extend into the family or the community? Where does school responsibility end and family or community responsibility begin? This will continue to be a nebulous issue as referral resources vary from community to community. Being able to define a range of responsibility would help keep the school counselor from being blamed—or held legally accountable—for all aspects of a student's development.

Are we as a profession doing too little or too much? This dilemma haunts the profession. Should counselors enhance their skills to be more versatile, or narrow their roles to do a few things well? Or should more services be offered but by different people, rather than expecting one diversely trained generalist to handle a complexity of problems?

Differences in counseling for various populations in diverse settings also need to be examined. How is elementary school counseling different from a middle school program? In too many situations, secondary models are imposed on elementary and middle schools, especially the latter. Rather than needing adaptation, perhaps we need altogether new models, especially for the intermediate level of schooling. And how is counseling different in a rural setting than in an urban setting? Should counselor preparation reflect these differences, or do we just assume an on-the-job refinement through trial and error—a painful, wasteful baptism?

Along with defining and refining the counselor's role, the wide range of technology available to counselors must be understood and used, so that counselors can use their time to do what the machines cannot do: counsel.

The areas discussed above imply some voids in the counseling literature. These questions could be answered through research and publication.

1. What are special needs of minority groups such as Hispanic and Oriental children? What is the school counselor's role with the refugee youngster who arrives destitute, speaking no English, having lost the majority of his family in war?
2. How can school counselors help teenaged parents? We do a lot with pregnant teens, but how can we support the teenager who finds the strength to continue school while mothering an infant? Do teen fathers need special help?
3. As schools open their doors and invite the community in, is there a school counselor responsibility for the new clientele? What counseling is to be

144

offered to the adult illiterate, for example, who enrolls in the adult education program?

4. Do gifted children have special counseling needs? Much has been written about counseling special education students and their parents, but as yet the topic of counseling gifted youngsters has received insufficient attention in the journals.

5. What is happening to school counselors with regard to the law? Most school law classes are aimed at administrators or classroom teachers, not counselors. How does a counselor keep up to date on legal requirements and pitfalls? Counselors feel very vulnerable; are they, in fact, being challenged in court, and if so, on what issues?

6. How do we use the technology? Most articles describe in very general terms what the capability of a computer is, but where does a counselor go to find out just what to do with it and how to adapt its functions to counseling tasks? Where are the counselor-hackers who can help us?

7. What financial resources do counselors need to budget for effective guidance and counseling programs? What should they ask for, how should they spend it, and how do they tell if the expenditure makes a difference?

8. How do we account for what we do so that we can show our worth to others? In the era of mastery learning, what is it that counselors help students master?

9. What are effective programs for students in the middle/intermediate/junior high schools? Are there techniques and strategies that are particularly useful for early adolescents? Although much attention has been given to elementary and high school counseling, much remains to be written on the middle school years.

10. What is the counselor's role in the whole excellence in education movement? How do counselors contribute to school excellence, and what is excellence in school counseling? Will we see an effective counseling movement to parallel the effective teaching emphasis currently in vogue?

These and many other topics deserve the attention of researchers and writers in the near future.

Summary

In some ways school counselors are like automobile seat belts. They both came on the market 20 some years ago as optional equipment, regarded by many as unnecessary expense and not personally useful. Just as we began to install seat belts in all cars, we began to install counselors in every secondary school and in many at the elementary level. Even though the need was clear, acceptance by many was reluctant. Now seat belt use is mandated by many states, just as counselor duties are described by state standards.

Perhaps we should learn from the seat belt by seeing how it differs from school counseling.

1. The seat belt is easy to use, and you always know where to find it. Are directions for counselor use as clear to their clients?
2. The function of the seat belt is clear. Do students and parents always know what the role of the school counselor is?
3. Seat belts work. In a crash, the seat-belted person is safer, research tells us. Can we use research to show that the school-counseled person is better equipped to survive an educational or psychological accident?

Seat belts may soon be replaced by air bags. Will the next generation of counselors be as different from us as air bags are from seat belts?

Scenario III—May 2007

Dr. Robin enters the office, throwing the master switch that turns on illumination devices, computers, and the beverage pot. Bright light, a soft glow and a pleasant hum from numerous terminals, and an aroma of fresh-ground, fresh-brewed, all-natural, no-aid, no-caffeine, calcium-enriched beverage fills the room. Dr. Robin thinks, "I really like this new job of guidance systems manager better than I did being a school family therapist. Maybe this family therapy thing is becoming passé anyway, with families being so hard to find nowadays. One half of our children come from divorced homes, and 70% of our Black children live in households headed by single women, with all too many of them living in poverty. Family therapy—what family?"

Dr. Robin glanced through the day's schedule on the daily prompt screen and mentally reviewed these activities for the guidance system manager's day.

9:00   Meeting of the entire department, all 20 of the Licensed Professional Counselors, career paraprofessionals, computer technicians, and parent-surrogates.
10:00   Meet with the parent-surrogates. Many people derided the addition of these people to the guidance system, but Dr. Robin believed they freed the professional counselors to do their real job. The therapists' time was too valuable to be spent with lonely children who just wanted adult company. With so many parents working all the time and absent from home, especially in one-parent households, the parent-surrogate surely filled a need. Dr. Robin realized that many taxpayers felt this was beyond the school's domain, but who else would help with the loneliness? Maybe they didn't belong in the guidance system, but Dr. Robin realized that many innovations became lodged in guidance systems just because nobody seemed to know what else to do with them.

11:30   Lunch with administration and computer people to see how many more terminals had been ordered and whether or not the locally developed software had been installed to interface the school division into the nationwide system for electronically transferring information. At last, no more transcripts on paper!

1:30   Meeting with the Licensed Professional Counselors. This would be a tough one. Dr. Robin couldn't understand why there was so much dissension among the therapists. Surely there was enough work to go around, with a case load of over 70 students for each professional person! Why couldn't they just stick to their own specialty area, without the substance abuse people believing that the family therapists were treading on their territory?

3:00   Meeting with the career and educational paraprofessionals. With the new computer terminals that allowed students to talk directly to colleges and prospective employers, having job interviews right in the counseling office really was convenient. Sometimes Dr. Robin thought maybe more attention should be given to this service, and less to therapy. However, the community surely demanded the other services.

Dr. Robin was glad to have the chance to be the guidance systems manager but wondered what the future would hold for the profession. Would guidance system managers, parent-surrogates, and therapists become obsolete or replaced by technology? Better keep up with the times. . . .

References

ACES. (1977). Standards for the preparation of counselors and other personnel service specialists. *Counselor Education and Supervision, 16*, 172–177.

ACES-ASCA Joint Committee on the Elementary School Counselor. (1966). *Report of the ACES-ASCA Joint Committee on the Elementary School Counselor.* Washington, DC: American Personnel and Guidance Association.

Alford, P., Martin, D., & Martin, M. (1985). A profile of the physical abusers of children. *The School Counselor, 33*, 143–151.

Arciniega, M., & Newlon, B. (1981). A theoretical rationale for cross-cultural family counseling. *The School Counselor, 29*, 89–96.

ASCA. (1977). The role of the secondary school counselor. *The School Counselor, 24*, 228–234.

Barry, R., & Wolf, B. (1963). *Modern issues in guidance-personnel work.* New York: Bureau of Publications, Teachers College, Columbia University.

Beale, A.V. (1986). Trivial pursuit: The history of guidance. *The School Counselor, 34*, 14–17.

Blum, D. (1987). Factors of social and economic change. In C.W. Humes (Ed.), *Contemporary counseling* (pp. 20–47). Muncie, IN: Accelerated Development.

Borow, H. (1964). Milestones of notable events in the history of vocational guidance. In H. Borow (Ed.), *Man in a world of work* (pp. 45–64). Boston: Houghton Mifflin.

Bowman, R.P. (1986). Peer facilitator programs for middle graders: Students helping each other grow up. *The School Counselor, 33,* 221–229.

Cangelosi, A., Gressard, C.F., & Hines, R.A. (1980). The effects of a rational thinking group on self-concepts in adolescents. *The School Counselor, 27,* 357–361.

Capuzzi, D. (1981). Family counseling: The school counselor's role. *The School Counselor, 28,* 165–235.

Carroll, M., & Gladding, S. (1984). Profiles of contributors to *The School Counselor* (1972–1981) by occupation, geographical location, institutional affiliation, and topic. *The School Counselor, 32,* 4–10.

Cole, C.G. (1986). From the editor's desk. *The School Counselor, 34,* 5–6.

Cole, C.G. (1987). Referral and collaborative working. In C.H. Humes (Ed.), *Contemporary counseling* (pp. 279–295). Muncie, IN: Accelerated Development.

Cole, C.G., & Anderson, N. (1979). Role statement for middle school counselors. *Middle School Journal, 10,* 8–9.

Corey, G. (1983). Group counseling. In J.A. Brown & R.H. Pate, Jr. (Eds.), *Being a counselor: Directions and challenges.* Monterey, CA: Brooks/Cole.

Davis, R. Johnston, P., DiCicco, L., & Orenstein, A. (1985). Helping children of alcoholic parents: An elementary school program. *The School Counselor, 32,* 357–363.

Devoss, J.A., & Newlon, B.J. (1986). Support groups for parents of sexually victimized children. *The School Counselor, 34,* 51–56.

Dinkmeyer, D., & Dinkmeyer, D., Jr. (1979). Holistic approaches to healthy. *Elementary School Guidance and Counseling, 14,* 108–112.

Dinkmeyer, D.C. (1968). The counselor as consultant: Rationale and procedures. *Elementary School Guidance and Counseling, 3,* 187–194.

Dougherty, A.M. (1986). Middle school counseling theme issue. *The School Counselor, 33,* 167–239.

Ellis, A. (1967). Rational-emotive psychotherapy. In D. Arbuckle (Ed.), *Counseling and psychotherapy.* New York: McGraw-Hill.

Gade, E., Hurlburt, G., & Fuqua, D. (1986). Study habits and attitudes of American Indian students: Implications for counselors. *The School Counselor, 34,* 135–139.

Gerler, E.R., Jr. (1977). The school counselor and multimodal education. *The School Counselor, 25,* 166–171.

Glasser, W. (1965). *Reality therapy: A new approach to psychiatry.* New York: Harper & Row.

Goodyear, R. (Ed.). (1984). *Personnel and Guidance Journal, 62,* 446–495.

Gorton, R., & Ohlemacher, R. (1987). Counselor evaluation: A new priority for the principal's agenda. *NASSP Bulletin, 71,* 120–124.

Hays, D. (1980). The buffalo, the dodo bird, and the whooping crane. *The School Counselor, 27,* 255–262.

Hendrick, S.S. (1985). The school counselor and bulimia. *The School Counselor, 32,* 275–280.

Hoyt, K.B. (1974). Professional preparation for vocational guidance. In E.L. Herr (Ed.), *Vocational guidance and human development* (pp. 502–527). Boston: Houghton Mifflin.

Humes, C.W. (1978). School counselors and PL 94–142. *The School Counselor, 31*, 229–238.

Hutchins, D., & Cole, C. (1977). A model for improving middle school students' interpersonal relationships. *The School Counselor, 25*, 134–137.

Hutchins, D.E., & Cole, C.G. (1986). *Helping relationships and strategies.* Monterey, CA: Brooks/Cole.

Hutchins, J.D., & Meo, K. (1987). Counseling theories and techniques. In C.W. Humes (Ed.), *Contemporary counseling.* Muncie, IN: Accelerated Development.

Kennedy, C.E., II. (in press). Techniques and technology. *The School Counselor.*

Krumboltz, J.D., & Thoresen, E.E. (1969). *Behavioral counseling: Cases and techniques.* New York: Holt, Rinehart & Winston.

Krysiak, G.J. (1985). Circle of friends. *The School Counselor, 33*, 47–49.

Krysiak, G.J. (1987). A very silent and gay minority. *The School Counselor, 34*, 304–307.

Levinson, E.M. (1985). Vocational and career-oriented secondary school programs for the emotionally disturbed. *The School Counselor, 33*, 100–106.

Lombana, J. (1985). Guidance accountability: A new look at an old problem. *The School Counselor, 32*, 340–346.

Martin, N.K., & Dixon, P.N. (1986). Adolescent suicide: Myths, recognition, and evaluation. *The School Counselor, 33*, 265–271.

Maultsby, M.C., Jr. (1984). *Rational behavior therapy.* Englewood Cliffs, NJ: Prentice Hall.

McComb, B. (1981). Special issue: Family counseling. *Elementary School Guidance and Counseling, 15*, 180–278.

McDaniels, C. (1964). *The history and development of the American Personnel and Guidance Association: 1952–1963.* Unpublished doctoral dissertation. Charlottesville, VA: The University of Virginia.

McDaniels, C. (1987). Career information. In C.H. Humes (Ed.), *Contemporary Counseling* (pp. 136–161). Muncie, IN: Accelerated Development.

Miles, J.H. (1976). Historical development of guidance. In T.H. Hohenshil and J.H. Miles (Eds.), *School guidance services* (pp. 13–15). Dubuque, IA: Kendall Hunt.

Miles, J.H. (1987). Consultation. In C.H. Humes (Ed.), *Contemporary counseling* (pp. 103–135). Muncie, IN: Accelerated Development.

Myrick, R.D., & Dixon, F.W. (1985). Changing student attitudes and behavior through group counseling. *The School Counselor, 32*, 325–330.

Odell, L.M. (1973). Secondary school counseling: Past, present, future. *Personnel and Guidance Journal, 53*, 151–155.

Omizo, M.M., & Omizo, S.A. (1987). The effects of eliminating self-defeating behavior of learning-disabled children through group counseling. *The School Counselor, 34*, 282–288.

Pardeck, J.A., & Pardeck, J.T. (1985). Bibliotherapy using a neo-Freudian approach for children of divorced parents. *The School Counselor, 32*, 313–318.

Patouillet, R. (1968). Organizing for guidance in the elementary school. In D.C. Dinkmeyer (Ed.), *Guidance and counseling in the elementary school.* New York: Holt Rinehart & Winston.

Perls, F. (1973). *The Gestalt approach and eye witness to therapy.* New York: Bantam.

149

Petrusic, J., & Celotta, B. (1985). What children want to know about their disabled peers: An exploratory study. *The School Counselor, 33,* 38–46.

Powell, R. (1987). Homosexual behavior and the school counselor. *The School Counselor, 34,* 202–208.

Purkey, W. (1978). *Inviting school success.* Belmont, CA: Wadsworth Publishing Company.

Ragan, L., & Hiebert. (1987). Kiddie QR (quieting reflex): Field testing a relaxation program for young children. *The School Counselor, 34,* 273–381.

Richmond, L. (1987). Computer applications in counseling. In C.W. Humes (Ed.), *Contemporary Counseling* (pp. 228–253). Muncie, IN: Accelerated Development.

Rousseve, R. (1985). Unwed adolescents with babies: A grim American reality. *The School Counselor, 33,* 85–87.

Seligman, L. (1981). Multimodal behavior therapy: Case study of a high school student. *The School Counselor, 28,* 249–256.

Shields, C. (1986). Good public relations is good for business (and guidance departments, too). *The School Counselor, 34,* 144–146.

Smith, A., & Brown, D. (1986). Designing and implementing an antismoking program. *The School Counselor, 33,* 379–385.

Super, D. (1970). *Computer-assisted counseling.* New York: Teachers College, Columbia University.

Traxler, A.E., & North, R.D. (1966). *Techniques of guidance.* New York: Harper & Row.

Walz, G. (1984). Role of the counselor with computers. *Journal of Counseling and Development, 63,* 135–138.

Wilcoxon, S.A., & Comas, R.E. (1987). Contemporary trends in family counseling: What do they mean for the school counselor? *The School Counselor, 34,* 219–225.

Wrenn, C.G. (1962). *The counselor in a changing world.* Washington, DC: American Personnel and Guidance Association.

Wrenn, C.G. (1965). *The counselor in a changing world revisited.* Teachers College Journal. Terre Haute: Indiana State College.

Response to The School Counselor: Image and Impact, Counselor Role and Function, 1960s to 1980s and Beyond

Courtland C. Lee

Associate Professor and Director, Counselor Education
University of Virginia, Charlottesville, Virginia

Dr. Cole has done an excellent job of surveying the past, present, and possible future of the role and function of school counseling professionals in her paper. She has, I believe, truly captured the essence of both evolution and revolution in school counselor role and function in the three creative scenarios presented. She has raised important issues for the counseling profession as a whole and the art and science of school counseling in particular. I would like to react to the issues Dr. Cole has raised from my perspective as a counselor educator in the business of training future counseling professionals, many of whom will apply their knowledge and skills to the school setting.

I think the one theme that stands out above all else in Dr. Cole's historical overview is the notion of *change* in counselor role and function. School counseling was, is, and no doubt will continue to be a dynamic profession: evolving from the Miss Lillians (the part-timers of the 1950s), helping young people get into college, into the social change agents of the 1960s and 1970s (challenging social ills), into the contemporary high-tech helpers armed with hardware and software on their way to becoming (if we are to believe futuristic pundits) Captain Kirks of the Starship Enterprise of human development in the schools of the next century.

If change is inevitable and constant in the profession, as Dr. Cole implies in her paper, then what of the present-day school counselor caught between the traditions of the past and the promise of the future? How does he or she define a professional role and what functions does he or she perform in the school setting? Dr. Cole has highlighted many questions that I know I am often asked by practicing school counselors in my travels. Questions such as: Am I a school counselor or a family therapist? How computer literate do I need to be in order to be effective in my work?, Will I need a doctorate to continue my career as a school counselor?, Do I need to be licensed/certified/registered *or what* to be a legitimate school counselor?, Do I really need all those newfangled methods/techniques to work with handicapped kids or minority kids? and so forth.

With questions such as these, is it any wonder then, as Dr. Cole has stated, that role confusion continues to exist among school counselors and that we see great diversity in counselor function, despite a solid and ever-growing base of theory, techniques, and technology? I share Dr. Cole's concerns about the 20-plus year search for identity among school counselors.

It is evident to me as a counselor educator that these questions and concerns, when considered within the context of Dr. Cole's paper, have some important implications for the future training of school counselors. Reflecting on the topics of importance to the school counselor over the last 20 years that Dr. Cole has identified, my initial reaction would be to call for sweeping curriculum changes in counselor education programs to ensure that new counselors receive the highly specialized training it is apparent they will need in the next 20 years and beyond. I might add that such changes would certainly help counselor education programs in their efforts to conform with the ever-increasing expectations placed on them by accreditation bodies.

However, upon further reflection, a major question that counselor educators must ask themselves is: Can a training program be all things to all people? Can we realistically train highly specialized school counseling professionals in 48, 51, or even 60 credit hour programs? Given the vast body of knowledge related to school counseling synthesized for use here by Dr. Cole, I think the answer to these questions is a realistic *no*. Perhaps the goal of counselor educators should be (as I suppose it always has been) to ensure that students receive the best general training possible—that they leave counselor education programs with solid counseling skills and a *basic* understanding of how to facilitate academic, career, and personal-social development in childhood and adolescence.

Beyond such basic training provided at the preservice level, the key to future specialized skills development on the part of school counselors will no doubt lie in comprehensive inservice training. It will be participation in such ongoing professional development efforts that will keep school counselors on the cutting edge of new theories, techniques, technology, and topics. What the changes over the last 20 years that Dr. Cole has identified make clear to me is that counselor educators must work closely with counselors in the schools, their supervisors, and the powers-that-be in local systems to develop comprehensive inservice training programs of high quality at the local, state, regional, and national level. Such programs, although offering credits for licensure or certification, should have as their primary focus providing counselors with the specialized awareness, knowledge, and skills to effectively define their mission as the primary mental health agent in present and future schools.

In another area, I am pleased, as a counselor educator who is interested in advancing the science of school counseling, that Dr. Cole, in discussing implications for the present and the future, has called for more research in the field. I join in her call for school counselors to form research partnerships with university-based counselor educators. The best way to state a case for the role and function of school counselors is to be able to present empirical evidence of what works and what does not. As I read Dr. Cole's analysis of professional trends, it became obvious to me that one important research imperative is in the area of program evaluation. As we continue into the future of school counseling it will be important to have empirical evidence on the effectiveness of models and methods. As Dr. Cole has stated, the literature is replete with descriptions of programs claiming to be successful, with little or no empirical evidence to support these claims. There are no doubt scores of successful school counselors with legions of model programs out there. It is incumbent upon us to help these counselors evaluate their programs and present the evidence to the profession.

Dr. Cole's observations on the impact of technology, particularly the computer on school counselor role and function, point out the need to make this impact an important aspect of program evaluation. In the next decade and beyond, we are going to need considerable systematic research on the impact of computer technology on human development in the school setting. The two basic questions we need to find answers to seem to me to be: Do computers make a difference in the development of youth? and, Do computers really enhance the role and function of the school counseling professional?

In closing my comments on Dr. Cole's excellent paper, I want to focus on "Mr. Reynolds," the counselor in her second scenario. Mr. Reynolds is the contemporary school counselor, the 20/20 counselor. He has the benefit of 20-plus years of school counseling knowledge and tradition behind him *and* 20-plus years of school counseling promise ahead of him. How Mr. Reynolds moves into the future will be representative of the image and impact of all school counseling professionals. He can go forward into the future unsure of his roles and function and have little impact on either the lives of young people or the counseling profession, *or* he can continue the process of evolution and revolution in school counseling, revealed for use by Dr. Cole, and move forward with a solid image and positive impact. Let us hope, in some measure, that we realize Dr. Cole's vision of the future.

Building Strong School Counseling Programs: Implications for Counselor Preparation

Thomas J. Sweeney

Coordinator, Counselor Education
Ohio University, Athens, Ohio

Context of Counselor Education: Past and Present

The papers of the major research reviewers offer a wide and varied view of school counseling over the last 20 years. Without attempting to document the history, one could easily provide a mirror reflection of what has been transpiring in counselor education during this period. Cole's view, for example, of the school counselor's office routine in the 1960s gives us an idea of how dramatically counselor education has changed as well. As tends to be true yet today, counselor educators came out of the ranks of education (Hollis & Wantz, 1984).

Like the school counselor of the 1980s, however, we have had to change and adapt to survive in a changing environment. Many of use comfortably aligned ourselves with the career education movement of the early and mid-70s. Less comfortably, we reoriented ourselves to a strong community-based counseling program as counselor positions in schools tended to level off and dry up with state and federal funds in the late 1970s and the 1980s. For counselor educators, developing community counseling programs, counselor licensure, accreditation of programs, national certification, and professional identity have been major issues and focuses of attention. Conversely, school counselor education has drifted to a lesser position in the minds of most counselor educators.

A content analysis of the ACES (Association for Counselor Education and Supervision) journal from 1961 to 1985 offers some collaboration of these perceptions (Hosie, 1986). There were 39 articles on school counselor role and function from 1961 to 1968. There were 13 such articles from 1968 to 1977. One article was published in the 1978 to 1980 series and none since. One might

155

conclude that counselor educators have solved the challenge of school counselor role! During this same time span, 28 articles appeared on school counselor programs and certification from 1961 to 1977. Only one article on school counselor certification has appeared since 1977.

There has been a revolution going on within counselor education. There have been casualties as well. The ACES membership peaked in the 1970s at just over 5,000 members. Today there are less than 3,000 members. And school counseling as a major force in most graduate programs is passé. In fact, some preparation programs are quietly being eliminated for lack of financial resources or evidence of need. This is not all bad. In some instances, programs are still preparing counselors for 1960s schools—these programs no longer meet the needs of most schools or young people.

With this brief background as a context, we can understand how few counselor educators are aware of the substantial threat to school counseling and, hence, school counselor education that exists today. In 1974, I authored an article on licensure as an essential issue for the survival of the profession. I believe that we may be at a similar point with respect to school counseling. Herr (1984) and Hohenshil (1987) have sounded the alarm about the implications of current educational reforms for school counseling.

Those of us in Ohio once again may be on the cutting edge of the issue. Last year, our state board of education modified school accreditation standards in such a way that there is no longer a mandated counselor-student ratio. It also has made it possible for bachelor-level social workers to be hired in lieu of counselors. In addition, apparently following the lead of some of the national reformers' recommendations, the board is requiring teachers to earn their master's degree in a subject area for advanced certification. It also has increased the teaching experience requirement from 1 year to 3 years. All of this and more was done despite sustained and substantive testimony to the state board by many different groups, including Ohio counselors and counselor educators. The board simply refused to take anything we had to say seriously. We were in good company. It also ignored the Ohio Education Association and other state professional associations.

The effect of these changes does not require much imagination. With the cost of one master's degree generally sufficient for the budget of most educators, who will be interested in working and paying for two master's degrees? As it stands now, there are no economic incentives to encourage such an effort even if one were willing to complete the requirements for two degrees. Left unchecked, Ohio will not be alone in this predicament nor will school counseling ever be the same. The real losers, however, will be the young people who the research presented at this conference indicates could benefit from effective school counselor services.

Rather than be discouraged, however, I see in these situations the seeds of what can become a renaissance for school counseling. We seem to have needed a clear and imminent danger, just as we had with the licensure of other professions in the early 1970s, to truly motivate us to action. As Herr (1984) and Hohenshil (1987) note, the absence of counseling services and counselors in most of the national education reform reports makes it clear that we must increase our efforts to acquaint policymakers with the contributions school counselor services make to the education and development of young people.

With this as a background, I will turn our attention to the observations of our research reviewers and the areas of service that school counselors offer that hold promise for winning the support of legislators, other educators, and parents. I will conclude with some observations about the implications that I see for counselor education. As the immediate past-chair for the Council for the Accreditation of Counseling and Related Educational Programs (CACREP), I wish to relate these to the Standards for preparation.

Learning to Love Learning

As I read the Krumboltz opening paragraphs, I wanted to stand up and cheer. They also reminded me of another writer's quip that, if God had known what schools were going to be like, he would have made children different. Krumboltz opens the door wide for counselors to speak a language parents and teachers understand well.

Stated another way, Naisbitt (1984) said that the big question we should all ask ourselves is, what business are we in? I think that we have contributed to some of our own role confusion, and confused others, by focusing too much on means and methods instead of goals and objectives. What business are we in? Are we service providers? Human development specialists? If you follow Krumboltz's thinking, I think you'll agree that we are in the "motivation" business. The simple question, "What is your goal?" should be the one to ask ourselves over and over again. If we agree that we want children to grow up enjoying learning, loving themselves, and knowing how to live positively with others, then our methods and techniques must conform to a different set of criteria than those that typically have been used in the past. Krumboltz illustrates this eloquently.

As he notes, parents want to hear that their children are enjoying school, that they are learning, and that they are excited by what they are discovering. Anyone who contributes to the successful attainment of these goals always will be in demand.

Another essential value that the research tends to support relates to cooperation. Children learn best when cooperation, not competition, is present. This, coupled with the findings related to internal versus external locus of control, raises the question of how counselor educators can successfully help counselors-in-training learn to contribute to these goals as consultants and counselors.

Although it may seem too simplistic, I believe that we should encourage these same values in graduate education and use modeling as our modus operandi. Showing instead of telling, followed by practice in methods and techniques found to foster joy and success in learning, could reinforce both the desired attitudes and behaviors. Encouraging more teaming and collaboration among students and staff would revolutionize many graduate programs.

Skills for the Future

When I returned to school counseling practicum and internship supervision after my term as AACD President in 1981, I had been away but a few years. Rural southeastern Ohio did not seem all that different by outward appearances. Our first few cases in group supervision seminar, however, sounded like those from the local community mental health center: one attempted suicide by a 14-year old girl, one drug overdose requiring the emergency squad, a depressed teacher with marital problems, one suspected pregnancy, and two cases of incest. We suddenly had urgent need for a crash course on legal and ethical implications! I wondered what happened to the day when we used the *Mooney Problem Checklist* to get a reading on student problems.

Capuzzi identifies the symptoms of discouragement among young people—depression, suicide, eating disorders, and substance abuse. As Cole notes, professional school counselors today would not need to administer a checklist to have the pulse of their own students. They know firsthand what is happening in the corridors, cafeteria, and streets at night.

The questions that run through my mind are, how can school counselors best use their time and talents to prevent these conditions when possible and, barring that, contribute to helping reorient students after problems already have developed? Although Capuzzi shares what we do know, he points out that there is still much we do not know. Teachers and counselors will be among those to uncover serious mental health problems.

Although neither will have the time or resources to provide ongoing, intensive counseling, there is much they can do. Like Gysbers, I believe that a well-articulated, comprehensive guidance program will have within it support groups, readiness activities, and educational and career exploration to help bring hope to what may seem like a hopeless situation for some youngsters.

On the other hand, we should teach school counselors to cooperate with others as referral agents and collaborators, and to establish the parameters within which counselors can function as primary, secondary, and tertiary care providers. In short, we should teach them not to play God and to practice responsibly in these stressful situations.

Conceptually, I also think that counselor educators must return to a somewhat forgotten area of counselor education, that concerning philosophy. Implicit in much of our observations are questions of values. If we treat only symptoms of suffering, we are doomed to fail. Without what Naisbitt (1984) calls a strategic vision, we can have no strategic plan. Each of us is sharing our view about the "facts" as we know them. How we use this information becomes a matter of priorities about what is most important, most relevant, and so forth.

How long has it been since any of us has participated in an informed, focused discussion on values, philosophy, and beliefs? It could be interesting and very helpful. It also would make ranking activities for priority more meaningful and, potentially, more effective. I do not believe that we can be all things to all people. We have been trying, and it is not solving the problems of children, the schools, or the school counselors who conscientiously try to fulfill the needs of our society through their efforts.

I also believe that this philosophical discourse should examine the values underlying the school, community, and government programs within which counselors are employed. For too long the helping professions including counseling have been shaped by change agents with goals, objectives, and methods that run contrary to those espoused at this conference. We will continue to be reactive if counselors are not among the policy shapers and managers. Such leadership will arise from among those individuals who articulate a vision based upon sound philosophy, research, and proven methods.

Career Guidance

Gysbers provides a compelling case for career guidance as an integrating and unifying focus for school counseling services. The heritage is there and, indeed, there is much to be said for its future in school counseling.

I have long believed that without hope for a good or better future, any human being will live in despair. A dream provides the proverbial "light at the end of the tunnel." I believe that the greatest gift we can offer to other human beings is encouragement in creating and realizing their dreams. For Hispanics, Blacks, women, and other minorities, this is no less important than for the abused child.

Two national reports, *Keeping the Options Open* (Commission on Precollege Guidance and Counseling, 1986) and *Frontiers of Possibility* (National College Counseling Project, 1986) place counselors and counseling services in a central role in the school reform movement. From the *Frontiers* report, the authors note:

> In examining the breadth and depth of counseling practices across the country, one cannot ignore the many imposing obstacles a student may face in achieving educational goals. . .The task of raising aspirations is crucial not only to inner city minority schools but also to many rural schools drawing students from lower income White families. . .The task may be reasonably clear, but the obstacles are great. Too often it is tempting to dwell on the difficulty—perhaps the impossibility—of accomplishing the task. . .We believed at the outset of our work, and have sub-

sequently confirmed in our research, that there are schools of every description that exhibit exemplary programs and practices. Many of these programs are succeeding in the face of seemingly insurmountable barriers.

Whether in a demoralized school emerging from the throes of defeat or in an already effective school moving to a higher level of attainment, schools on the move recognize the crucial role of the counselor. Also, we found that schools on the move recognize the importance of raising student aspirations toward higher education. While James Bryant Conant's vision of the counselor's role is not yet a reality across the nation, we believe it still represents the best view of what is important and attainable. Most importantly, we now believe that this frontier of possibility exists realistically for every school and every student. (pp. 3–4)

Clearly, the career studies cited by Gysbers also provide evidence to support the counselor's role in helping young people to raise their aspirations and to find the means to realize them. Equally important to those of us interested in school counseling, there are other organizations and groups who already are aligned with our desire to ensure that counselors attain a central role in the school.

School Counselor Role: 1980s and Beyond

I have been pondering the question of what is the central role of the counselor in the school. At the risk of oversimplifying, I attempted stating our reviewers' comments into a sentence. Krumboltz suggests that the counselor's central role is working with others to improve academic achievement for young people by fostering a lifelong joy for learning. Capuzzi offers a case for helping young people to develop personal and social competencies, so that what I call the symptoms of discouragement would be ameliorated. Gysbers believes that following our roots and success with career guidance is a sound foundation for even better counseling in the future. Cole posits the idea that the counselor's role will change emphasis over time and be shaped by the needs of the students and community. In this latter case, I chose to select one of the three positions Cole offered because it was the most persuasive to me.

At this point, I will digress a moment to share what I believe is a relevant, if not funny, story. Two youngsters were having an argument and the mother asked the father to help settle it. The father took each youngster aside and listened intently to each child's side of the story. In each case when the child was through explaining his position, the father said empathetically, "You're right!" Whereupon each child skipped off happily. Over hearing all this, the mother was exasperated and said, "You told both of those children that the were right! They can't both be right!" And he said, "You're right!"

Fortunately, our reviewers are not in a competition nor are they in disagreement. If we listen to each, without the other's positions in mind, we can say empathetically, "You're right!!" Schools and the children within them have the same basic needs but the blocks to achieving these needs vary dramatically from one community to the next and from one area of the country to the next.

Cole asked the question, are we, as a profession, doing too little or too much? This is, indeed, a dilemma that haunts the profession. I believe that the answer is, "Yes," on both counts. The question that needs to be answered is, what services can the counselor provide in his or her individual school that best further the goals of children in realizing their physical, social, emotional, educational, and career development potential? In the absence of a reasonable approximation of an answer to this question, we will no doubt continue to witness a diversity of counselor functions and criticisms for not doing more or in the right proportions.

We do know what significant others think and what they prefer. For example, I do not think that I have ever heard a single complaint about a counselor being too involved with teachers in the classroom. I have yet to hear that the counselor's help with a parenting group or substance abuse program was unnecessary. I cannot recall a single instance in which a student or parent thought the school counselor was providing too much career counseling or precollege planning assistance. I have tried to think of one occasion when a school principal objected to the counselor providing too much leadership for the counseling services.

I have heard of persons who held counseling positions doing too much of many things that we agree are not counseling functions. We have all heard the war stories of the counselors who offered bad advice or a seemingly unwarranted judgment of a student's future potential. Bad news dies hard. And it doesn't take much to keep it around.

Before we despair, I ask that you consider the other professions. Name one that goes unblemished! None is without its critics and none is without its challenges.

Let us choose to focus on what we know has been effective, what we know is well-received, and what we know needs to be done within the realm of counseling. With that as an orientation, let us proceed to additional implications for school counselor education.

Implications for Counselor Education

I wish to preface this section with a brief statement about the mission of our accreditation agency and its potential for significantly affecting school counselor preparation.

CACREP and its Mission

The Council for the Accreditation of Counseling and Related Educational Programs (CACREP) is a corporate affiliate of the American Association for

Counseling and Development (AACD). As such, it is the accrediting agency for the world's largest association for counseling. It has recognition from the Council on Postsecondary Accreditation (COPA). COPA is the official agency accepted by the higher education community for the purpose of regulating postsecondary accreditation. COPA's position is that accreditation serves the professions by:

1. Providing a means for the participation of practitioners in setting the requirements for preparation to enter the professions;
2. Contributing to the unity of the professions by bringing together practitioners, teachers, and students in an activity directed at improving professional preparation and professional practice.

To be accredited by CACREP includes the following:

1. The program is located in and supported by an educational institution accredited by one of six regional accrediting bodies recognized by COPA.
2. The institution staff has completed a thorough self-study and voluntarily applied for a verification of its programs as having met or exceeded national standards. This review process required months of preparation involving faculty, students, administrators, graduates, employers, clinical supervisors, and others who influence or are influenced by this program. The site visit team has conducted an indepth verification of the fact that standards have been met or exceeded.
3. The program was thoroughly reviewed by the Council and determined to have met or exceeded the Standards.

Implicit in the process of accreditation is not only the attainment of a goal or status but rather a commitment to the continual striving for excellence in the preparation of future practitioners. Sustaining the accreditation status becomes one goal of these programs. Regular program review, attention to measures of outcome, and external verification are among the hallmarks of CACREP accreditation.

The long-standing concern of AACD and its divisions (including American School Counselors Association (ASCA) and ACES as the original partners in the development of preparation standards) has been for high quality professional services to the public. By giving official sanction to this process, the associations encourage more institutions to follow the good example of the pioneers and benefit not only others, but the institutions themselves in their goal toward excellence.

For these reasons, I believe that we should affect school counselor preparation through accreditation at both the state and national levels. By using the CACREP core categories for preparation, I will share further observations based upon our reviewers' papers.

Core Areas of the CACREP Standards: Implications for the Future

The CACREP Council has adopted policies and practices that are important for us to know. First, aside from indicating that an institution must have a 2-year program with a minimum of 48 semester (72 quarter) hours, there is no reference to courses, per se. I mention this because the Council allows the institution to explain and identify where and when specific content is taught. This avoids the tendency to expect a separate course for every content area mentioned within the Standards.

Second, in keeping with COPA philosophy, the Council has been encouraging programs to articulate counselor competency objectives and to establish outcome measures of these through practicum, internship, and follow-up of graduates. The most recent revision of the Standards has been designed to facilitate this process for self-study and review. I believe that these are sound practices for all programs and will do much to improve counselor education in the future.

There are presently eight core areas in the Standards. Without great specificity, the following outline will illustrate how our reviewers' observations and recommendations can be imbedded within the existing Standards.

1. Human Development:
    a. Students (counselors-in-training) will be able to identify and use methods that foster:
        1. enjoyment of learning;
        2. positive self-reference; and
        3. internal locus of control orientation.
    b. Students will be able to assist others in the process of:
        1. setting appropriate learning goals for children including those with special needs;
        2. structuring time management;
        3. teaching relaxation and stress/distress management; and
        4. understanding learning styles and the application of this knowledge in designing learning experiences.

2. Helping Relations
    a. Students will be able to function effectively as consultants to others in:
        1. establishing a cooperative class/school environment;
        2. teaching methods of peer assistance activities;
        3. intervening with crisis management methods;
        4. networking with community agencies; and
        5. making effective referrals.

   b. Students will be able to provide short-term supportive counseling related to:
     1. helping manage family discord;
     2. dealing with unwanted pregnancy;
     3. dealing with feelings of depression; and
     4. confronting unhealthy behaviors such as substance abuse, eating disorders, etc.

3. Career Development
   a. Students will be able to help design and implement a comprehensive, developmental guidance curriculum that includes:
     1. career development modules infused within the general school curriculum;
     2. continuous and sequential career development activities designed to help young people conceptualize a career identity;
     3. educational exploration through precollege, apprenticeship, and related postsecondary educational opportunities including sources of financial aid; and
     4. placement and follow-up services to ensure effective adjustment of graduates.
   b. Students will be able to help others in the selection and use of career computer software and related technology for the purpose of furthering career development objectives and activities.

4. Appraisal
   a. Students will be able to apply their knowledge of both normal and abnormal human development through diagnosis by accurately identifying and taking appropriate action through crisis intervention and referral in cases of mental health issues requiring intensive or long-term care.
   b. Students will be able to assist young people to understand their educational and career potential through the interpretation of tests and inventories.

5. Group
   a. Students will demonstrate mastery of group methods for:
     1. classroom management, career guidance groups, democratic classroom meetings, and age-level-appropriate social problem solving; and
     2. structured teacher and parent study and consultation groups.
   b. Students will be able to establish leadership training for cooperative peer group activities.
   c. Students will be able to establish support groups and related group guidance based upon special needs of young people with similar learning impediments or talents.

6. Social/Cultural Foundations
   a. Students will be knowledgeable about and able to structure activities for others that promote empathy for minorities and their special needs.
   b. Students will be able to provide counseling services designed to promote minority participation and benefit for personal, educational, and career development.
   c. Students will be able to conduct needs assessments from which to design and implement guidance and counseling activities suited to differences in ethnicity, language, family circumstances, sex, etc.
7. Research
   a. Students will be able to design, implement, and effectively report the results of a comprehensive program evaluation.
   b. Students will be able to use computer-generated statistical packages to treat data and evaluate results.
   c. Students will be able to conduct literature searches, derive implications, and use these in the design of program activities.
8. Professional Orientation
   a. Students will be able to develop and effectively present a plan and budget for a comprehensive, developmental program including the philosophy, rationale, needs assessment and related data, goals, objectives, activities, timelines, and required resources.
   b. Students will have a thorough familiarity with the professional ethical code, state credentialing requirements, statutes pertaining to privileged communication, and related matters concerning client welfare.

Although these objectives are by no means exhaustive, I believe that they are representative of many of the activities that the research reviewers have reported to be important or shown to be effective in school counseling. By emphasizing them in the statement of standards, there is a much greater likelihood that they will more quickly and systemmatically be found in future counselor education curricula throughout the country.

Building on this as a method for more quickly and systemmatically affecting graduate education, I further suggest that advocates for better use of counselor services seek to incorporate similar changes in school administrator and teacher certification and preparation accreditation standards. So long as these groups remain unaware of the legitimate functions of the counselor, we are still talking to ourselves in a proverbial vacuum.

Conclusion

The implications of this conference should reach far beyond statements about research. To be effective, they must find their way into practice. They must be the foundation for new research. They must help shape the preparation of new counselors and the inservice of those already in practice. Counselor educators will need to be active participants for this to be possible. I wish to underscore an opinion shared by Krumboltz relative to the research findings on cooperative group learning. Because there are other instances where I believe that the same remarks are applicable, I wish to paraphrase them in a broader context.

There is still much research to be done. The evidence already available in several areas, however, is so promising that little harm and much good can be derived from starting sooner, rather than later, to encourage teacher and counselor use of the promising methods and techniques.

No less important, counselor educators will want to consider ways of providing inservice programs for practicing school counselors using the data and suggestions from this conference as a foundation. We should not be surprised that many of the counselors graduated in the 1960s and 1970s will welcome substantive programs addressing the issues and needs that they find in today's schools. Many counselor educators will find this a pleasant return to our roots.

Counselor educators also will do well to pursue educational administration faculty in order to present courses or modules on the professional role of the school counselor. We can hardly be justified in critizing school counselors for accepting quasi-administrative functions when research has indicated that administrators receive little preservice preparation in this area.

Finally, we counselor educators have been partners in leadership with school counselors on many important issues in the past. We need to mobilize that potential again in order to create legislation establishing the professional role of school counselors such as Cole reports exists in Virginia. Imperfect as such legislation can be, our licensure laws already are demonstrating that it enhances the respect we require.

If properly managed, I believe that our licensure laws, national certification, and accreditation can be used to help forge new and stronger respect for the professional role of the school counselor. This will require that all counselors, regardless of setting, rally to this cause. I believe that this conference and the wide distribution of its results can provide the rationale and impetus for this movement.

References

Capuzzi, D. (1988). Personal and social competency: Developing skills for the future. In G.R. Walz (Ed.), *Research and counseling: Building strong school counseling programs*. Alexandria, VA: American Association for Counseling and Development.

Cole, C.G. (1988). The school counselor: Image and impact, counselor role and function, 1960s to 1980s and beyond. In G.R. Walz (Ed.), *Research and Counseling: Building strong school counseling programs*. Alexandria, VA: American Association for Counseling and Development.

Commission on Precollege Guidance and Counseling (1986). *Keeping the options open.* College Entrance Examination Board, New York: Author.

Herr, E.L. (1984). The national reports on reform in schooling: Some missing ingredients. *Journal of Counseling & Development, 63,* 217–220.

Hohenshil, T.H. (1987). The educational reform movement: What does it mean for counseling? *Journal of Counseling & Development, 66,* 57–58.

Hollis, J.W., & Wantz, R.A. (1986). *Counselor preparation 1986–89.* Muncie, IN: Accelerated Development.

Hosie, T.W. (1986). A content analysis of counselor education and supervision: The formative years. *Counselor Education & Supervision, 25,* 271–283.

Krumboltz, J.D. (1988). The key to achievement: Learning to love learning. In G.R. Walz (Ed.), *Research and counseling: Building strong school counseling programs.* Alexandria, VA: American Association for Counseling and Development.

Naisbitt, J. (1984). *Megatrends.* New York: Warner.

National College Counseling Project (1986). *Frontiers of possibility.* Burlington, VT: National Association of College Admissions Counselors.

Is "School Counseling Research" an Oxymoron?

Larry C. Loesch

Professor and Graduate Coordinator, Counselor Education
University of Florida, Gainesville, Florida

The history of the school counseling profession is testimony to the magnan-
imous, diverse, and extensive efforts school counselors have made in attempting
to help children lead happier, more productive, healthier, and fuller lives. The
four primary papers in this monograph attest to this contention. Cole (1988) has
summarized effectively both the length and scope of these efforts. Capuzzi (1988)
has elaborated successfully on some of the major problems with which school
counselors have helped children cope. Gysbers (1988) has elucidated the school
counseling profession's ongoing focus on helping children become productive,
and therefore self-sufficient and contributing members of society. Krumboltz
(1988) has provided a cogent example of the potentially far-reaching effects of
school counseling. Thus, there is no doubt that the school counseling profession
strives toward noble and lofty goals and that its members have invested untold
effort towards those goals. However, one major and nagging question remains:
Is there *evidence* that the school counseling profession's efforts have been, are,
or will be successful?

In keeping with the approach of the ERIC-CAPS/AACD "20/20" conference,
this important question can be addressed from two perspectives. The first is
historic; how successful has the school counseling profession been in providing
evidence that its efforts have been (and therefore presumably are) effective? The
second is futuristic; can or will it be established that those efforts are effective?
Before responding to the major question from each of these two perspectives,
it should be noted that "evidence" is used here in a literal sense to mean *empirical*
results from properly conducted research investigations. Certainly there is a
multitude of testimonials to the "good things" that have been done in the school
counseling profession. However, if school counseling truly is a profession (and

I believe that it is), then testimonials are not sufficient "proof" of effectiveness. Rather, effectiveness must be determined on the basis of *empirical* evidence.

> *History is a nightmare from which we are trying to awaken*—James Joyce

The sad fact of the matter is that there exists a relative dearth of research specific to the school counseling profession, and most research that exists in not very good. Compared to other professions, school counseling has very little empirical data to show that its activities are helpful and successful. Apparently, research has not been valued, emphasized, or endorsed as an important role function for school counselors. There are several bases for this conclusion. First, even casual perusal of back issues of the two professional journals directly pertinent to the school counseling profession (i.e., *The School Counselor* and *Elementary School Guidance & Counseling*) reveals that (empirical) research articles constitute a small, perhaps insignificant, portion of the articles published in those journals. Moreover, even those published are often relegated to "special" sections of the journals, thus furthering the perspective that research activities are outside the "mainstream" of school counseling activities. Editorial decision-making policies (rightfully) reflect the interests of the readership. Therefore, it is logical to conclude that most school counselors do not have demonstrated interest in (i.e., value) research articles and activities.

A second basis for the conclusion can be derived from examining the nature of professional preparation practices for school counselors. For example, Schaeffer and Atkinson (1983) obtained information from 189 school counselor preparation programs and found that only a mean of 4.9% of the required credit hours in those programs was in the area of "scientific research." Similarly, Ibrahim and Thompson (1982) investigated training practices for secondary school counselors and concluded that they receive a disproportionately low amount of training in research methods and applications. Ibrahim and Thompson also found that research courses were taken as electives relatively infrequently by school counselor trainees. And, in an all too telling study, Hosie and Mackey (1985) surveyed school counselor preparation programs to determine differences in preparation activities and courses for elementary and secondary school counselors and *didn't even inquire about preparation in research*! This lack of emphasis on research in school counselor preparation programs persists despite numerous pleas in the professional literature for improved research skills among school counselors (e.g., Pine, 1981; Remer, 1981; Sprinthall, 1981). It also persists despite the fact that school counselor preparation program accrediting agencies, such as the Council for the Accreditation of Counseling and Related Educational Programs, identify "research" as a "core curriculum" preparation area and give evaluation of its instructional effectiveness equal prominence with areas such as counseling theories and practice, career development, and group counseling in their accreditation decision-making processes.

State-level school counselor certification, as distinguished from school counselor preparation program requirements, provides a third basis for the conclusion. Only a very, very few of the sets of state-level certification or recertification requirements include preparation in research.

Finally, a fourth basis can be derived from role-and-function statements produced by professional organizations. Although most school counseling role-and-function statements include allusions to a research function, sometimes under the guise of an "accountability" component, the attention given to research is at best minimal. For example, the 1981 American School Counselor Association (ASCA) statement entitled *The Practice of Guidance and Counseling by School Counselors* contains only one statement about research activity by school counselors. "[(In part) the school counselor's responsibility to the profession] fosters the development and improvement of the profession by *assisting* with appropriate research and participating in professional association activities at the local, state, and national levels" [emphasis added] (ASCA, 1981, p. 12). If research is an important activity for school counselors, why is it that only "assisting with," as opposed to taking the lead in conducting research is advocated? If research is important, why are research and professional organization involvement couched within the same sentence? Other professional statements contain similarly obtuse references to research activities by school counselors (cf., ASCA, *The Role of the School Counselor in Career Guidance: Expectations and Responsibilities*, 1984). Clearly, professional organizations have done little to foster a research orientation among school counselors. Commenting on the nature of accountability activities by school counselors, Lombana (1985) wrote that "for too long, counselor functions that do not fit into a direct counselor-client scheme have been denigrated" (p. 341). This poignant statement seems equally applicable to the research function in school counseling.

If research is not valued, emphasized, or endorsed by school counselors but there *is* research in school counseling, from where does the research come? Apparently it comes from counselor educators interested in the school counseling profession. Again, perusal of back issues of *The School Counselor* and *Elementary School Guidance & Counseling*, as well as other pertinent journals such as the *Journal of Counseling and Development, Measurement and Evaluation in Counseling and Development*, the *Career Development Quarterly*, and *Counselor Education and Supervision*, reveals that the vast majority of research articles having anything at all to do with school counseling have been contributed by counselor educators. Obviously, incentive and motivational factors are in operation. Counselor educators are at least encouraged, and more frequently required, to "make research contributions to the professional literature" in order to enhance their opportunities for professional advancement (e.g., academic promotion and tenure). Conversely, there is little or no reward for practicing school counselors to engage in research or publish research results. Research activities by school counselors are rarely rewarded/reinforced by local school systems and also are not required for recertification by state departments of education. Moreover, research activities are not strongly endorsed by professional organizations, so school counselors engaging in them can't even derive a sense of professional fulfillment from conducting research. To borrow a bastardization of the English language often used in the field of economics, an "effective system of disincentives has been established" for research by school counselors!

One of the implications of the decided imbalance in research activities among counselor educators and practicing school counselors relates to the respective proportions of "basic" and "applied" research in the school counseling profession. In *very* general terms, "basic" research involves investigations of theoretical propositions whereas "applied" research involves investigations of effects of activities. Because of their theoretical orientations as well as their professional employment situations, counselor educators *tend* to do "basic" research. Conversely, those practicing school counselors who do research *tend* to do "applied" research. Taking liberties with generalizations, school counselors tend to try to find out *if* something works whereas counselor educators try to find out *why* or *how* something works. Therefore, to the extent that these generalizations are true, the majority of published research in school counseling should be "basic" research. Given the many authorities bemoaning the lack of "applied" research by school counseling practitioners (e.g., Anderson & Heppner, 1986; Goldman, 1978; Pine, 1981), it seems that such is the case.

The "conclusion" that the majority of research in school counseling is "basic," as opposed to "applied," in turn leads to several other "conclusions." First, the extant research in school counseling has done little to influence or provide direction for propositions about what should be the nature of the school counseling profession. For example, current school counselor role-and-function statements have been derived from (albeit well-intentioned) "think-tanks" of professionals rather than from empirical bases. However, just because it is proffered that something "should" be done, it does not necessarily follow that the something is *needed* to be done, that it *can* be done, or that it will be done *effectively*. Second, school counseling research has failed to influence significantly the nature of professional preparation programs for school counselors. There is scant research on what school counselors actually do in their day-to-day activities and there is even less on what "significant others" (e.g., students, parents, teachers, administrators, and policymakers) in the lives of school counselors want and need school counselors to do. How then can fully appropriate school counseling preparation programs be developed? Finally, school counseling research has failed to demonstrate, to any significant extent, that school counseling activities are effective and successful. The professional school counseling literature is replete with descriptions of the many things school counselors do, but is almost devoid of evidence that those activities make *identifiable* and *demonstratable* differences in peoples' lives. Is it any wonder then that many professionals have warned of pending doom for the school counseling profession?

> *We have to live today by what truth we can get today and*
> *be ready tomorrow to call it falsehood*—William James

In commenting on previous research in the school counseling profession, it is appropriate to examine not only the amount but also the nature of that research. Unfortunately, here again there is mostly "bad news." Indeed, a considerable number of criticisms have been leveled at research in the school counseling profession.

Goldman (1976) wrote that adherence to strict research paradigms was one of the reasons that (school) counseling research "has, on the whole, been of little value as a base or guide for practitioners" (p. 543). Mehrens (1978) agreed with Goldman's conclusion, but countered that *lack* of adherence to proven research paradigms was the basis for it. Thus school counseling research has been criticized for being both "too rigorous" and "too lax" in methodologies used. Both of these criticisms are appropriate. Some research in school counseling is so "tightly" controlled that the results are meaningless outside of very strictly defined limits whereas other research is so "loosely" controlled that attributions of causation are impossible.

The breadth of topics researched in the school counseling profession also has been the subject of criticism (e.g., Goldman, 1978). All too often, school counseling research studies have been restricted to specific procedures, provided by school counselors having specific skills, applied to specific groups of students, in specific settings, having specific characteristics, and so forth. In other words, many research studies in the school counseling profession are limited at best, and fully lacking in generalizability at worst (Anderson & Heppner, 1986; Minor, 1981).

A third, and closely related to the second, criticism of school counseling research is the definitive lack of program evaluation studies. Lombana (1985) wrote that:

> It is no secret that school counselors have resisted efforts to systematically plan, implement, and evaluate their guidance programs. In the past several years, numerous authors . . . have decried counselors' aversion to program accountability and stressed the need for change, lest guidance programs face extinction. (p. 340)

With few exceptions, such as the career development program evaluation studies cited by Gysbers (1988), the "portents of doom" apparently have gone unheeded because reports of program evaluation studies are rarely found in the school counseling literature.

In 1981, The April, May, and June issues of the *Personnel and Guidance Journal* were devoted (almost) exclusively to research in the counseling profession. The 27 articles related to research included in those issues described an incredibly wide variety of research approaches applicable in the counseling profession. Furthermore, numerous examples, as well as reference citations for additional examples, were couched within the research methodologies described. Unfortunately, the truly amazing aspect of this comprehensive coverage of research in counseling was that very few of the examples were from the school counseling profession. This situation exemplifies yet another criticism of school counseling research; specifically, that it tends to rely too heavily upon a few "traditional" research approaches and ignores many "innovative" but potentially fruitful research methodologies.

Another appropriate criticism of school counseling research is the almost total lack of replication of findings. The school counseling profession has apparently adopted the perspective that if a research finding is published, it must be "true" and it must "remain true." One of the fundamental characteristics of "good" research is that it is replicable (Kerlinger, 1986). That is, in order for the results of a research study to be considered as "scientific truth" (or "fact"), essentially the same results must be found each time the study's research methodology is replicated. Unfortunately, the "truths" of the school counseling profession emanating from its research have rarely been subjected to the test of replication.

Want to engage in an exercise in futility? Search the school counseling research literature for reports of school counselor activities that didn't work (i.e., didn't produce the desired results). Common sense, as well as principles of learning, suggest that school counselors can learn just as much from reports of what "doesn't work" as they can from reports of what does (vis-a-vis learning what *not* to do). Nonetheless, the school counseling profession maintains its passionate love affair with the asterisk (used to signify "statistically significant" results), and thus continues to use inappropriate or ineffective activities through sheer lack of shared knowledge. Therefore, the school counseling profession can be criticized legitimately for failing to validate fully even those few research bases upon which it is founded.

Finally, the school counseling profession can be criticized for its failure to manifest the potential benefits of the use of computers for research purposes. The benefits derived from incorporation of computer technology into the work of school counselors have been lauded by numerous authors as well as by professional organizations. For example, in 1983 ASCA published a monograph entitled *Microcomputers and the School Counselor* (Johnson, 1983). The contributors to that monograph identified numerous ways computers were being (and could be) used by school counselors. However, the use of computers for research purposes was not among them. Similarly, reports of school counselors using computers for research purposes (other than for data analyses) are almost non-existent in the school counseling literature. It seems that school counselors have systematically ignored a potentially powerful research tool. In so doing, the school counseling profession has both limited and hindered its research efforts.

The preceding discussion has focused on criticisms of research approaches and methodologies in the school counseling profession because those criticisms transcend various topics in the profession. However, the discussion should not be construed to be a "blanket condemnation" of school counseling research. Although it is true that the general criticisms can be applied to all topics researched in school counseling, it also is true that much has been learned or "proven" from school counseling research. For example, it has been reasonably well established that school counselors can help improve students' self-concepts, reduce students' discipline problems in school, facilitate students' development of effective (life skills) coping behaviors, foster better relationships among students and their families, improve students' interracial relationships, enable students to avoid or cope with personal stressors and problems (Capuzzi, 1988; Cole, 1988), increase students' career maturity, improve students' career decision-making processes, facilitate students' development of effective life styles (Gysbers, 1988), and become better, more active, and self-motivated learners (Krumboltz, 1988). Thus, although the scales of professional opinion remain heavily weighted toward the negative side of school counseling research, there is weight on the positive side. The challenge ahead is to compel a radical shift in the balance.

> *The farther backward you can look, the farther forward*
> *you are likely to see*—Winston Churchill

Pine (1981) eloquently described the importance of research in the school counseling profession:

> While it has always been assumed that counseling research and practice should be intimately tied together, research and practice seem to have become alienated from each other. School counselors seldom conduct research and often question the relevance and importance of research. In the face of the questions, demands, and problems challenging counseling and guidance, the profession can no longer afford a separation between research and practice. Indeed, it never could! The reintegration of research and practice is essential if any genuine progress is to be achieved in addressing pressing and important issues in school counseling. (p. 495)

Pine addressed the need for research in school counseling from the perspective of self-preservation of the school counseling profession. That need also is imperative from another perspective. A solid empirical research base is one of the hallmarks of a true profession. If school counseling is to assume a position of full respect and recognition among professions, it must establish its empirical bases.

To achieve the (re)integration of research and practice that Pine described, the school counseling profession must take several decisive actions. First, it must "legitimize" research as an appropriate, needed, and important role function for school counselors. Professional organizations, such as ASCA, are in a primary position to spearhead this action. For example, research functions should be incorporated into school counselor role-and-function statements. This would emphasize to school counselors that research is not an adjunct professional activity, but rather an integral part of professional functioning. Professional organizations also should encrourage and reward school counseling research dissemination in professional journals and at professional meetings. And finally, professional organizations should exemplify the incorporation and use of research data in their decision-making processes.

A second action that must be taken is that more and better attention must be paid to research skills training in school counseling preparation programs. Accreditation standards for school counseling preparation programs already stipulate the need for training in research. School counselors and their professional organizations should support and demand effective implementation of those research preparation standards. It is likely that such action would call for new research training emphases and methods in those programs. Fortunately, some innovative methods for teaching research skills have been proposed already (e.g., Barkley, 1982; Heppner, Gelso, & Dolliver, 1987). Those methods need to be tried and carefully evaluated; others need to be developed and tested.

A third action that must be taken is for current school counseling practitioners to become more involved in the conduct and dissemination of research. There are several components to this action. First, many current school counselor practitioners should be afforded opportunity for (re)training in research approaches and methods. Again, school counseling professional organizations are well suited to provide leadership for such activities. Unstructured or semistructured research learning activities, such as the collaborative action research plan described by Pine (1981), also are well-suited training methods for practitioners. Second, school counseling practitioners must be encouraged and rewarded for professional publication and presentation of research activities. Professional organizations should spur such activities by inviting research to be conducted and by providing support and encouragement for the research. Third, school counseling practitioners should be encouraged, again primarily by professional organizations, to replicate previous research. This approach not only would serve to provide a reasonably safe, guided way for practitioners to "get into" research, but also would help to establish the credence of existing research.

School counseling practitioners also should explore and use a greater variety of research approaches. This fourth step is particularly needed to stimulate interest in research activities among practitioners. All too often school counselors have adopted the perspective that there are just a few "right" ways to do research. In point of fact, there are many, many different, but valid and effective, research approaches and methods. School counseling practitioners must seek out those methodologies that are appropriate to their respective individual needs, professional interests, and personal characteristics and abilities. If school counselors can come to understand that research methodologies should be fitted to their circumstances rather then their having to "fit" or adapt to research methodologies, research should become less disdainful, and more personal, interesting, pleasant, and satisfying for them.

The final action that needs to be taken is that school counseling practitioners need to be encouraged, by professional organizations and by their colleagues, to focus upon "applied" research. Berdie (1972) referred to (school) counselors as "applied behavior scientists," a phrase that aptly describes the school counselor's work. If school counselors are primarily involved in *applications* of principles of human behavior, why should they engage, to any substantial extent, in research activities inconsistent with their primary activities?

These suggestions are large and comprehensive, and their general discussions belie the many intricacies and difficulties in their implementation. However, if they were to be implemented, the school counseling profession would be well served and far better off for the effort expended.

> *Long-range planning does not deal with future decisions,*
> *but with the future of present decisions*—Peter Drucker

Assuming the nature of school counseling research can be changed as has been suggested, the next important question is what topics should be researched? The four articles to which this article is in part a response provide the best answer to this important question.

Cole (1988) and Capuzzi (1988) have fulfilled effectively the unenviable task of attempting to project important trends and needed activities in the school counseling profession in the next 20 years. Their responses were by necessity comprehensive because that is the nature of the school counseling profession. Therefore, any attempt to project school counseling research needs also must necessarily be comprehensive. Indeed, all the questions raised by Cole and all the trends identified by Capuzzi need to "researched" in order to determine valid answers. However, a few merit additional comment. For example, family counseling activities are becoming prominent among school counselors yet very little is known about the effectiveness of family counseling processes and techniques. Similarly, school counselors' roles as consultants to teachers, parents, and others seem to be increasing rapidly, but their effectiveness in these roles remains largely unknown. School counselors also seem likely to increase their developmental/preventative guidance activities. Longitudinal research is needed to determine if those activities are successful. Finally, it is likely that school counselors will continue to focus many of their efforts on students with "special" or "unique" characteristics (e.g., pregnant teenagers, gifted students, or students with learning difficulties). Such students require special and unique school counseling interventions. The effectiveness of those interventions must be determined so that service provision can be maximized and "wasted time" can be minimized.

Gysbers's (1988) task was different from that of Cole and Capuzzi in the sense that the topic addressed was, in some senses, narrower in scope. It also was different because most of the school counseling research has been done in the area of career development and counseling. That's the "good news." The "bad news" is that it is often more difficult to synthesize somewhat disparate research findings than it is to synthesize professional opinions. Fortunately, he was successful in his efforts. Again, only two of the general trends he addressed can be commented upon, and then in only equally general terms. First, each of the multitude of tools, techniques, resources, and programs available to school counselors for career development and counseling need to be carefully evaluated (i.e., "researched" in terms of effectiveness). The task at hand is nothing short of monumental, yet it needs to be accomplished lest students at best not be helped and at worst be harmed by use of inappropriate or invalid methods and resources. Second, the conceptualization of career development as a lifelong process and the attendant implications for the nature and scope of career counseling and education activities emphasize the need for *both* short-term and longitudinal evaluations of the effects of those activities. Short-term effects are often of immediate concern to students (and to their parents), and therefore deserve research attention. However, adherence to a developmental perspective requires that long-term effects also be investigated.

Krumboltz's (1988) article represents a "back-to-basics" perspective and in it he effectively discusses a concept that has been "lost" in the school counseling profession. The school counseling profession has long promulgated the position that its primary goal is to help students become better people. However, the primary goal of schools is to help students learn information and skills. Therefore, because school counselors work in (or with) schools, it would seem that *the* primary goal of school counseling should be to help students become better learners. This is an important perspective, but one not frequently found in the school counseling literature. The significance of that state of affairs here is that it reflects a typically neglected, but tremendously needed, area of research in school counseling. That is, if school counseling is to continue to exist as it apparently desires to, the profession must be able to demonstrate that it helps all types of students become better *learners*. Accountability in terms of being able to show that school counseling helps students become better learners is the type that has the greatest potential to be well received by parents, administrators, and others who have significant influence on the future of the school counseling profession.

Finally, within the context of conducting research on the many important topics in school counseling, the profession must focus on human characteristics indicators that are readily interpreted. That is, although it is valuable to establish that school counselors can influence positively, for example, students' "self-concepts," "attitudes toward school,'" or "career maturity," the value is restricted to those who are in consensus with the respective researchers about the *operational* definitions of those constructs. Unfortunately, such consensus is rarely achieved. A far better tactic would be for school counseling researchers to concentrate upon the behavioral manifestations of abstract constructs. For example, if a school counselor's intervention truly improves a student's "locus of control," the student's *behavior* should change in *observable* ways. A focus on readily observable, behavior-change outcomes is the best way to demonstrate that school counseling activities do indeed make differences in students' lives.

About the Title of This Article. . .

An "oxymoron" is a figure of speech in which incongruous or contradictory terms are combined (e.g., "a deafening silence"). Are "school counseling" and "research" incongruous or contradictory? The answer is a "definite maybe" (another oxymoron). Historically, school counseling and research certainly have not been fully integrated and combined, but they also have not been distinctly separate. This indefinite state of affairs is both undesirable in and unhealthy for the school counseling profession. Thus the profession is rapidly approaching a major choice-point. It must either embrace research as an integrated aspect of its existence or find a way to exist as a "profession" even though it lacks a strong empirical basis.

References

Anderson, W.P., & Heppner, P.P. (1986). Counselor applications of research findings to practice: Learning to stay current. *Journal of Counseling and Development, 65*, 152–155.

American School Counselor Association. (1981). ASCA role statement: The practice of guidance and counseling by school counselors. *The School Counselor, 29*, 7–12.

American School Counselor Association. (1984). *ASCA role statement: The school counselor in career guidance: Expectations and responsibilities*. Alexandria, VA: Author.

Barkley, W.M. (1982). Introducing research to graduate students in the helping professions. *Counselor Education and Supervision, 21*, 327–331.

Berdie, R.F. (1972). The 1980 counselor: Applied behavior scientist. *Personnel and Guidance Journal, 50*, 451–456.

Capuzzi, D. (1988). Personal and social competency: Developing skills for the future. In G.R. Walz (Ed.), *Research and counseling: Building strong school counseling programs*. Alexandria, VA: American Association for Counseling and Development.

Cole, C.G. (1988). The school counselor: Image and impact, counselor role and function, 1960s to 1980s and beyond. In G.R. Walz (Ed.), *Research and counseling: Building strong school counseling programs*. Alexandria, VA: American Association for Counseling and Development.

Goldman, L. (1976). A revolution in counseling research. *Journal of Counseling Psychology, 23*, 543–552.

Goldman, L. (1978). *Research methods for counselors: Practical approaches in field settings*. New York: Wiley.

Gysbers, N.C. (1988). Career guidance: A professional heritage and future challenge. In G.R. Walz (Ed.), *Research and counseling: Building strong school counseling programs*. Alexandria, VA: American Association for Counseling and Development.

Heppner, P.P., Gelso, C.J., & Dolliver, R.H. (1987). Three approaches to research training in counseling. *Journal of Counseling and Development, 66*, 45–49.

Hosie, T.W., & Mackey, J.A. (1985). Elementary and secondary school counselor preparation programs: How different are they? *Counselor Education and Supervision, 24*, 283–290.

Ibrahim, F.A., & Thompson, D.L. (1982). Preparation of secondary school counselors: A national survey. *Counselor Education and Supervision, 22*, 113–122.

Johnson, C. (Ed.). (1983). *Microcomputers and the school counselor*. Alexandria, VA: American School Counselor Association.

Kerlinger, F.N. (1986). *Foundations of educational research*. New York: Holt, Rinehart & Winston.

Krumboltz, J.D. (1988). The key to achievement: Learning to love learning. In G.R. Walz (Ed.), *Research and counseling: Building strong school counseling programs*. Alexandria, VA: American Association for Counseling and Development.

Lombana, J. (1985). Guidance accountability: A new look at an old problem. *The School Counselor, 32*, 340–346.

Mehrens, W.A. (1978). Rigor and reality in counseling research. *Measurement and Evaluation in Guidance, 11*, 8–13.

Minor, B.J. (1981). Bridging the gap between research and practice: Introduction. *Personnel and Guidance Journal, 59*, 485–486.

Pine, G.J. (1981). Collaborative action research in school counseling: The integration of research and practice. *Personnel and Guidance Journal, 59*, 495–501.

Remer, R. (1981). The counselor and research: Introduction. *Personnel and Guidance Journal, 59*, 567–572.

Schaeffer, J.L., & Atkinson, D.R. (1983). Counselor education courses in program evaluation and scientific research: Are counselors really being prepared for the accountability press? *Counselor Education and Supervision, 23*, 29–34.

Sprinthall, N.A. (1981). A new model for research in the service of guidance and counseling. *Personnel and Guidance Journal, 59*, 487–494.

Future Directions for Elementary/Middle School Counseling

Patricia A. Ferris

Coordinator of Guidance and Counseling
Center School District, Kansas City, Missouri

The future directions for elementary and middle school counseling can be considered from many vantage points. One view is dependent upon the meaning of the term future. Although it is not known what will happen in the future, the meaning given to the term "future" could make a difference in the direction of school counseling. Several definitions of the future are found in the literature. Inbody (1984) reviewed various concepts of the future and school counseling. In particular he reviewed several ways to think about the future. First, the "probable future" is what will likely be if we take no action to attempt to shape the future. Second, the "possible future" is what may be if one considers the alternatives. Third, the "plausible future" is what may be expected, if a systems theory approach is used. Finally the "perferable future" is considered by some as the ultimate future. It is from the vantage point of the "preferable future"— proposing desirable images—that this paper approaches the topic—future directions for elementary and middle school counseling.

Although the major focus of the 20/20 Conference: Building Strong School Counseling Programs is to project the future based on the reviews of research, there are some recent events, trends if you will, that would seem to influence the images to be proposed. First, there is evidence that an increase in the number of school counselors at the elementary and middle school levels can be expected in the next few years. A number of states have approved legislation that provides ratio requirements for elementary school counselors. In some cases these may include middle school levels. Several other states have legislation pending that would require elementary school counselors. This legislation and a general acceptance of the importance of elementary and middle school counselors will likely increase the number of counselors in relation to the number of students served. Images of the future based on lower ratios will give opportunity to provide adequate and complete programs. The way the programs are envisioned will be an important element of the future. Adequate and complete programs will require ratios to reflect the needs of the students served and the specific objectives to be met in the counseling program.

Second, some state departments of education are reviewing certification standards for school counselors at all levels. The intent of the review is the enhancement of the requirements. In response, counselor education programs and professional development activities will reflect the changes that are generated. The increased number of school counselors at these levels and the change in standards have created a need for careful attention to school counselors' education, certification, and professional development. The manner in which these changes are envisioned will have an important impact upon the future programs provided by elementary and middle school counselors. Education and professional development programs need to assist counselors to have the skill and knowledge for the implementation of the future school counseling programs.

Third, it is known that the number of students available for college is lower than in recent years. Even though there is a high number of minorities, a lower percentage of minorities is entering college. Many rural youths, in some cases from failing family farms, are not seeking college enrollments. Consequently, there is a national effort to provide precollege guidance to students during middle school years. The Commission on Precollege Guidance and Counseling (1986) report, *Keeping the Options Open*, and the National College Counseling Project (1986) report, *Frontiers of Possibility*, make recommendations for school counseling programs to include precollege counseling at the seventh grade. The National Institute of Independent Colleges and Universities (1986) developed a video program and parent booklets to assist school counselors in providing meetings for parents to begin planning during their child's seventh-grade year for their child to go to college. Based upon this information, it is evident that school counseling programs need to develop a strong curriculum for students to learn to plan for the future. In particular early planning is needed to help students become aware of college possibilities.

The future school counseling programs provided by elementary and middle school counselors will be influenced by these trends and by the background of the student population and the local school setting. As a backdrop against which the future programs will be envisioned, consider this brief description of the student population and the educational structure.

Recently, Hodgkinson (1985) reported the demographics of education and suggested that educators must consider educational programs from the vantage point of the students who will populate the schools. The number of students is expected to remain low; however, an increase is expected in the number of students from minority backgrounds. The family status of students in the year 2001 was described as follows: only 41 of every 100 sutdents born in 1983 will have reached age 18 with the original family intact. The percentage of teen suicides, teen homicides, teen arrests, teen drug/alcohol use, and teen pregnancies has steadily increased since 1960.

It was suggested that our schools will have more students at risk as a result of the high number of babies born to teenage mothers. Children born to teenage mothers are often susceptible to poor health and learning problems and may continue to live in a single-parent family. Children of single parents are more likely to live in poverty and be of "latchkey" status. In addition, with the educational excellence movement, graduation standards have been raised without sufficient funds to provide support for the less able students. It is conceivable that this will mean a higher number of dropouts. If the projections regarding the student population are correct, school counselors will be needed to provide programs to attempt to prevent what could happen in our schools as a result of the life circumstances of the students. The school counseling programs envisioned must consider the needs of the population in the 1990s and beyond.

Themes for Future Directions

Several themes were noted in the four research reviews that would seem to suggest the future directions of elementary and middle school counseling. Some of these themes represent practices or ideas that are not really new. In fact they may be in operation in some schools now. The themes for elementary and middle school counseling programs are:

1. To expand the school counseling program to include the facilitation of the positive mental health of the significant adults involved in the child's education.
2. To expand the consulting role to promote the use of techniques that promote a safe, secure, positive learning environment.
3. To establish and manage a comprehensive school counseling program.
4. To establish specific delimited student competencies for which school counselors will assume responsibility.
5. To utilize group methods and techniques for counseling and classroom activities.
6. To enhance leadership skills to develop with other staff members cooperative programs that provide guidance-oriented activities as a part of the regular school curriculum.
7. To use technological advancements to assist in the management of the program and in the delivery of services to students.
8. To secure and maintain current information concerning societal trends, status of students, and community situations for program planning.

9. To develop programs and activities that will specifically provide greater understanding of the multicultural population and the variety of family structures.

Each of the four reviews provided information that was used as a basis for each of these trends. All four papers provided substantial information to draw upon. The trends and the position suggested by each of the reviewers are as follows:

1. *To expand the school counseling program to include the facilitation of the positive mental health of the significant adults in the child's education.* School counselors have been identified by the reviewers as providing activities that could be viewed as facilitating the mental health of significant adults in the learning environment. Stress management for both students and teachers as discussed by Dr. Capuzzi suggests that school counselors can provide assistance to staff members who are experiencing stress. Dr. Krumboltz's recommendations for consulting are to encourage giving choices, setting appropriate performance standards, structuring better ways to manage time, and accepting credit for student accomplishments. When carried out, these recommendations will contribute to the positive mental health of all individuals in the school. The review by Dr. Cole listed a trend toward working with the family of students experiencing difficulty. Through parent education, counseling groups, and family counseling, the counselor assists parents to gain knowledge about child development, to enhance communication, and, with single parents and step parents, to resolve issues related to their special family structure. Dr. Gysbers briefly alluded to the use of consultation with administrators, staff, and parents. All of these approaches are ways to affect the mental health of both students and adults.

2. *To expand the consulting role to promote the use of techniques that encourage a safe, secure, positive learning environment.* As reviewed by Dr. Cole, the consulting role of the school counselor has been an important aspect of school counseling programs since the 1960s and 1970s. However, the review of the research by Dr. Krumboltz has revealed some specific ways in which the school counselor can consult with the teacher to enhance learning. To help build the feeling of being valued and important, Dr. Krumboltz recommends encouraging teachers to give choices, set appropriate performance standards, structure better ways to manage time, and accept credit for student accomplishments. He further suggests that the counselor can encourage teachers to build teamwork and cooperation through the use of teams in class and peer tutoring. Dr. Capuzzi discusses the impact of school environment on self-esteem and recommends that teachers need to maintain a positive view of students. There is a relationship between the positive view of students by teachers and the positive view students have of self. Although Dr. Gysbers does not specifically refer to the type or content of the consultation, he does include consultation as a method of working with the other members of the guidance team.

3. *To establish and manage a comprehensive school counseling program.* Dr. Gysbers presented a structured and highly organized K–12 guidance program that uses a broad definition of career development. The comprehensive K–12 program is a significant contribution in the development of elementary and middle school guidance programs. Perhaps it is this more organized model that will resolve the dilemma, discussed by Dr. Cole, concerning the confusion of the counselor's role. The organized and specific program proposed by Dr. Gysbers could make a clear statement about the role of the school counselor. The recommendations of Dr. Krumboltz for students to accept responsibility, take tests wisely, and adapt to their individual learning style, and of Dr. Capuzzi to work to prevent blocks to personal and social competency and to resolve the blocks when they develop are examples of the activities to be included in the comprehensive K–12 model.

4. *To establish specific student competencies for which school counselors will assume responsibility.* As discussed by Dr. Cole, much of what the school counselor does is based upon student needs within the larger framework of societal needs and community situations. Although it may be important to some extent for the school counselor to respond to whatever these demands seem to be, it could lead to the confusion of role and functions of the school counselor. Dr. Gysbers proposes that even though counselors are sensitive to the times, a lasting program must have continuity and stability of purpose. The establishment of a set of student competencies for which the school counselor would assume responsibility would allow the counselors to be more direct and accountable. In the opinion of this writer, the competencies for which the counselor is responsible need to be basic skills that are essential to meeting life's experiences. During the elementary and middle school years students need to develop an awareness of self and others and have an adequate view of self; to gain knowledge about age-appropriate life roles; to develop effective communication skills and establish age-appropriate interpersonal relationships; and to learn problem-solving, planning, and decision-making skills. The focus of these skills is to prepare students to enter high school and continue through life with success. Dr. Krumboltz encourages competencies in relation to learning that would cause children to accept responsibility for their outcomes, take tests wisely, and adapt to their own individual learning style. As Dr. Cole points out, delimiting the counselor's role will allow the counselor to perform in a more accountable manner. The identification of competencies to be achieved within the framework of the comprehensive guidance program will provide direction and specification for the school counselor's role.

Dr. Capuzzi's material on personal and social competency provides a wide range of problem areas that needs remedial counseling services. In many cases, early preventive activities could avoid the problems. These problem areas, along with those discussed by Dr. Cole, need the attention of the school counselor as a part of the overall plan to serve all students in the comprehensive K–12 guidance program. Gaining skill and knowledge to be professionally competent to counsel with students experiencing the problems discussed by Dr. Capuzzi is essential.

5. *Utilize group methods and techniques for counseling and classroom activity.* Dr. Krumboltz identified the importance of group work with students for counseling as well as learning in teams. Dr. Gysbers makes reference to group counseling and suggests that classroom activities be carried out as a part of the guidance curriculum that assists students to learn appropriate knowledge and skills. As reported by Dr. Cole, group methods have been an established approach for many counselors; however, in some cases counselors do not have appropriate preparation to counsel in groups. Special professional development activities will be needed to assist all school counselors to be knowledgeable and have the skills to work with groups.

6. *To enhance leadership skills to develop with other staff members cooperative programs that provide guidance-oriented activities as a part of the regular school curriculum.* Dr. Cole presents an image of the future in Scenario III in which the school counselor functions as a guidance systems manager. The description shows the school counselor coordinating the work of several other guidance workers. Dr. Krumboltz's recommendation for the counselor to work in ways to enhance the learning climate in the school is an example of the leadership role that the school counselor will need to achieve. Dr. Gysbers's guidance team approach with all staff involved and the infusion of careers and development of self into curricular areas places the counselor in a leadership role. Dr. Gysbers discusses the importance of the team approach for the comprehensive program. However, he cautions that the professionally certified counselor must remain the program coordinator. Such an approach would require that the school counselor be prepared, as a team leader, to assume both a coordination and consultation role. The special knowledge and skill to take a leadership position in the school community will be an important component of the future counselor education programs.

7. *To use technological advancements to assist in the management of the school counseling program and in the delivery of student activities.* Dr. Cole discusses the different types of technological advancements that school counselors have available to them. Much of the work of the counselor can be reduced and made easier by the use of the computer and other machines. The program proposed by Dr. Gysbers could certainly be monitored in an easier manner by a counselor using a computer. It is important to find more efficient methods of maintaining the program record system.

8. *To secure and maintain current information concerning societal trends, status of students, and community situations for program planning.* Although Dr. Cole suggests that school counselors could be too responsive to societal trends, it is important that school counselors be aware of the factors in the environment that affect students' lives. Dr. Gysbers also cautions that even

though school counselors must be sensitive to the times, they need to use caution to avoid overresponding and failing to meet the important goals of their total program. Assessing the needs of students, parents, teachers, and the community is one method of understanding the current trends and situations in a community.

9. *To provide programs and activities that will specifically enhance students' and the staff's understanding of multicultural issues and the variety of family structures.* Based upon the knowledge that the number of minority students in schools will increase and single parents and blended families will be in the majority, school counselors need to provide activities that assist students, parents, and staff to understand and interact for optimum mental health.

Future Directions for Research

Each of the four major papers for the 20/20 Conference: Building Strong School Counseling Programs suggested research directions. For the last few years, this writer has proposed that the American School Counselor Association establish a research team to assist practicing school counselors to carry out organized and coordinated research projects. With the recommendations for needed research, an ASCA team or research center could provide the strength of leadership needed in school counseling research. Although school counselors have the real life situations in which to conduct research, they often do not have the time and perhaps lack the expertise to design a research project and prepare the statistical report. However, they may be in a position to pretest, carry out the treatment, and posttest. Dr. Cole suggested that school counselors work with a counselor educator/research person to conduct research. One extention of this idea would be to organize a team to design a series of research projects and provide assistance in obtaining the measurement instruments. Such projects could then be replicated in a variety of settings—urban, rural, small school, or large school—and with participants from various socioeconomic situations and levels of ability. After collecting the data for the proposed research project, school counselors could send the data to the research team for statistical analysis and report preparation. This cooperative method of research could fulfill the broad gap in research related to the effect that school counseling programs have.

Based upon the many recommendations included in the papers by Dr. Capuzzi, Dr. Cole, Dr. Gysbers, and Dr. Krumboltz, there is a great deal to accomplish to develop new skills, change school counseling programs, and investigate the various facets of school counselors' work. School counselors need to take charge of their future, take action together to establish effective school counseling programs, and conduct research to show the effect of school counseling activities. By working together and envisioning positive programs, the preferable future will be reached.

References

Commission on Precollege Guidance and Counseling. (1986). *Keeping the options open.* New York: The College Board.

Hodgkinson, H.L. (1985). *All one system: Demographics of education, kindergarten through graduate school.* Washington, DC, Institute for Educational Leadership.

Inbody, N. (1984). Futurism and school counseling. *The School Counselor, 31*(3), 215–222.

National College Counseling Project. (1986). *Frontiers of possibility.* National Association of College Admissions Counselors.

National Institute of Independent Colleges and Universities. (1986). *Paving the way.* Washington, DC, National Institute of Independent Colleges and Universities.

Building Strong School Counseling Programs: Future Directions for Secondary School Counseling

Thelma Thomas Daley

Guidance Supervisor, Baltimore County Public Schools, Towson, Maryland

The past is indeed prologue. According to Cetron and O'Toole (1982), we live in a time of such endless change that anxiety attack has become a part of our everyday speech. To be able analytically to review secondary school counseling for the past 20 years is a revealing process. Moreover, to propose action steps and priorities for the next 20 years based on the research is both challenging and exciting. As a synthesizer my two-fold charge is:

1. To highlight the important implications and amplifications of the past 20 years of research and development in the selected four conference topics as related to secondary school counseling; and
2. Based upon the implications, outline priorities and key steps for secondary school counseling for the next 20 years.

The papers by John Krumboltz, Dave Capuzzi, Norman Gysbers, and Claire Cole have implications for the student, the client, and the counselor. Figures 1 and 2 give a telescopic view of major themes amplified in the research papers. The research clearly supports the need for counseling services for adolescents and young adults in the more than 16,000 secondary school systems.

To some degree counseling is envisioned as being capable of influencing changes, but there are not enough empirical data to substantiate the outcomes. In fact Cole's historical chronology implies a rather amoebic nature of counseling with the social milieu acting as the protoplasmic flow altering the shape of counseling, or as Cole says, "shaped by what is happening in society," and refueling the debate on the counselor role and function. In the words of Cole, "the issue of role identity persists."

FIGURE 1
Research Themes Related to the Counselor

Roles
   Managing/Coordinating
   Consulting
   Counseling
   └Modalities
     └Process
       └Outcomes
         └Skilled Delivery

Image
Expectations
   Systems Used
   Tools; Technology
   Involvement in the Learning Process
   Population Needs
   Evaluative Process
   Climate
   Policies
   Needed Research
   Planned Curriculum
   Multicultural Approaches

FIGURE 2
Research Themes Related to the Student

Self-Image
Depression
Loss
Abuse
Planned Parenthood
Eating Disorders
Suicide
Stress

- Developing over the life span
- Coping/Handling/Managing
- Making Transitions
- Developing in Stages with
  Intermittent Critical Events

- Learning with Joy
- Feeling/Reaching
- Feeling Good About Self
- Valuing

Collectively the data support the counselor in facilitating the growth and development of the student:

- as a learner;
- as a valued human being; and
- as a person in the process of developing over the life span—a total development sustained throughout the period of integrity (or despair).

In the secondary school, generally the principal is considered the instructional leader and the overall leader of the school. However, the principal is by no means the sole decision maker nor the sole influencing factor in the school's climate. A challenging school environment should help students to explore and expand ideas and abilities; extend critical and creative thinking; and increase social responsibility (MSDE, 1985). The climate of a school is directly influenced by interpersonal relationships between students and their counselors and their teachers (Myrick, 1987).

Krumboltz's research relates to the student as a learner, a learner in a supportive, motivating, challenging, valuing, cooperative, and enjoyable school environment. He posits the counselor in the hub of the educational process and views the counselor as that school facilitator who helps the student to pull it together. Krumboltz's premise is that education should excite and inspire students to want to learn, to explore, to discover, to achieve, and to acquire knowledge and skills as a lifetime process. Counselors play a role in both the cognitive and affective domains. As Myrick (1987) implies, the counselor teaches, coaches, tutors, instructs, informs, and counsels as a part of the helping process. Myrick further parallels Krumboltz's philosophy as he states,

> Developmental counselors base their work on helping students learn more effectively and efficiently. Counselors are concerned with the personal problems of students because they can detract from learning. More effective and efficient learning is the essence of counseling and guidance, no matter the counseling theory or intervention. (Myrick, 1987, p. 136)

Counselors devote a great deal of time toward the improvement of how students see and feel about themselves because self-esteem is a direct correlate of school achievement. Krumboltz reviews those barriers that counselors see as diurnal stumbling blocks to achievement: grading, class rank, labels, tests, restrictive policy, and interpersonal relations—all affecting the self. For "we are selves, and everything we do is to satisfy or fulfill ourselves" (Bloom, 1987, p. 173). Thus, counselors help the underachievers, facilitate goal setting, facilitate the instruction of test-taking skills, and encourage teaching adapted to the child's style of learning. All, once again, underscore the counselor's role as a manager, consultant, and coordinator as well as counselor.

In the learning process as researched by Krumboltz, the data suggest that counselors do not just assist students in adapting to high school but influence changes in the learning environment, the policies, the methodologies, the attitudes, the curriculum, the academic and social policies, and whatever other force that may negatively influence the learning milieu. Bradley (1975) suggests that the concerns to be addressed may be as simple as the attendance policy or admission requirements or as complete as sexism, racism, or declining academic achievement.

Personal and Social Competencies

In 1986, the American Association for Counseling and Development once again was on the cutting edge as it sponsored the conference entitled, "Powder Kegs in America: Counseling Interventions" (Alexander & Rose, 1986). Congresswoman Patricia Schroeder, in addressing the conference, emphasized that powder kegs are pervasive in our society. It seems that Dave Capuzzi's research focused on nine powder kegs relating to the self and the family. The evolution of counseling as also viewed by the other researchers, Gysbers and Cole, points up the changing nature of counseling. The pervasiveness of personal and social issues knows not the meaning of state or region, ethnicity, sex, economics, or specific age. In some systems such as mine, children as early as the primary grades are exposed to educational programs designed to increase their awareness of and fortification against sexual and physical abuse.

Although self-esteem is an age-old topic for counselors to address, Capuzzi highlights the need to address this important area from a multicultural perspective. In fact the research seemingly implies that self-image is a thread that is interwoven throughout eating disorders, suicidal tendencies, proclivity for abuse, management of stress, and strength in coping with separation or divorce. This synthesizer reinforces Capuzzi's assumption that counselors can do a better job of helping students to develop coping skills as they face the myriad of personal and social concerns that subject them to being "at risk" in an educational system where apocalyptic statements seemingly prevail. Capuzzi clearly calls for better research and greater use of stress management both by teachers and counselors as they collectively assist students with personal and social issues.

Career Guidance

Norman Gysbers, in addition to a comprehensive recap of the development of career guidance, moves toward a refreshing sphere. His analysis of the later research points us toward a comprehensive developmental guidance program K–12, with a distinct and identifiable career dimension. He connects with Krumboltz's learning environment and Capuzzi's personal and social competencies when he cautions that "if we don't attend to the overall structure and formulation of all of guidance in the schools, then whatever is popular for the time will be emphasized. Although guidance must be sensitive to the times, there also must be continuity and stability of purpose and program." Cole says, "The counseling profession has been shaped by what is happening in society. . . .Those entering the profession must be capable of and willing to acquire new sets of skills as their client demands change. Although a teacher can remain perhaps marginally effective with little change from year to year, the school counselor cannot."

Myrick (1987) supports Gysbers's approach as he posits that "developmental guidance and counseling assumes that human nature moves individuals sequentially and positively toward self-enhancement. It recognizes there is a force within each of us that makes us believe that we are special and there is nobody like us. It also assumes that our individual potentials are valuable assests to society and the future of humanity" (p. 31).

The counselor's role in the total environment is again a major thread as Gysbers proposes that guidance programs are built on a team approach. Grade level teaming has become institutionalized at the middle school level, but the high school remains subject-oriented and departmentalized. Since the inception of P.L. 94–142, students with handicapping conditions are subjected to a sophisticated teaming analysis through the ARD (Admission, Review, and Dismissal) process at all levels. Unfortunately, due to time, and both human and fiscal resources, this team approach is not yet foreseeable for all high school students, though it is badly needed as an approach to customize the educational program based upon the needs and individual learning and development styles of students.

Image and Impact: Counselor Role and Function

Cole, in her exploration of research related to the image and impact of the school counselor, sharpens one's awareness to the change as she describes three counseling scenarios ranging from 1960 to 2007. She clearly documents the chronology of the social forces "shaping" counseling. Cole's second scenario represents the 1980s in a middle school (gleaned from the statement on meeting with parents of incoming elementary school students). Even for the 1980s, there is a poignant statement, "and the question to be answered is . . . Is Guidance and Counseling free to execute its own mission, its own curriculum?" Cole's overall scenario should be applauded for including paraprofessionals, computers, advisory committees, community outreach, and student involvement. However, she writes, "the program to print final grades was up and running." The latter represents those administrative priorities that impede the best designed sequential, comprehensive, developmental programs. Cole helps us to be very pragmatic as she highlights the telephone and the copying machine as major counseling tools.

Although secondary schools are on varying levels of computer use, the majority of high schools have some form of a micro or mainframe system.

The research highlights the trend to work with parents, that is, parent groups, but a question remains as to how far this goes. Additionally, Cole's analysis of the image and impact underscores involvement in the personal and social areas, including the handicapped, the gifted, ethnic minorities, and women. The research also seems to indicate emerging use of certain techniques such as peer counseling, relaxation, and bibliotherapy. There has never been a void in finding questions as to the counselor's role, which remains debatable. Bradley (1978) sums it up by inferring, first, that counselors are trained in a setting unaware of the counselor's obligation to the organizational setting of the school. Second, she cautions that counselors are usually trained to counsel within the four walls of an office, to emphasize remediation, and to perform without fully understanding the mission, goals, and objectives of the high school. The role confusion gives greater credence to Gysbers's call for a systematic, sequential, comprehensive program evaluated for outcomes, as well as to Cole's characterization of counselor accountability.

Cole's scenario for the year 2007 emphasizes the managerial role; highlights certification and technology; alludes to better ratios through the reference to a large department; and notes our movement to have parent-surrogates on board. Some of the inferences, however, are frightening, in particular the references to families and the inquiry, "what family?"

The emerging statistics remind us that 60% of today's three-year olds will have been raised by a single parent by the time they are 18. The family will not be the traditional mother and father with Dick and Jane. BUT, IT WILL STILL BE A FAMILY, whether it be poor, Black, Asian, from a divorced home, or a single-parent home. As counselors we may need to change our lenses because a new structure is rapidly emerging. Harold Hodgkinson, a senior fellow at the American Council on Education, said, "It's a demographic given that if we don't do something new, it's going to get worse. The education system is the only system left that seems to function in a way that we can get a handle on it. The family, church . . . all have gone through striking changes" (*Washington Post*, October 11, 1987, p. A23).

Facing the Future

As we think of the next 20 years, we are also thinking about another century. The preschool and kindergarten students I see in my administrative-supervisory role as I work with the counselors in elementary settings within the Baltimore County, Maryland, schools are part of the projected statistics of our college graduates and workers of the 21st century. The high school students are the projected workers and the annuitants. Harold Hodgkinson, former director of the National Institute of Education, has addressed the demographics and the effect of demographics on education. His comprehensive report is entitled, *All One System: Demographics in Education, Kindergarten through Graduate School* (1985). Other reports appear in *Principal* (1986) and the *Education Digest* (1985).

Some of the realities counselors will be facing according to the demographics as drawn from Hodgkinson's studies are as follows:

- 7% of the children come from homes with the working husband, the housewife, and two children;
- 85% of White students and 75% of Black students complete high school;
- 30% of children are "latchkey" children;
- 15% speak another language;
- 40% will be living with a single parent by their 18th birthday;
- of the 4 million children born in the United States each year, the majority are White, with a rising number born as the first child to mothers over 30, of which half are college graduates;
- in comparison to a decade ago, there are some 400,000 fewer White students and 280,000 more Black children;
- the Mexican-American population is the fastest growing, and due to immigration, the Asian-American population is rapidly increasing. (In 1985, two-thirds of all the immigration in the world was to the United States according to Hodgkinson, 1986);
- by 1992, there will be as many college students 25 years old and older as there will be 24 years old and younger;
- in the first 2 decades of the 21st century there will be a scarcity of youth and a growing population of those over 65; and
- a major concern to be faced and seriously addressed by this nation is the continuing decline in the number of minority high school graduates applying for college despite the increase in the number of Black middle class students in the school system. Richard Berendzen, President of American University, cited this factor as a serious concern as he addressed administrators and supervisors in the Baltimore County School System during their 1987–88 series of professional study.

Change is inevitable! Whether intentional or unintentional, counseling in secondary schools in 2007 will be different! How different depends on many factors. However, even with the brightest galaxy and the best orange-pekoe tea leaves, it is difficult for us to describe in exact terms the profession, the roles, the environment, the people, and the processes 20 years in the future.

One cannot outline the future of guidance and counseling at the secondary level without giving adequate attention to guidance and counseling at the elementary and middle school levels—for each is related. Boyer (1983) reminds us that high schools do not work in isolation. Being connected, they are shaped by such connections. Hodgkinson (1985) goes so far as to say, "If people begin to see the educational system as a single entity through which people move, they may begin to behave as if all education were related."

Ferguson (1980), in establishing the framework for the transformation of our consciousness in her *Aquarian Conspiracy*, alludes to a 1979 futures conference bulletin that seems appropriate now for a preface.

> Our first great challenge is to create a consensus that fundamental change is possible . . . to create a climate, a framework, which can integrally organize and coordinate the forces which are today striving for growth along separate paths. We will create an irresistibly vibrant vision, a new paradigm for creative . . . action . . . .Until we have created that master context, all talk of strategy is meaningless. (p. 40)

Marvin Cetron and Thomas O'Toole in *Encounters with the Future* (1982) further emphasize a need to face change as they write:

> The year is 1990 and the world population exceeds 5.3 billion souls, all striving to get through the next ten years and into the 21st century. Electric cars dart through the streets of New York, the first city to wire one million computers into the workplace. The silicon chip drives elevators and subways, turns thermostats, runs operating rooms, and changes traffic lights. The jobs people have, the games they play, the purchases they make, the funds they transfer, even the food they cook start with the silicon chip. (p. 139)

Proposals for the Future

1. Strategic Planning

With or without effort, there will be change either by transmission, that is, without some intentional force, or by transformation that is through a conscious effort both inwardly and outwardly. Thus the counseling profession must embark upon strategic planning with an anticipation of the changes. Planned organization change is important. In a period of educational reform as school systems debate their newly revised curricula, guidance and counseling, and how they will "fit," should be a part of the debate. Proposed is a major forum and study on counseling within the school structure in the 1990s and beyond. Instructional leaders need to experiment with therapeutic and developmental models and combinations of both. Is there time and a way to "fit" a solid developmental program—a guidance curriculum—into a seven-period day, a 35-period week as the curriculum develops rigor, and more rigor? This question must be answered or high school counselors will remain in the bind of trying to work with students on a "hit-miss" piecemeal basis. Students will continue to be penalized for "missing a class" because they were in a counseling session. Counselors will continue to work with students mostly on a one-to-one basis because logistically it is easier.

In the reform movement, school systems have examined their programs for increased mathematics and science; for a core curriculum; for the addition of the humanities; for creative ways to offer instruction to the basic, the gifted, the learning disabled student; for learning incentives such as the offering of certificates of achievement for the accumulation of credits and quality points; however, none has seriously examined "how" guidance and conseling will be delivered to the students. Everyone expects it to get done, but no one finds the most enhancing structure. This is an issue that must be debated not only by counselors and counselor educators. It must be addressed in a forum in concert with school administrators, chief state school officers, and other policymakers who are responsible for designing the overall school structure and ensuring the delivery of quality services to students. Until this issue is addressed, school counseling at the secondary level, the high school level to be specific, will continue to be in a dilemma. The question is, does the guidance and counseling program fit the organization of the high school, or vice versa?

2. Structural Enhancement

Future programs should and will be structurally enhanced through expanded technology, the employment of technicians, and use of a systems approach. Modern technology will be employed to bring the latest information on college, careers, trends, programs, and the like to counselors, students, and teachers. Technology will provide students with access to employers, employment services, colleges, and community agencies. Employment assessment and interviews will be conducted within the friendly environment of the school via technology connecting with the potential employer. Technicians will execute the career information systems, the electronic mail, and other activities that will free the professional counselor to be accessible to the students. Via improved computers, a variety of computerized assessment stations will allow students to expeditiously search, clarify, and plan.

Currently computers have not alleviated laborious paperwork associated with program planning and scheduling. Although scheduling is clearly an administrative task, in some schools computerized scheduling has caused the counselor to face increased mounds of paper and thousands of squares to be "bubbled" or darkened for the machine. In spite of these negative aspects, each counselor can expect a brighter day.

Within a very short time span, there will be online diagnosis and a desktop communication system in the counselor's office. Technology will provide mass storage with minimum space and will serve as an electronic resource for records and student information. It will provide linkages with agencies, business and industry, and mental health centers. Technology will be a carrier of images—collecting, collating, and disseminating. Technology's artificial intelligence will give the professional counselor the long-awaited space, time, and support for the execution of a role commensurate with the training.

3. Outcome Based

The counseling program should be planned, organized, and managed with full attention to the execution of both process and impact evaluation. Student growth and development should be assessed and directed toward specific outcomes. To be outcome directed presupposes that the guidance program has a defined mission, is an integral part of the total educational program, recognizes the unique qualities of all the students, and has clearly defined goals and objectives based upon evidenced and established student needs. Additionally students exiting from high school will be expected to have major life-planning skills: decision-making and coping skills—including skills to self-assess, self-manage, self-monitor, and self-mediate.

4. Parental Guidance

Boyer (1983) intimated that we, as educators, are part of the blame for the gap between home and school. Parents have questions. Few understand the changing financial aid scenario, and concomitantly, the majority want to know and to be a part of their child's plans, progress, and critical encounters. It is proposed that cable be used to provide home guidance to parents: information on financial aid, dates for tests and plans, and helpful hints to assist them in understanding the routine growth, the instructional arena, and pressures and stresses adolescents face. Today, robots are used to call parents when children are absent. Robots can call to give a helpful guidance message.

5. Certified Counselors

This is the era of credentialing, an evolving process. The next 20 years will witness NBCC (National Board for Certified Counselors) certification as a given minimum requirement for all school counselors. Additionally, NBCC will have completed, it is hoped, the school counseling specialty, and employers will be searching for and hiring counselors who are NCCs (National Certified Counselors) with an NBCC school counseling specialty. As counselors enhance their therapeutic and identification skills and become integrally involved in the learning process, credentials, as a "good housekeeping" stamp, will become more and more important. Only the approved will practice.

6. Member of the Instructional Team

As a viable member of the instructional team, the counselor's role as a consultant will be evident and expected. As consultant, the counselor will bring about change in the school environment, the organization, the practices, the curriculum. As a consultant to teachers, administrators, and parents the counselor will bring about change that will affect the lives of many students. It is the emerging role. Brown et al. (1979) see the consultant as one who:

- stimulates education and innovation;
- enhances human relations;
- facilitates professional interchange to stimulate students' growth;
- solicits untapped resources; and
- is a viable force within the learning environment.

7. New Initiatives

As more students come to school from low-income families or single-parent homes or as teenage parents themselves, counselors as organizational change agents will take steps to research, establish the need, and work with appropriate powers to:

- Create programs to assist low-income families with college.
- Design improved college counseling, particularly in light of the continued decline in the number of Blacks seeking college. During the last 20 years, high school graduation rates have improved for Black students, but since 1975 the college attendance and completion rates have declined. Blacks are underrepresented among graduate and professional school students (The College Board, 1985).
- Stimulate the school and community to provide day care programs so the increasing number of teenage mothers and single parents will have nursery care as they attend school, work, or both. The counselor's ongoing research will bring this to fruition.
- Provide crosscultural models (Sue, 1981) and maintain culturally effective counselors. Twenty years from now school enrollment will resemble colorful mosaics, and even the superintendent, principals, and a majority of the teachers may be non-White. Counselors will be called to help faculties deal with different cultures, adapt learning styles, and design learning modalities that enhance each population.

8. Models

We must design a school counseling model that will integrate proficient personal counseling with an organized, sequential developmental program. This issue remains debatable as some urge counselors to abandon all efforts of therapeutic models (Bradley, 1978), although some (Hohenshil, 1981) imply that counselors involved in the developmental approach are not adequately prepared to provide extensive counseling services, particularly for populations such as the handicapped.

Proposed is a model (Figure 3) that brings about changes in training that will parallel conceptual changes in the organization of the secondary school. The

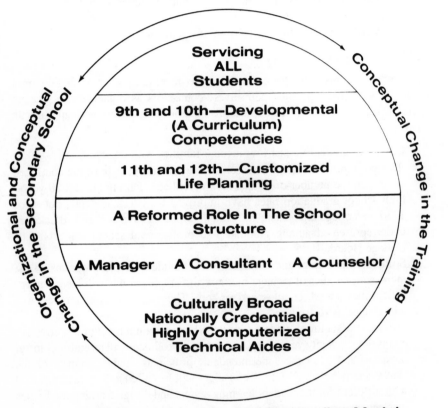

Factors to Consider in a Counseling Model

FIGURE 3A

Role And Impact

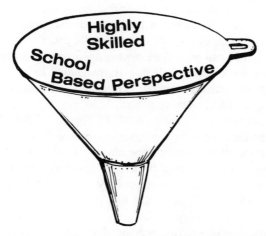

Ingredients for a Successful High School Model

- **Management, Organization, and Planning**

- **Measurable Student Growth and Development**

- **Didactic and Therapeutic**

- **School Team Member**

- **Human Resource Developer**

FIGURE 3B

model proposes equitable service to all students with a clearly defined developmental program in grades 9 and 10—built upon the K-12 program. At grades 11 and 12, the emphasis is tailored to individual planning, the refinement and application of decision-making skills, and the honing of coping skills. The NBCC certified counselor is a manager, a consultant, and a counselor. A curriculum is available to facilitate the developmental thrust.

Additionally, the counselors will have training in cognitive models—Bruner, Asubel, and Gagne. The nature of the career development curriculum will be enhanced by the counselor's instrumental skills and the translation of tested theories and models into practice. Drawing upon Jerome Bruner, the counselor will bring into the lesson the client's surroundings, living environment, and cultural amplifiers, sensing, finding, organizing, and relating the client's own milieu to the established learning goals.

The counselor may well explore Asubel's concept of the advance organizer in planning the career development curriculum and in searching for an information process model as a way of presenting. In another direction, the counselor has long been accustomed to a behavioral approach, and Gagne's stimulus-response model offers another methodology for presenting and teaching. The model stresses the learner, the event that stimulates the learner's senses, the learner's retrieval of memory of data, and the responses. It entails motivating the student, building objectives, apprehending the data, attending so as to understand, giving clear instructions, and acquisition. To the learner it means coding and hooking the new knowledge to the old. It is generalization and application.

The counselors will be highly skilled in working with the emerging personal-social problems as vividly described by Capuzzi. What can counselors do? What can outside psychological agencies do? It is time for a coordinated and integrated approach to the plethora of youth concerns. Indeed it is estimated that 90% of persons with eating disorders have mild forms of an affective disorder (depression), to cite one accelerating concern. Counselors must be adept in detecting symptoms, adverse clues, and changes in student behavior. They should facilitate parent and teacher awareness. Early detection increases the likelihood of positive treatment for adolescents.

Helping students with self-management and communication is a reasonable approach. However, the provision of an open, trusting environment should be a priority.

In the future, the enrollments may be smaller and schools might well maximize their resources by allowing the community mental health unit to be housed in a wing of the school. Like the HMOs, one stop will cover the needs. As stated earlier, a day care center will be a part of the facility, now an expected service. The entire school will have a partnership with business, industry, and postsecondary institutions.

Drawing upon their human resources development training, counselors will be conducting more inservice sessions for teachers, helping them to build expectations and integrate the affective with the cognitive emphases.

Summary

The counselor of the future will teach, coach, model, mentor, manage, consult, and counsel. The counselor of the future, fortified with a broad theoretical base, will select from a variety of identification, assessment, helping, and evaluation strategies. The goal will be synonomous with the school's goals: a fully functioning educated person.

References

Alexander, S., & Rose, M. Eds. (1986). *Powder kegs in America: Counseling interventions and conference proceedings*. Alexandria VA: American Association for Counseling and Development.

Bloom, A. (1987). *The closing of the American mind*. New York: Simon & Schuster.

Boyer, E.L. (1983). *High school: A report on secondary education in America*. New York: Harper & Row.

Bradley, M.K. (1978). Counseling past and present: Is there a future? *Personnel and Guidance Journal, 57*, 42–45.

Brown, D., Wyne, M.D., Blackburn, J.E., & Powell, W.C. (1979). *Consultation*. Boston: Allyn & Bacon.

Cetron, M., & O'Toole, T. (1982). *Encounters with the future: A forecast of life in the 21st century*. New York: McGraw-Hill.

The College Board (1985). *Equality and excellence—The educational status of Black Americans*. New York: College Entrance Examination Board.

Ferguson, M. (1980). *The Aquarian conspiracy: Personal and social transformation in the 1980s*. Boston: Houghton Mifflin.

Hodgkinson, H.L. (1985). *All one system: Demographics in education, kindergarten through graduate school*. Washington, DC: Institute for Educational Leadership.

Hodgkinson, H.L. (1985, November). What's right with education? *Education Digest*, 170–173.

Hodgkinson, H.L. (1986, January). What's ahead for education? *Principal*, 6–11.

Hohenshil, T.H. (1981). The future of the counseling profession. *Personnel and Guidance Journal*, 1960, 133–134.

Maryland State Department of Education (1985). *Recommendations of the Maryland Commission on Secondary Education: School administration/climate*. Baltimore: Maryland State Board of Education.

Myrick, R.D. (1987). *Developmental guidance and counseling: A practical approach*. Minneapolis: Educational Media Corporation.

National College Counseling Project (1986). *Frontiers of possibility*. Burlington, VT: National Association of College Admissions Counselors.

Sue, D.W. (1981). *Counseling the culturally different*. New York: John Wiley.

Reflections and Projections

Garry R. Walz

Professor, College of Education
University of Michigan, Ann Arbor, Michigan

Throughout the 20/20 conference we emphasized the word research. For many practitioners, the word suggests a complicated process that frequently produces little of real or immediate value to the counselor. I would suggest a different perspective for understanding research. If we break the word into "re," meaning anew, and "search," meaning to seek out, research becomes the process of seeking out ideas and information anew, of gaining fresh insights into human behavior.

In this perspective one need not be a white-coated specialist to do research—a person who is seeking new insights and understandings regarding human behavior is a researcher. Many of us who do not think of ourselves as researchers are, by focused searching, actually performing as practicing researchers. It is a process that many counselors perform and can use to improve their practice. In using this definition, all of us can and should be researchers.

A number of significant implications emerge from the excellent papers presented at the 20/20 conference. These implications refer to whether and how we will use the findings from our 20 years of counseling research.

1. We must view information about counseling as essentially a body of *friendly facts*. Over 2,000 studies were identified in the preparation of conference papers, and the authors cited 600 of them. It is clear that each paper can serve as a highly useful reservoir of facts and ideas. If we are to benefit from this body of ideas, insights, and experiences, it is essential that individually and collectively we view data as something to be sought and used. Unless a positive attitude toward data exists, they will remain potentially useful, but practically useless.

2. Guidance research must be directed toward and contribute to *major priorities and commitments*. We can improve the utility of our research if we can focus it on the topics and issues that are of primary interest and need to counselors and counseling. Making hard decisions about what is important can help us undertake research that makes it a viable intervention, not an academic exercise.

3. *Counselors need to practice copycat creativity—the acquisition and utilization of ideas and resources from disparate sources.* The focus of counseling is extremely broad in terms of problems addressed and the means of response. To acquire fresh ideas and approaches we need to look consciously and systematically for what is promising and proven in other fields. One of our major goals should be to acquire those programs and practices that have worked well for others and to adopt and adapt them to our own circumstances. In particular, we need to seek ways to improve upon what others have developed and are using. We can become copycats of others but creatively improve upon their efforts.

4. *Marketing moxie will become an increasingly important factor* in determining public acceptance and support of counseling programs and practices. There is increasing competition among service providers for the public dollar. Only those services that effectively communicate with the public are likely to prosper. A key to winning public support is the ability to demonstrate that a given service is unique and superior to competing services in meeting student needs and interests. Marketing can play a crucial role in communicating our uniqueness and superiority.

5. *Change and improvement in counseling will occur only if we have gutsy guys and gals.* Research can point the way to what needs to be done, but the impact of research depends upon whether counselors will work to implement research findings even without administrative support. We need a "hot cognition," an aggressive response to implementing significant research findings. A laid-back, dispassionate approach will not bring about the needed changes.

6. We have reached the point where we need to think about *changing for the sake of changing.* If we wait for clear, documented evidence that change is needed we will be too late. Continuous renewal of our programs and practices is a must if we are adequately to use the new ideas and resources generated by research and development. We are unlikely to change too often—the greater problem is that we will wait too long before we introduce new ideas and practices, thus producing a gradual erosion in the quality of our programs.

If we adopt these six perspectives on implementation, we may make more mistakes but, more important, we are likely to heighten the vigor and effectiveness of the services to which we are committed. Doing research is a necessity, but making a commitment to its effective utilization is equally imperative.